# FUNDAMENTALS OF CATHOLICISM
## VOLUME II

# FUNDAMENTALS OF CATHOLICISM

VOLUME II

by

KENNETH BAKER, S.J.

IGNATIUS PRESS    SAN FRANCISCO

Imprimi Potest: Thomas R. Royce, S.J.
              Provincial, Oregon Province
              of the Society of Jesus
              Portland, Oregon

Imprimatur:   +Thomas J. Welsh
              Bishop of Arlington, Virginia

Cover design by Riz Boncan Marsella


© 1983 Kenneth Baker, S.J.
All rights reserved
ISBN 0-89870-019-1
Library of Congress catalogue number 82-80297
Co-published by Ignatius Press, San Francisco
and Homiletic & Pastoral Review
86 Riverside Drive, New York, N.Y. 10024
Printed in the United States of America

# CONTENTS

## Part I: UNITY OF GOD

| | | |
|---|---|---|
| 1. | Our Knowledge of God | 13 |
| 2. | Man Can Know God with Certainty | 16 |
| 3. | On Proving the Existence of God | 19 |
| 4. | Two Ways to God | 22 |
| 5. | God Is Known through Creatures | 25 |
| 6. | Our Imperfect but True Knowledge of God | 28 |
| 7. | "By Your Light We See the Light" | 32 |
| 8. | What's in a Name | 35 |
| 9. | God's Absolute Perfection | 38 |
| 10. | There Is Only One God | 41 |
| 11. | God Tells Nothing but the Truth | 44 |
| 12. | No One Is Good but God Alone | 47 |
| 13. | "Before Abraham Ever Was, I Am" | 50 |
| 14. | "Where Could I Flee from Your Presence?" | 53 |
| 15. | God and Intelligence | 56 |
| 16. | Prayer and God's Knowledge of the Future | 59 |
| 17. | God's Will and the Problem of Evil | 62 |
| 18. | For God Everything Is Possible | 65 |
| 19. | God Is Infinitely Just | 68 |
| 20. | His Mercy Is Everlasting | 71 |

## Part II: TRINITY

| | | |
|---|---|---|
| 1. | The Most Holy Trinity | 77 |
| 2. | God Is Both One and Three | 80 |
| 3. | The Fatherhood of God | 83 |
| 4. | The Son and the Holy Spirit | 86 |
| 5. | The Origin of the Son and the Holy Spirit | 89 |

|     |                                              |     |
| --- | -------------------------------------------- | --- |
|  6. | Jesus Is the Perfect Image of the Father     |  93 |
|  7. | The Origin of the Holy Spirit                |  96 |
|  8. | Three Divine Persons—One God                 |  99 |
|  9. | What Is a Divine Person?                     | 102 |
| 10. | "The Father and I Are One"                   | 106 |
| 11. | The Works of the Trinity                     | 109 |
| 12. | Father, Son and Holy Spirit Dwell in Us      | 112 |
| 13. | The Trinity Is an Absolute Mystery           | 115 |

### Part III: CREATION

|     |                                              |     |
| --- | -------------------------------------------- | --- |
|  1. | God Created the Heavens and the Earth        | 121 |
|  2. | Why Did God Create the World?                | 124 |
|  3. | The Best Possible World?                     | 127 |
|  4. | The Beginning of the World                   | 130 |
|  5. | God Keeps the World in Existence             | 133 |
|  6. | The Divine Plan for Creation                 | 136 |
|  7. | The Origin of Man                            | 139 |
|  8. | All the Children of Adam and Eve             | 142 |
|  9. | Body and Soul                                | 146 |
| 10. | Where Does the Human Soul Come from?         | 149 |
| 11. | The Idea of the Supernatural                 | 152 |
| 12. | Adam and Eve before the Fall                 | 155 |
| 13. | The Sin of Our First Parents                 | 159 |
| 14. | The Transmission of Original Sin             | 162 |
| 15. | What Is Original Sin?                        | 165 |
| 16. | Never Make Light of Sin                      | 168 |
| 17. | Do Infants Dying Without Baptism Go to Limbo? | 171 |
| 18. | Angels by the Millions                       | 174 |
| 19. | What Is an Angel?                            | 177 |
| 20. | The Angels Were Tested Too                   | 181 |
| 21. | Where Did the Devil Come from?               | 184 |
| 22. | Each Person Has a Guardian Angel             | 187 |
| 23. | The Power of the Devil                       | 190 |

## Part IV: CHRISTOLOGY

1. Jesus Christ Is True God — 197
2. Jesus' Divine Knowledge and Power — 200
3. The Divinity of Jesus in St. John's Gospel — 203
4. St. Paul on the Divinity of Jesus — 206
5. Jesus Christ Is Truly Human — 210
6. The Perfect Man — 213
7. Jesus Is a Divine Person — 216
8. Jesus Is Both God and Man — 219
9. The Two Wills in Christ — 222
10. His Kingdom Will Have No End — 225
11. The Hypostatic Union — 228
12. The Whole Trinity Brought about the Incarnation — 231
13. "We Adore Thee, O Christ . . ." — 234
14. Heart of Jesus, Burning Furnace of Love — 237
15. Talking about Jesus — 240
16. Jesus' Soul Possessed the Immediate Vision of God — 243
17. Jesus' Suffering and Glory — 247
18. Did Ignorance or Error Exist in Christ? — 250
19. Jesus Possessed Both Infused and Acquired Knowledge — 253
20. Jesus Was Free from All Sin and Could Not Sin — 257
21. Jesus Possesses the Fullness of Grace — 260
22. The Power of Christ — 263
23. Jesus' Suffering and Human Feelings — 266
24. Why Did God Become Man? — 269
25. Jesus Christ—Redeemer and Liberator of Mankind — 273
26. Fallen Man Cannot Save Himself — 276
27. The Divine Teacher — 279
28. King of Kings, and Lord of Lords — 282

| | | |
|---|---|---|
| 29. | Jesus Is a Priest Forever | 286 |
| 30. | Jesus' Sacrifice on the Cross | 289 |
| 31. | What Do We Mean by "Redemption"? | 292 |
| 32. | Jesus Died Not for Himself but for All Men | 295 |
| 33. | Jesus Merited Grace for Us | 298 |
| 34. | The Descent of Christ into Hell | 301 |
| 35. | Jesus' Glorious Resurrection | 304 |
| 36. | The Ascension of Jesus | 308 |

## Part V: MARIOLOGY

| | | |
|---|---|---|
| 1. | Church Teaching about Mary, the Mother of God | 315 |
| 2. | Mary Is a Gift of God | 318 |
| 3. | Mary, the Immaculate Mother of God | 321 |
| 4. | Hail Mary, Full of Grace | 324 |
| 5. | Mary Was Free from All Evil Desire | 327 |
| 6. | Mary, Our Sinless Sister | 330 |
| 7. | Mary's Fullness of Grace | 333 |
| 8. | Joseph and Mary, Husband and Wife | 337 |
| 9. | Mary, the Mother of God | 340 |
| 10. | Mary Freely Said Yes to God | 343 |
| 11. | The Virginal Conception of Jesus | 346 |
| 12. | Mary's Virginity during Childbirth | 349 |
| 13. | What about the Brothers and Sisters of Jesus? | 353 |
| 14. | Our Spiritual Mother | 356 |
| 15. | Mary, Our Go-Between | 359 |
| 16. | Mary Cooperated in Our Redemption | 362 |
| 17. | Mary Prays for All of Us | 365 |
| 18. | The Dormition of Mary | 368 |
| 19. | The Assumption of the Blessed Virgin Mary | 372 |

| | |
|---|---|
| 20. Hail, Holy Queen | 375 |
| 21. Mary Is Our Sure Way to Christ | 378 |
| 22. The Immaculate Heart of Mary | 381 |
| 23. Mary, Mother of the Church | 385 |

# PART I

# UNITY OF GOD

I

## OUR KNOWLEDGE OF GOD

One of the basic problems currently confronting American society is that of belief in a transcendent God who is the Eternal Judge of each person. I for one do not doubt that loss of belief in a personal God (that is, atheism) is at the root of many of our social problems, such as abortion, divorce, pornography, murder, drug addiction, and so forth.

Our modern technological society, which has helped produce an affluent life style for a large proportion of the population, has been accompanied by a significant decline in church attendance and belief in God. There is nothing new in the observation that man tends to forget his Creator when he is prosperous. That stands out very clearly in the Bible, especially in the Old Testament.

I don't know how obvious it is to you, but it is certainly obvious to me, that atheism has become much more common in the past twenty years than it was before. Of course, there are different kinds of atheism. There are explicit theoretical atheists who will give you arguments why they think there is no God—usually the arguments are based on the presence of evil, disease, poverty, war, and so forth.

In this country, with a long and strong tradition of religious belief, perhaps what is known as "practical atheism" is much more prevalent. The practical atheist is the person who gives some kind of verbal assent to the existence of God but lives as if God did not exist and as if he did not have to give an account of his stewardship to God after his death. For every theoretical atheist, such as a convinced Marxist, there are dozens of practical atheists.

It is strange but true that it often takes great suffering or tragedy to bring men back to a realization of their total dependence on God the Creator. Cancer, blindness, paralysis, imminent death often are much more effective than homilies, C.C.D. classes or college theology courses.

One of the reasons for the growing loss of faith in God is the all-pervading secularism that surrounds us. In this context "secularism" means the exclusion of God from public life and public affairs. The national government, cities and corporations are run as if God did not exist and as if the persons in charge would not have to give an account of their actions to God Almighty on the day of judgment.

I have been teaching university students for almost twenty years. Over ten years ago I began to notice the mounting skepticism among Catholic students about the existence of God and especially about the ability of the human mind to be certain about the existence of God and to grasp universal principles of morality. It came to me as something of a shock in 1968 to discover that over ninety percent of the Catholic college students I was teaching held some form of situation ethics, that is, a theory of moral relativism which holds that no moral act (such as adultery or fornication) is always and in all circumstances evil.

It seems to me that much of this skepticism and practical atheism flows from a lack of clear knowledge of some of the basic principles of philosophy and theology. It is not necessary for me here to belabor the point that in many of our schools Catholic doctrine and faith are not taught with the clarity and conviction that they once were.

In the magnificent Catholic tradition there are immense treasures of wisdom and knowledge available to all who take the trouble to look for them. I am convinced that the Catholic who knows his faith well possesses adequate weapons to defend himself against all the attacks of our contemporary secularism.

What I hope to do in the following essays is simply to expound the Church's teaching on what we can know about God by the natural light of reason and what we can know about him from faith and divine revelation.

## 2

## MAN CAN KNOW GOD WITH CERTAINTY

As Catholics, most of us were taught about God from early childhood. Our parents taught us how to make the Sign of the Cross; they told us about Jesus, Mary and Joseph, especially in reference to Christmas. So we learned about God from others—from parents, relatives and teachers in grade school. The question I wish to propose today is the following: Granted that we learned about God from others, is the human mind capable of knowing something about God through the use of its own power?

There are those who say that man cannot know anything about God, since we perceive only material things and by definition God must be spiritual or essentially above material bodies. He may exist, they say, but we can never know for sure, and we can know nothing definite about such a Being. People who hold such views are often referred to as "agnostics" or "skeptics".

Then there are the atheists who explicitly deny the existence of God. They are usually pragmatists and materialists. Convinced Marxists and communists fit into this category. They go beyond the agnostics since they affirm with certainty that God does not exist.

In the history of the Church, especially in the nineteenth century, we find a group of intellectuals called "traditionalists" who maintained that the only way we can know about God with certainty is from a divine revelation. In order to explain why all primitive peoples had and have a belief in God of some kind, they claimed that an original revelation given to Adam and Eve was handed down from one generation to the next. That explains, they said, the universal belief in a god of some kind. This view was condemned by Pope Gregory XVI and Pope Pius IX.

What does the Catholic Church say about the ability of man's mind to know God? In 1870 the First Vatican Council made the following official declaration: "Holy Mother Church holds and teaches that God, the origin and end of all things, can be known with certainty by the natural light of human reason from the things that he created" (see *Denzinger* 1785, 1806). What does this mean? It means that the mature human mind has the capability within itself to conclude to the existence of God by considering the wonders of creation, such as the sun, moon, stars, flowers, ocean, animals and plants.

The definition is a general statement, so it does not say that every person has this capability. Many are defective for one reason or another; some have been corrupted by environment and education. The Church merely says that the human mind can do it—without saying how many or how few can do it. Please note also that, according to Vatican I, God's existence can be known "with certainty". "Certainty" is much more than a hunch, an opinion or a guess. The source from which God's existence is deduced is the multiplicity of "things that he created". Created things are finite; they are moved or produced by another. Since there cannot be an infinite series of finite beings moving another, there must ultimately be one infinite or unmoved source of movement in all the others. That first "unmoved mover" we call God. St. Thomas Aquinas develops this argument at length and we will return to it later.

According to the testimony of the Bible the existence of God can be known from nature. Wisdom 13:1–9 is a good passage to read on this point, especially verse 5: "Through the grandeur and beauty of the creatures we may, by analogy, contemplate their Author." St. Paul in his Letter to the Romans says: "For what can be known about God is perfectly plain to them since God himself has made it plain. Ever since God created the world his everlasting power and deity—however invisible—have been there for the mind to see in the things he has made" (1:19–20).

The Fathers of the Church often stressed the ability of the human mind to know God. They pointed out that there are two kinds of knowledge of God: one from faith and the other from reason, but knowledge from reason precedes that from faith. They also insisted that man's natural knowledge of God is *obvious* both from the physical world and from the moral order of conscience. Thus the knowledge of God in man is so basic that one could almost say that it is innate, at least in the sense that the principles for discovering God are innate to man.

According to St. Paul, man cannot violate God's law and then claim ignorance. "Such people", he says, "are without excuse; they knew God and yet refused to honor him as God or to thank him; instead, they made nonsense out of logic and their empty minds were darkened" (Rom 1:20–21).

3

# ON PROVING THE EXISTENCE OF GOD

Can the human mind *prove* the existence of God? That is a basic question which has perplexed many thinkers and many Christians. Of course, there are many atheists, agnostics, skeptics, fundamentalists and sentimentalists who, for various reasons, assert that man cannot prove the existence of God. Some say that the only things we can know are material; since God by definition is infinite being—and therefore spiritual—it follows, they say, that we cannot know anything about him. Others claim that we do know something about God, but that our knowledge comes only from faith or revelation or tradition; these explicitly deny that man can rationally prove the existence of God.

What does the Catholic Church say about this question? You should know, first of all, that Catholicism has a high regard for nature—for everything that God created, including man, and especially man. Hence, the Church has great respect for man's intelligence and will. A basic principle of Catholic theology is that grace builds on nature, that is, nature (which is good) comes first; then grace is added to nature and perfects nature. This means that man's reason precedes faith. Logically, before man can have faith in God and believe in divine revelation, he must have at least some vague idea about the existence of God and thus the possibility of God speaking to him, i.e., divine revelation.

Accordingly, the Church clearly teaches that the existence of God can be proved, so that one can know for certain by the use of the natural light of reason that there is a supreme being. The Bible says the same thing (see Wis 13 and Rom 1:20). St. Paul summarizes the basic argument succinctly by stating that the invisible God is known from the visible things he created.

In the nineteenth century some Catholic intellectuals denied that the human mind can prove the existence of God. The Pope took action aganst them. Professor L. Bautain was required by Pope Gregory XVI in 1840 to subscribe to the following proposition: "The reasoning process can prove with certitude the existence of God and the infiniteness of his perfections" (*Denzinger* 1622). A. Bonnetty was required by Pius IX in 1855 to affirm: "The reasoning process can prove with certitude the existence of God, the spirituality of the soul, and the freedom of man" (*Denzinger* 1650).

Have you ever heard of the "Oath Against Modernism"? It was drawn up by Pope St. Pius X and published on September 1, 1910. The saintly Pope imposed that oath on all clergy to be advanced to major orders, on pastors, confessors, preachers, religious superiors, and on professors in philosophical and theological seminaries. The oath remained in effect until the Second Vatican Council. I can remember clearly that our seminary professors took the oath each year in the sanctuary of our chapel in a solemn ceremony; I was required to take it before my ordination to the priesthood in 1960. I don't know exactly when the requirement to take the oath was dropped. There may be some few seminaries where it is still required, but for the most part it is a dead letter.

With regard to proving God's existence, note what the oath says: "And first of all, I profess that God, the origin and end of all things, can be known with certainty by the natural light of reason from the created world (see Rom 1:20), that is, from the visible works of creation, as a cause from it effects, and that, therefore, his existence can also be demonstrated" (*Denzinger* 2145).

From the above, then, it is clear that the Church teaches that the human mind can prove the existence of God. The documents do not say that every person can do it—just that it can be done; this means that at least *some* can do it. Actually, this truth flows from what was said previously, namely, that God can be known with certainty by the natural light of reason from created things. Thus, the difference between "natural knowledge" and philosophical "proof" or "demonstration" is one of degree, not of kind. As St. Paul says, we all know something about the invisible God from his visible effects—the creatures all around us, from our own finiteness and limitations, from our conscience, from the beauty and transience of the world. To put all of this together into a structured proof requires some philosophical training and insight.

As St. Thomas Aquinas pointed out in his great *Summa* (*Summa Theologica*, I, q. 2, art. 3), the heart of the various arguments for the existence of God is *causality*, that is, we see the effects and argue from them to the cause. The effects usually employed in such arguments are such things as physical motion, contingency, degrees of perfection, order or finality in the universe, and the testimony of the human conscience. The conclusion of these arguments is: GOD EXISTS.

4

## TWO WAYS TO GOD

There are different ways to know the same object. I can know something about whales from personal experience, having seen them and touched them. I can also know about whales through the testimony of others—teachers, parents, reading and pictures. The latter method is based on human faith or trust. A large part of our ordinary knowledge of the world and human affairs is based on human faith or the testimony of others.

When we begin to reflect on our knowledge of God, we may be surprised to discover that here also there are two sources. I have already explained the Church's teaching that man can know for certain about the existence of God from the things he has created. That is often referred to as our natural knowledge of God.

God's existence, however, is not merely an object of natural rational knowledge; it is also an object of supernatural faith. This means that the affirmation of God's existence can be the result of a free gift of God's grace and faith in him. Knowledge of God through faith is on a higher level than natural knowledge; it is also much more certain and clear.

Consider that at the beginning of all the professions of faith stands the fundamental statement: "I believe in one God." The First Vatican Council teaches: "The holy, Catholic, apostolic Roman Church believes and professes that there is one true and living God, the creator and lord of heaven and earth" (*Denzinger* 1782). Looking at the question from another point of view, the denial of God's existence is condemned as heresy by the same Council (See *Denzinger* 1801).

According to Hebrews 11:6, faith in the existence of God is absolutely necessary for salvation: "Without faith it is impossible to please God; for he who wishes to approach God must believe that he is and that he is a rewarder to them that seek him." But the Council of Trent in the sixteenth century stated clearly that only supernatural faith in revelation is effective for eternal salvation (see *Denzinger* 798).

What all of this means is that a merely primitive natural knowledge of God, based on human investigation and reason alone, is not sufficient for a man to attain the end for which God created him. For, God has destined man for a *supernatural end*, that is, one that totally surpasses what his natural powers can ever attain. That supernatural end is the face to face vision of God which involves the fullness of personal knowledge and love. Here is found the perfection of the mutuality of love.

In addition to the testimony of God found in nature, in the course of human history God has revealed himself and his will to man through the prophets, and especially through his Son, Jesus Christ. So we also know about

God's existence through revelation. Revelation means that God speaks to man and makes known to him on a personal level what he expects of him. Thus, God revealed himself to Abraham, Moses, David, Isaiah, St. John the Baptist, and so forth.

Our natural knowledge of the existence of God is increased and strengthened by supernatural revelation. Also, since many human beings, for one reason or another, do not have the mental equipment to discover much about God, divine revelation makes certain knowledge about God accessible to all. Note what the First Vatican Council officially stated on this point: "It is owing to this divine revelation, assuredly, that even in the present condition of the human race, those religious truths which are by their nature accessible to human reason can easily be known by all men with solid certitude and with no trace of error" (*Denzinger* 1786). Thus, by his revelation God assists man to come to the knowledge of eternal things that he desperately needs for his eternal salvation—easily, with certainty and without error.

It is a disputed point among theologians whether one and the same person can at the same time have both knowledge and faith in the existence of God. St. Bonaventure and St. Albert the Great affirmed the possibility; St. Thomas Aquinas denied it. The problem is that knowledge rests on insight, while faith rests on the testimony of another. Thus, it is possible that the same truth can be known by one person and believed by another; this is a very common phenomenon in human affairs.

Aquinas seems to resolve the difficulty when he says that it is possible for the same person at the same time to have a natural knowledge of the existence of God as the originator of the natural order, and a supernatural faith in the existence of God as the source of the supernatural order. The reason for this is that faith embraces truths which are not contained in natural knowledge, so the object of the knowledge in each case is different (see *Summa Theologica*, II–II, q. 1, art. 5).

According to the teaching of the Church, therefore, we have both natural knowledge of God's existence from observation, and supernatural knowledge of his existence from faith.

5

# GOD IS KNOWN THROUGH CREATURES

There is a big difference between knowing *what* something is and knowing *that* it really exists. For example, I may have a clear idea of the Mobil flying red horse—a combination of horse and bird that is fiery red; but we all know that such an animal does not exist in reality outside the mind. Someone created it mentally and then gave it external artistic expression. The same process is used constantly by Walt Disney Productions and similar companies.

In the present series we are considering our knowledge of God. I have already explained some of the ways by which we come to know the existence of God, or that he exists. The next question to take up is: What kind of knowledge of God can we attain in this life?

In the nineteenth century there was much agitation over this problem. A number of Catholic thinkers, called "ontologists" (= knowledge of being), taught that, even in this life, we possess by nature an intuitive, immediate knowledge of God, and that in the light of this immediate knowledge of God we come to know created things. In other words, they said that we know God first and creatures second.

The theory of ontologism runs counter to the clear teaching of the Bible that we know God from his works and the things he has created (see Wis 13, Rom 1:20). Moreover, this doctrine is in direct opposition to the teaching of the Council of Vienne (1311–1312); it was also rejected by the Magisterium of the Church under Pius IX and Leo XIII. In 1861 the Vatican rejected the following proposition: "An immediate knowledge of God, which is at least habitual, is so essential to the human intellect that without that knowledge it can know nothing. It is the light of the intellect itself" (*Denzinger* 1659).

Ontologism is the product of philosophers who have lost contact with ordinary, everyday life. We all know from the daily experience of our own consciousness that we know very little about God. We know that he exists, but what he is in himself—what his inner nature is—escapes us.

Once again, in this matter as in so many other important facets of our lives, the holy Catholic Church comes to our aid. Popes, bishops and theologians have reflected on this problem for many centuries. Their conclusion, and the one that is supported by the Church, is that our natural knowledge of God during our life in this world is not an immediate, intuitive cognition, but a mediate, abstractive knowledge because it is attained through the knowledge of creatures. So we know creatures first; from them we can conclude to certain perfections in the Creator, since every effect has some resemblance to its cause.

In order to have immediate or intuitive knowledge of anything the mind must have direct access to it; it must come in direct contact with it. God, however, is wholly spiritual, while we are a unity of spirit and matter. The only things that we can know directly are material things, since we are dependent on our bodily senses for whatever reaches the mind. The five senses are the five "gateways" to the human intellect. Since God is not the object of our senses, it is clear that we cannot have direct or "immediate, intuitive" knowledge of him.

Let us now return to our original question: What kind of knowledge of God can we have in this life? It should be clear from the above that it must be, because of the nature of our mind and the nature of God, a knowledge that is mediate (i.e., deduced from creatures) and indirect. Catholic philosophers and theologians call such knowledge "analogical" or "analogous".

The word "analogy" (analogical, analogous) means "proportionate" or "similar". We can say, for example, that there is a certain analogy between a boy's toy car and a real automobile. There is a proportion there; there is both a similarity and a difference between the two.

The same relationship holds for our knowledge of God in this life. It is analogous. For, in our knowledge of God we apply concepts gained from created things to him on the basis of a certain similarity of them to him as their Creator and efficient cause. Thus, all perfections found in creatures must also be in their creator, though not necessarily in the same way.

Pure perfections of being which imply no imperfection and limitation in their concept can be attributed to God. Hence, we can say that God is truth, being, knowledge, love, goodness, wisdom. But a being that contains matter in its basic concept is thereby limited; this means that it cannot be attributed directly to God. God created the horse, but we cannot say that God is a horse; nor is he an elephant, or an eagle or a whale. Such creatures are in the mind of God but their qualities can be attributed to him only metaphorically. So we can know a great deal about God, but we cannot know his nature or essence directly. Our knowledge of God, therefore, in this life is analogical.

6

## OUR IMPERFECT BUT TRUE KNOWLEDGE OF GOD

We have been considering our knowledge of God. We have touched on the questions of his existence and his nature, that is, what he is in himself. We saw that, since our knowing is essentially dependent on the senses and a number of material factors, we cannot have immediate, intuitive knowledge of God. What knowledge we do have, therefore, must be mediate, abstractive and analogous.

A basic insight of Catholic teaching about God and our knowledge of him is that our knowledge must be "analogous". Analogy is proportion or similitude. It is based on the relation of effect to cause. Thus, there is a special relationship between a son and his father by reason of generation; so also there is a relationship and similarity between creatures and the Creator, since an effect must be pre-contained in the cause, at least in some way.

Since the sixth century Catholic theologians have repeatedly pointed out that our knowledge of God is arrived at by three different mental procedures: the three ways are called "affirmation", "negation" and "eminence". The way of *affirmation* (or causality) proceeds from the consideration that God is the efficient cause of all things, and that the efficient cause contains in itself every perfection which is in the effect. It follows logically from this that God possesses every true perfection found in creatures.

Perfections which do not involve limitation or imperfection can be attributed directly to God. In this category are such things as unity, truth, goodness, wisdom, justice, love, mercy, knowledge, life. Perfections of creatures which contain something finite or material in their concept cannot be attributed directly to God but only in a metaphorical sense. In this category are such things as earth, fire, water, horse, bird, sun, moon, man, and so forth.

In speaking about God we often say what he is not. This is called the way of *negation*. By negation we deny to God every imperfection and limitation which is found in created things. For us, it is much easier to say what God is not than it is to say what he is. Every negation of an imperfection in him implies an affirmation of some perfection. For example, when we say that God is infinite, we mean that he has no limits whatsoever; this is the equivalent to saying that he is the fullness of being. We often deny imperfection in God. Thus, we say that he is *im*mutable (not subject to change), *im*measurable (he cannot be measured), eternal (not subject to time).

The third way of speaking about God is the way of *eminence*. It is similar to the way of affirmation, but goes beyond it and says that God possesses the pure perfections of being in an infinitely higher manner than they are possessed by creatures.

These three ways of knowing God obviously complement one another. For, the attribution of a perfection to God, like life or love, requires the attribution of it to him eminently, and the negation of every imperfection.

We are treading here on very mysterious ground, which is an indication of how very limited our knowledge of God really is. Some of the Fathers of the Church, fully aware of this situation, have made the following statements or something like them: God is not being, not life, not light, not love, not good, not spirit, not wisdom, not mercy. Such statements might at first shock us, but their purpose is not to deny these perfections to God. They mean that these perfections do not belong to God in the same way as they do to creatures, for he possesses all of them in an infinitely higher manner.

It should be obvious from the above that our knowledge of God in this world is a composition of many inadequate concepts; therefore, it is necessarily limited and imperfect. Some of the ecumenical councils of the Church have declared that God's nature is "incomprehensible" to men (Fourth Lateran in 1215; Vatican I in 1870). We might also recall here what St. Paul says in Rom 11:33: "How incomprehensible are his judgments, and how unsearchable his ways!" When the Bible and the Church say that God is "incomprehensible", they do not mean that he cannot be known in any way; they mean that he cannot be known perfectly or exhaustively by a created mind.

St. Augustine said: "Our thinking about God is more true than our statements about Him, and His Being is more true than our thoughts about Him." Thus, only God possesses a comprehensive knowledge of himself, for only an infinite intellect can comprehend infinite being.

Even though our knowledge of God in this life is imperfect, it is still true as far as it goes. For, God truly possesses the perfections we attribute to him. Also, we are basically aware of the limited and analogous character of our knowledge of God and our statements about him.

7

## "BY YOUR LIGHT WE SEE THE LIGHT"

Up until now we have been talking about our *natural knowledge* of God. For the Catholic there is also another way to know God; it is called our *supernatural knowledge* of God. In this type of knowing the human mind is elevated by the grace of God to a new dimension so that it knows by divine faith. The source of the mind's knowledge is God's revelation in Jesus Christ. What is known or the object of this knowledge is the triune God himself, just as he is. Through the supernatural gift of faith we know mysteries hidden in God from all eternity and we know them with infallible certitude based on the authority of God himself.

The life of grace in this world is a preliminary stage and a preparation for the glory and happiness God has in store for us in the next life. Christian, supernatural faith on earth is in orientation to the immediate vision of God in heaven. In a certain sense, faith is a kind of anticipation of the vision of God in the world to come.

Knowledge acquired by faith, of course, remains imperfect, because the basic truths of Faith, such as the Trinity—three Persons in one God, are beyond the comprehension of human reason. In this regard we might reflect on those words of St. Paul: "We walk by faith and not by sight" (2 Cor 5:7); and, "Now we are seeing a dim reflection in a mirror; but then we shall be seeing face to face" (1 Cor 13:12).

If our knowledge of God in this life suffers from a lack of clarity, what can we say about the saints in heaven right now, such as St. Paul, St. Augustine, St. Teresa, St. Elizabeth Seton and all the rest? Are they any better off than we are? The Church teaches infallibly that the blessed in heaven possess an immediate intuitive knowledge of the divine essence, that is, of God as he is in himself. God shows himself to them nakedly, clearly and openly; they do not know him indirectly through reflections or images, but immediately as he is in himself. Describing that future state, St. John says, "We shall be like to him because we shall see him as he is" (1 Jn 3:2).

In describing this mystery Church documents and theologians often use the words "immediate vision" of God. God of course, since he is absolute Spirit and infinitely removed from matter, cannot be *seen* with the eyes of the body, either in this life or with the eyes of the glorified body after the resurrection. The words "vision" and "light" refer to understanding or seeing with the mind. Literally, they do not "see" God the way we look at a sunset or a beautiful painting; it is more like grasping with the mind, as when we understand that 2 plus 2 equals 4.

It is important to stress that the immediate vision of God in heaven exceeds the natural power of cognition of the human soul and is therefore *supernatural*. This is a truth of Faith that was solemnly proclaimed by the Council of Vienne in the year 1312. God is infinite; man is finite. In the beatific vision God shows himself to man in an embrace of love. Love by its very nature must be free; it cannot be demanded. The immediate vision of God is a gift that absolutely transcends the natural power of every created intellect, man and angel, and therefore it is wholly supernatural. The Bible says the same thing. In 1 Tim 6:16 we read that God lives "in inaccessible light: no man has seen him and no man is able to see him." At the end of his Prologue St. John says: "No one has ever seen God; it is the only Son, who is nearest to the Father's heart, who has made him known" (1:18).

The reason for man's inability to see God immediately is the weakness of his intellect. We can know things only according to the innate power of our mind. Anything that exists on a higher level than our mind is out of reach, so to speak. Since God is infinite and we are finite, he is out of reach. We find something similar in certain animals who are superior to man in one area. Thus, elephants are stronger than we are, dogs hear much better, eagles see farther and so forth. In order to see God, therefore, the mind must be elevated to the realm of God.

That elevation takes place in this life through divine grace and in the next life through what is called "the light of glory". The light of glory is necessary for man in order to attain to the immediate vision of God. St. Thomas Aquinas says that it consists in a lasting, supernatural perfecting (= habit) of the human power of cognition through which it is inwardly strengthened for the vital act of the immediate vision of God. The expression "light of glory", which first appears in the writings of St. Bonaventure and St. Thomas, is based on the interpretation of Psalm 35:9: "Yes, with you is the fountain of life, by your light we see the light."

Do the saints in heaven fully understand God or comprehend him? Both the Bible and Church documents repeat that God is incomprehensible to the created intellect, even after the light of glory has been granted to it by the grace of God. Since God is infinite being, his knowability is inexhaustible. This means that the saints in heaven can always know more about God for all eternity and still there will always remain more to know. It is rather simple: the finite mind cannot comprehend infinite being. The finite spirit, which is man, can understand the infinite essence of God in a finite manner only. We can sum up the above by saying: The blessed in heaven know the infinite God, but they do not know him infinitely.

8

## WHAT'S IN A NAME?

So far I have explained Catholic teaching on the two kinds of knowledge we have of God—natural and supernatural. By reason we can learn much about God from the things he has made. By faith and revelation we attain to a higher knowledge of God as he is in himself.

In order to speak about things we know, we have to put names on them. The purpose of a name is to signify what a thing is. Thus, we can speak in general about "trees", or more specifically about "oak trees" and so forth. As we all know, names are important.

The answer to the question, "What's in a name?" is that it attempts to convey to another, at least in some way, the nature of the thing named. With that in mind, the question I will try to answer in this short essay is: Of the many names applied to God, which one best signifies his inner nature or what he is?

Since the nature of God cannot be adequately conceived by the human mind, it cannot be expressed in a perfectly corresponding name. For this reason some of the Fathers referred to God as "unnameable", "inexpressible" and "nameless". The Old Testament applies many names to God, but most of these refer to his activities in the created world and not to his inner nature. Thus the Old Testament refers to him as The Strong One, The Lord of Hosts, Judge, All Highest, The Holy One.

The real name of the true God in the Bible is "Yahweh". It is derived linguistically from the Hebrew word "to be" and means: HE WHO IS. According to the book of Exodus, this is the name that God gave himself in his conversation with Moses from the burning bush:

> Then Moses said to God, "I am to go, then, to the sons of Israel and say to them, 'The God of your fathers has sent me to you.' But if they ask me what his name is, what am I to tell them?" And God said to Moses, "I Am who I Am. This", he added, "is what you must say to the sons of Israel: 'I Am has sent me to you.'" And God also said to Moses, "You are to say to the sons of Israel: 'Yahweh, the God of your fathers, the God of Abraham, the God of Isaac, and the God of Jacob, has sent me to you.' This is my name for all time; by this name I shall be invoked for all generations to come" (Ex 3:13–15).

Therefore, in the Hebrew Bible "Yahweh" or what is called the tetragrammaton (YHWH) is the proper name of God. And it means "I AM" or "HE WHO IS". This name was considered so sacred by later generations that, out of reverence, it was not even pronounced. Wherever it occurred in the Bible the word "Adonai" was pronounced instead (meaning "Lord").

The New Testament takes over some of the names of God used in the Old Testament. But Jesus transformed the name "Father", which occurs only in a few places in the Old Testament, into the principal name for God in Christian revelation. We see this clearly in the beautiful prayer that Jesus gave to us, the "Our Father".

In more philosophical-theological terms, what is the basic determining factor of the divine essence to which the names God, Yahweh and Father refer? It must be the fundamental characteristic of the Deity which both distinguishes it from all created things and which is the source of all the other divine perfections.

In answer to this question some have replied that it is God's infinity or his spirituality. The opinion best founded on the Bible, and most often affirmed by the Fathers and outstanding theologians like St. Bernard and St. Thomas Aquinas, is that what is most characteristic of God is that he is absolute being or subsistent being (*ipsum esse subsistens*). In God there is no difference or distinction between his essence and his existence. His essence is to be, to exist, to live. All created things, such as horses, birds, stars, suns, moons and men, have received their being or existence from another. God has his being of himself and from himself and through himself by virtue of his own essence. He did not cause himself or create himself, *because he always is*.

As pointed out above, God revealed his proper name to Moses as: "I AM WHO I AM." God is therefore purely and simply being. Later biblical texts express the absolute being of God by referring to Yahweh as the First and the Last, the Alpha and the Omega, the Beginning and the End. St. Bernard said: "One may call God good or great or blessed or wise or whatever one will, but all is contained in the phrase 'He is.' "

The notion of "subsistent being" distinguishes God fundamentally from all created things which only participate in being, but which are not being itself. The being of created things is a limited being, and in comparison with the being of God it is more non-being than being. So the name that best captures the nature of God is: HE WHO IS.

9

GOD'S ABSOLUTE PERFECTION

We have seen that God is absolute and subsistent being. The Old Testament calls him "Yahweh" or "He who is". In our English translations we find the name "Lord". The question I want to pursue next concerns the various attributes or properties or perfections of God. We say that God is good, loving, almighty, wise, infinite, eternal and so forth. Because God is the fullness of being, and absolute spirit, we do not grasp him entirely in one concept; this is due to the fact that we can know only what we perceive through our senses—and God cannot be perceived by the senses. It is also due to the weakness and limitation of our intellect.

Accordingly, since we know that God created all things, that he is their source and originator, and since we know that every effect must be pre-contained in its cause in some way (otherwise the cause could not produce it), it follows that the many and varied perfections or attributes of creatures must exist also in the Creator —at least in some way.

Even though we attribute many different perfections to God—love, goodness, wisdom, mercy, power—we should not conclude that there is multiplicity in God. Since God is absolute being, he is simple; that means that there is no composition of any kind in God. We are composed of body and soul, mind and emotions and so forth, but God is perfectly simple. For this reason the various perfections we attribute to God are really identical among themselves and they are also identical with the divine being. Because of the weakness of our minds, our knowledge of God is derived from reflection on God's effects, that is, the creatures he produced. Here we discover many different perfections. We attribute them all to God under different names, but they all signify the same reality. The various names, however, are not synonymous because they signify the divine being under many and different aspects.

We are not able to consider all of God's attributes, but we will treat some of them. First, let us reflect a moment on his perfection and infinity. It is an article of Catholic faith, taught by the First Vatican Council, that God is absolutely perfect. What is meant by "perfection"? That is "perfect" in which nothing is lacking which, according to its nature, it should possess. Thus, we speak of a perfect diamond, a perfect shot in golf, a perfect pass in football, a perfect score in an examination. Jesus tells us in Matthew 5:48, "You must therefore be perfect just as your heavenly Father is perfect."

The Fathers of the Church base the absolute perfection of God on his infinite fullness of being. St. John Damascene said: "The Divine Essence is perfect, is in no way deficient in goodness, in wisdom and in power. It is without beginning, without end, eternal, boundless—in short, absolutely perfect." St. Thomas Aquinas said that, since God is the First Cause of all created things, he contains in himself all the perfections found in creatures. Obviously, however, they do not pre-exist in him in the same way in which they exist in creatures. As I mentioned before, the pure perfections of being, such as love, truth, wisdom, knowledge, exist in him formally but in a higher way than they exist in creatures; mixed perfection, that is, those that include matter in their concept such as elephant or rose, do not exist in God formally but only in the sense that he knows them and can create them. Thus, we cannot say truthfully that God *is* an elephant, but we can say that he is love.

Vatican Council I says of God that in reason and will and in every perfection he is infinite. We read in Psalm 147:5, "Our Lord is great, all-powerful, of infinite understanding." What does the word "infinite" mean? The infinite is that which has no limits, no end, no boundaries. The infinite can be distinguished according to potentiality and according to actuality. The potentially infinite, like numbers, can be multiplied infinitely, but the reality is finite and limited. God's being or reality is actually infinite.

The Fathers of the Church call God infinite and uncircumscribed. St. Gregory of Nyssa said that God is "in every way without limit". The absolute infinity of God is based on the fact he is absolute being. Since God did not originate from another being or was not caused by another, and since he is not composed of parts in any way, there is absolutely no basis in him for a limitation of his being. Therefore, the Church says with her full authority that God is actually infinite in every perfection.

## 10

## THERE IS ONLY ONE GOD

In the last essay we saw what the Church means when she says that God is actually infinite in every perfection. One of the functions of the Teaching Authority of the Church is to preserve and defend the true notion of the nature of God and his special attributes or characteristics. During the past few centuries atheists and atheistic humanists of many different colors have attacked the Christian idea of God from every angle. They have tried to erase from men's minds the very idea of a transcendent God who is above this material world and totally independent of it.

To meet this challenge Vatican Council I in 1870 issued a unique profession of faith which is just as valid today as it was over a hundred years ago:

> The holy, Catholic, apostolic and Roman Church believes and professes that there is one true and living God, the Creator and Lord of heaven and earth. He is almighty, eternal, beyond measure, incomprehensible, and infinite in intellect, will and in every perfection.
>
> Since he is one unique spiritual substance, entirely simple and unchangeable, he must be declared really and essentially distinct from the world, perfectly happy in himself and by his very nature, and inexpressibly exalted over all things that exist or can be conceived other than himself (*Denzinger* 1782).

This useful profession of faith gives us a checklist of faith in God without whose existence the other truths of Christianity have no meaning.

Now I want to concentrate on two of God's attributes from the above list, namely, that he is *simple* and *one*.

In the course of history men have fashioned many different ideas about the supreme being, some quite accurate and others quite foolish. A rather common and foolish idea is that God is a body. Some think that he is identified with the material world, while others have thought of him as the sun or as a man or as an animal.

The great Catholic tradition, relying on the Bible, the insights of the Fathers of the Church and the saints, has steadfastly denied that God is a body. The reason for this is that a body is necessarily composed of various parts. A mountain or a rock can be broken into smaller pieces. A man is composed of head, trunk, arms, legs, etc. Anything that is composed must be put together by another. But God is the absolute being and the first cause, as we saw before. Therefore it follows that there is no composition in God, for example, of body and soul, of bodily members, of substance and accidents, of essence and existence, of nature and person, of power and action, of passivity and activity. Another way of saying this is to assert that God is *absolutely simple*—and this is the traditional language of the Church.

In the revelation of the New Testament God's being is often identified with his attributes. Thus Jesus said of himself, "I am the way, the truth and the life" (Jn 14:6), and we read in 1 John 4:8, "God is charity."

We conclude from the above, then, that God is a pure spirit, that is, he is neither a body nor a composition of body and spirit. It is true that the Old Testament often represents God in a visible human form by the use of anthropomorphisms (for example, God walks and talks with Adam in the Garden of Eden). This is a human way of speaking. The Old Testament also affirms God's spirituality and transcendence by describing him as the Creator of all things and supreme over the world. Jesus says explicitly in John 4:24 that "God is spirit."

To Catholics it is obvious that *there is only one God*. But millions of human beings believe and have believed in a multiplicity of gods. A belief in two or more gods is directly opposed to both Catholic faith and reason. What do we profess to believe in the Creed at Mass every Sunday? "We believe in *one* God. . . ." The most basic doctrine of the whole Bible, both Old Testament and New Testament, is that there is only one God. Thus, we read in Deuteronomy 6:4, "Hear O Israel: The Lord our God is one Lord." St. Paul, the Apostle of the Gentiles, was constantly opposing all forms of idol worship and polytheism. Thus, he wrote in 1 Corinthians 8:4, "We know that idols do not really exist in the world and that there is no god but the One."

St. Thomas shows in his writings that a multiplicity of gods is an impossibility. God, he says, is the supreme being. If we suppose that there are two of them, then each would have to be distinguished from the other by some characteristic. This means that one would have something the other did not, and vice versa. On this supposition neither would be the supreme being or the fullness of all being. So there can be one God only. The oneness of God also follows from his absolute simplicity and the infinity of his perfection—points which we have already shown.

11

# GOD TELLS NOTHING BUT THE TRUTH

In this essay I wish to offer for your consideration a few ideas about truth in God or God's truth. Truth is a good of the mind that we are seeking constantly. We all know what it is, but many find it difficult to explain to others what is meant by "truth". It is one of those basic experiences of human life that is so simple that it is hard to find words to explain.

Let us begin by noting that there are different levels or degrees of truth. Thus, there is 1) the truth of things, 2) the truth of thought, and 3) the truth of speech and action.

The "truth of things" consists in the agreement of a thing with its idea. It is the reality of a thing insofar as it is knowable. Thus, a perfect circle is a true circle. Often when we experience something that measures up perfectly to our idea of what it should be, we say that it is "true". We might say, for example, that our automobile is a "true car". In this sense, the one God we considered previously is also the true God. Vatican Council I said explicitly that there is only one true God. The God of Christians is the true God because he alone fully realizes the idea of God. As the Creator of all things, God gives all of them both their being and their knowability. Thus every created thing is the realization of a divine idea. By knowing them we get some idea of God himself.

The divine ideas, which created things mirror in some way, are identified with the divine nature which God knows perfectly. Therefore God is not only infinite being but also infinite truth. He knows all things.

Many readers may not be familiar with the above line of thought—it presupposes a certain familiarity with philosophy. The kind of truth we are more familiar with is the "truth of thought" which consists in the agreement of thought with things. Objective, extra-mental reality is the measure here. If I experience a horse and so come to know what a horse is, and if I then see a four-legged animal that corresponds to that idea and recognize it as such, I have a true idea.

Some intellects are more powerful than others because they exist on a higher level. Accordingly, angels have a power of intelligence higher than that of men because they are not confined to a body and so are not dependent on the five senses for their information. God possesses an infinite power of cognition according to the teaching of Vatican I. Also, we read in Psalm 147:5, "Our Lord is great, all-powerful, of infinite understanding." Since in God the knowing subject, the object of knowledge and the act of knowledge are identical, it follows that God is absolute truth. By knowing himself perfectly he thereby knows all things. Thus, every possibility of error is excluded from God. Accordingly, Vatican I again said that God "can neither deceive nor be deceived".

Truth of speech and action can also be called "God's moral truth". Moral truth comprehends truthfulness or veracity which is the agreement of speech with thought, and fidelity which is the agreement of action with speech.

God is truthful—in his revelation he speaks only the truth. Vatican Council I said that it is impossible for God to deceive anyone. By faith we accept what God has told us as absolutely true. The Bible bears witness to the truthfulness of God and the impossibility of his being a liar. Jesus says in John 8:26, "The one who sent me is truthful, and what I have learnt from him I declare to the world." Paul writes in his letter to Titus 1:2 that God "does not lie". Again, in Hebrews 6:18 we read that "it is impossible for God to lie." Thus, since God is absolute truth or truth itself, he cannot lie or deceive.

In addition to being truthful, God is also faithful. One is faithful who carries out in deed what has been promised with words. In many places the Bible extols the fidelity of the Lord. "The Lord is faithful in all his works" (Ps 145:13). "We may be unfaithful, but he is always faithful, for he cannot disown his own self" (2 Tim 2:13). While affirming the end of the world and his own Second Coming our Lord said, "Heaven and earth will pass away, but my words will never pass away" (Mt 24:35). So just as God is completely truthful so also is he absolutely faithful.

One of my favorite texts from the New Testament is: "If you make my word your home you will indeed be my disciples, and you will know the truth and the truth will make you free"(Jn 8:32). To know Jesus and his word is to be made free. But Jesus does not merely speak the truth—he is the truth, as he tells us in John 14:6, "I am the way, the truth and the life." Therefore, those who believe in Jesus and live according to his Word are in possession of God's truth. And he himself tells us that they are the ones who are really free in this life.

12

## NO ONE IS GOOD BUT GOD ALONE

We often hear it said, or even say ourselves, that "God is good." Some utter, almost as an ejaculation, "Good God!" It is also worth noting that, in the English language, the word "good" is formed by adding an extra "o" to "God".

The point I want to make here—the thought I want to leave with you to mull over—is that God is absolute, perfect goodness, both in himself and in relation to others. Some people deny this because of the obvious evil in this world. The main reason for this is that they cannot see or explain how a good God could permit so much evil. But that is another problem which we will consider later. At present I will try to clarify the notion of "good" and give reasons for saying that God is absolutely good.

I would like to impress upon you that the idea of "good" is very closely associated with "being" and "perfection". Thus, a thing is good to the extent that it exists or is perfect. For example, a car that does well all that a car is supposed to do, is often referred to as "a good car". If it will not start, or if it breaks down often, it is said to be "a bad car" or a "lemon". In a similar way, we say that tools, plants, animals, machines and so forth are "good" if they live up to expectations. Therefore, the more perfect or "well made" they are, the better they are.

The Church teaches in Vatican Council I that God is infinite in every perfection. Since goodness is a perfection of being, it follows that God is infinitely or absolutely good. The same Council also teaches that in the act of creation God communicates his goodness to creatures. This means that all created things are good only insofar as they participate in the goodness of God. Thus, we read in Genesis 1:31, "God saw all he had made, and indeed it was very good." In the same vein, the Psalmist sings in 136:1, "Give thanks to the Lord, for he is good, his love is everlasting!" Likewise, Our Lord says in the Gospels that "No one is good but God alone" (Mk 10:18; Lk 18:19). By this statement Jesus means that only God is perfectly good of himself, while others are good by participating in the goodness of God.

In addition to the objective goodness of God, there is also the matter of his moral goodness or his holiness. What do we mean by "moral goodness"? It means freedom from sin in any of its forms. And the ultimate basis of "freedom from sin" resides in the agreement of the will with the objective moral norm. Therefore, God is absolute moral goodness and holiness because he is absolutely perfect and also because the divine will is identical with the divine being which is the supreme moral norm. Accordingly, the absolute sinlessness of God is not merely a factual state of being free from sin; it also means that it is intrinsically impossible for God to commit sin.

One of the major themes of the Bible is that God is the Holy One. This is especially true in the writings of Isaiah the prophet. In 6:3 he stresses the absolute holiness of the Lord by repetition: "Holy, holy, holy is the Lord of hosts. His glory fills the whole earth." Also, we read in Psalm 22:3, "Yet, Holy One, you who make your home in the praises of Israel, in you our fathers put their trust." The four animals before the throne of God, as described in the book of Revelation 4:8, day and night never stop singing, "Holy, holy, holy is the Lord God, the Almighty, he was, he is and he is to come."

The word "holy" expresses God's sublimity over all worldliness and sinfulness, as the comparison between his holiness and the sinfulness of the prophets shows (Is 6:5–7). The infinite chasm between the holiness of God and the sinfulness of man is brought out by the expression used by Isaiah and the Psalms, "the Holy One of Israel" (see Is 1:4; Ps 71:22).

All things are good to the extent that they exist. Since they are creatures and therefore receive their being from God, it is obvious that their goodness also comes from God who is the supreme good. St. Thomas Aquinas is noted for stressing "desirability" as the peculiar aspect of the good. He said that "the good is what all men desire". If you reflect on your own desires for a few moments, you will soon notice that you desire that which is good—either for yourself or for another. Wishing evil on another is called "hatred", but the one who hates another is motivated by the desire of some (at least apparent) good for himself, namely, the punishment or removal of the other person.

The good is what all men desire—it is what you and I desire. We perceive the good as perfective of our own lives; through the good we achieve our fulfillment as persons. One of the basic problems in this life is choosing the right goods at the right time and in the right way. Since God is the supreme good, only he can satisfy us completely. St. Augustine said, "Our hearts were made for Thee, O Lord, and they will not rest till they rest in Thee."

# 13

# "BEFORE ABRAHAM EVER WAS, I AM"

In order to understand better who God is, we have been considering some of his attributes or characteristics. We learn about these from Holy Scripture, from the official teaching of the Church and from the insights of philosophers and theologians. I would ask you to reflect for a few moments on two qualities of God that indicate how different he is from us. Let us consider his immutability (unchangeability) and his eternity.

A thing is changeable if it goes from one condition to another. We experience each day in our body and in our mind that we are changeable. We grow older each day. We sleep and then awake. We are happy and sad, vigorous and tired, hungry and full. In fact, everything we experience is changeable. When a thing changes it loses one perfection and gains another; or it goes from a state of not having something to having it, for example, when we learn mathematics we go from a state of not knowing math to knowing it.

What about God? Does he change too? The Church teaches as a dogma of faith that God is absolutely unchangeable or immutable. Vatican Council I said that God is "entirely simple and unchangeable" (*Denzinger* 1782).

The notion of God's immutability appears often in the Bible. Thus, we read in James 1:17, "with him there is no such thing as alteration, no shadow of a change." The Psalmist says in 102:27, "yourself, you never change, and your years are unending." And the prophet Malachi indicates that the divine name itself contains the basis of God's absolute immutability when he says, "For I am the Lord and I do not change" (3:6).

St. Thomas Aquinas sees the basis of God's absolute immutability in his absolute being, simplicity and infinite perfection—attributes of God that we have considered in previous essays. The point of Thomas' argument is that all change involves losing something and gaining something. Since God is the fullness of all being and perfection, he cannot lose or gain. It follows therefore that God is absolutely unchangeable.

You might wonder at this point whether or not God changes when he creates the world, or when he creates each new human soul at the moment of conception. The answer is that God himself does not change, but there is a new realization in time of the eternal resolve of his divine will to create. The change is not in God but in the effect which, since it is in the created world, is temporal and changeable.

The immutability of God leads naturally to the consideration of his eternity. First of all, what is meant by the word "eternal"? Eternity is a type of duration in being without beginning and without end, without sooner and later; it is a "permanent now". In other words, the essence of eternity is the *absolute lack of succession* of moments. It is very difficult for us to grasp the correct notion of eternity, since we are totally caught up in *time* which is a succession of one moment after another.

The Bible and the Church teach that God is eternal. The Fourth Lateran Council in 1215 and Vatican I in 1870 teach that God is absolutely eternal. The notion also occurs in the famous "Athanasian Creed" (*Quicumque*, D 39) from the fifth or sixth century: "The Father is eternal, the Son is eternal, and the Holy Spirit is eternal. Nevertheless, there are not three eternal beings, but one eternal Being."

Holy Scripture bears witness to the divine eternity. Thus, Psalm 90:2 says that God has no beginning or end: "Before the mountains were born, before the earth or the world came to birth, you were God from eternity and for ever." We noted that "lack of succession" is essential to eternity. This notion is seen in Jesus' remarkable words, "I tell you most solemnly, before Abraham ever was, I AM" (Jn 8:58).

When we say that God is eternal, therefore, we are saying that he always existed, that he will always exist, that he has no beginning or end. To say that God is eternal is to deny that he is subject to *time* in any way. Whatever is in time is changeable, and we saw above that God is totally unchangeable. Hence, he is eternal. St. Augustine said that God's eternity is a constant present: "The eternity of God is his Essence itself, which has nothing changeable in it. In it there is nothing past, as if it were no longer; and nothing future, as if it had not yet been. In it there is only 'is', that is, the present."

## 14

## "WHERE COULD I FLEE FROM YOUR PRESENCE?"

When we were little children we learned that God is everywhere, that he sees us all the time, whether in the daylight or in the darkness. We learned, and we have since come to experience, that no place is hidden from the sight of God—not even the innermost depths of our own conscience. Thus, we know that God sees not only our external, visible actions, but also that he sees into our hearts and reads our thoughts and desires. In this essay I propose to offer you a few reflections on the omnipresence or ubiquity of God.

We have already considered the fact that God is infinite in all perfections. He is absolute being, truth, goodness;

he is unchangeable and eternal. Another question can be raised here about God: How is he related to the world and to the whole material universe? Some have said that after he created the world he more or less turned it loose and forgot about it (Deists); others said that angels are subject to his power but not material things (Manichaeans).

The Bible praises God as being present everywhere, but it also insists that he is not limited by the world. Our existence is limited to a certain place and for a certain time. God is not limited either by space or by time. This means then that he cannot be measured or "packaged". Nothing can contain God because he is infinite, that is, he exists in a way that is wholly different from our way of existence. Thus, King Solomon says in his prayer, "If heaven and the heaven of heavens cannot contain you, how much less this house which I have built" (1 Kings 8:27). And the Lord says through the prophet Isaiah, "Heaven is my throne, and the earth my footstool" (66:1).

That God is everywhere present in created space has been taught by the Church from the beginning; in fact, it is a dogma of the Catholic faith. Holy Scripture teaches the same thing often in picturesque language. Consider the following passage from Psalm 139:7–10: "Where could I go to escape your spirit? Where could I flee from your presence? If I climb the heavens, you are there, there too, if I lie in Sheol. If I flew to the point of sunrise or westward across the sea, your hand would still be guiding me, your right hand holding me." In his famous sermon in Athens St. Paul said, "In fact he is not far from any of us, since it is in him that we live, and move and exist" (Acts 17:27–28).

It is obvious that the Bible proclaims the omnipresence of God, almost, one might say, on every page. But it is one thing to state the fact, and another thing to understand how it is so. I think that the clearest explanation was given by St. Thomas Aquinas in his great *Summa Theologiae* I, q. 8. Thomas argues that every cause must be in contact with or be present to its effect. That is a basic principle of all reality. God, however, is infinite being and the Creator of all finite beings. Since God is the source of the being of all creatures, it is not sufficient that he give them their being initially; he must also constantly keep them in existence, or conserve them. Otherwise they would drop back into nothingness. This means that wherever finite things exist, whether they are spiritual or material, God must be present to them keeping them in existence. It is obvious then that, since every "place" is composed of finite beings that are kept in existence by the power of God, God must be in every place, that is, he is everywhere (i.e., omnipresent or ubiquitous). Therefore, God sees and knows everything. As the Psalmist says, "Where could I flee from your presence?"

Another thought worth considering is that, even though God is everywhere present, he is not present to each creature in the same way. For example, his presence in purely material things like rocks is not the same as his presence to intellectual or spiritual creatures like angels and men. Also, we must distinguish between his presence in the order of nature, and his presence in the supernatural order of divine grace. For, by his grace he communicates himself to the spiritual creature in an act of personal love.

In the natural order God keeps us in existence and

knows all we do. In the order of grace he is present to us also in different ways. Consider, for example, how Our Lord is present in the Blessed Sacrament of the altar in a very special way. He is present in the soul of the baptized, justified person in a different way. He is also present in the Christian community, in the proclamation of the Word of God, in the administration of the sacraments of the Church.

It is important to remember that God is everywhere —nothing is hidden from his view. But at the same time we must not forget that God is not simply identified with the world; in fact, he is infinitely elevated above it so that it is, in the words of Isaiah, his "footstool".

## 15

## GOD AND INTELLIGENCE

"God knows all things." We have heard that since we were children and most of us have probably repeated it ourselves many times. In our own conscience we know that God sees everything we do, that he reads the innermost secrets of our heart.

One might wonder whether or not there is intelligence in God. This question has been raised more than once in the course of human history. Actually, the answer is rather simple, at least for the Christian believer. For, according to the relation of cause and effect, the effect must be pre-contained in the cause, at least in some way. Thus, since intelligence exists in man, and man was created by God, it follows that intelligence must be in God. In fact, God must be infinite intelligence since, as we have seen before, he is infinite in every perfection and the power of intelligence is one of the highest perfections of being.

That God is intelligent is obvious also from the order, beauty and finality of everything we see in the created universe. To see this point all we have to do is reflect for a few moments on the complexity and order in the functioning of our own bodies. We did not produce ourselves; much of the current science is directed to trying to understand the marvels of the human body and mind.

When thinking about God we might ask ourselves: Does God know things the same way I do? The correct answer is that he does know; in fact, he knows all things perfectly, but he does not acquire his knowledge the same way I do. My knowledge comes from the outside; what I know are things and realities outside of myself. Gradually, through a growing knowledge of other things, I also come to some knowledge of myself. With God it is just the other way around. His being and knowledge are absolutely identified. This means that he perfectly comprehends himself, and by knowing himself he knows all other things outside of himself. For, as we have seen, he is the Creator of all things; he is the source of the existence of everything distinct from himself. For us, things have to exist before we can know them; for God, things exist because he knows them.

For those of a more philosophical bent, we might point out that the basis for all knowing is immateriality.

Thus, the reason we can know past and present and also anticipate the future, which does not yet exist, is that the human mind is immaterial; this means that it transcends the limits of both time and space. St. Thomas argues that the degree of the power of knowing is determined by the degree of immateriality. Thus, animals have sense knowledge, but they are totally limited by time and space; you may have noted that they have no knowledge of the future. Since man is a unity of spirit and body, he attains the lowest level of immateriality. Angels are spirits without bodies, so they have a higher degree of intelligence than man. God is pure being and pure intelligence. This means that there is no multiplicity of ideas in God; so he knows everything in one single simple act. Since man's mind is united to matter in the body, it is dependent on matter and material things for its knowledge. This gives rise to multiplicity in our manner of knowing and in our ideas. Since God is absolutely immaterial, he knows all things in one act.

Since God's power of knowing is infinite, it follows that he knows himself perfectly. Another way of saying the same thing is to say that he comprehends himself. This truth is asserted in many passages in the Bible. Thus, we read in 1 Samuel 2:3, "The Lord is an all-knowing God and his is the weighing of deeds." St. Paul says in 1 Corinthians 2:10, "The Spirit searches the depths of everything, even the depths of God."

The divine intellect is identified with the divine essence. Therefore, by knowing himself God knows all other things; he knows himself perfectly and everything to which his divine power extends. So God is not determined by the things he has created; he determines them. God knows extra-divine things in his own essence, since he is both the exemplary and the efficient cause not only of all real things but also of all possible things.

Since God knows himself perfectly he has exhaustive knowledge of his own creative causality and everything that flows from it. Thus, we read in the Holy Bible in 1 John 1:5, "God is light and in him there is no darkness."

# 16

# PRAYER AND GOD'S KNOWLEDGE OF THE FUTURE

We have already considered some of the differences between God's knowledge and our knowledge. To the believer it is obvious that God's knowledge is infinitely perfect, while ours is very limited. Also, what we know is determined by reality outside of ourselves; we take in knowledge similar to the way in which a bucket receives water that is poured into it. With God it is the other way around: finite things exist because he knows them.

As Christians we believe that God knows all things. Since his knowledge is identified with himself, what God knows directly and primarily is himself. By knowing himself perfectly he knows all the possible ways in which created things can reflect various aspects of the divine being. This means that created or extra-divine things are only the secondary object of the divine knowledge. As I pointed out before, it is important to note that God's way of knowing is very different from the human way of knowing.

There are different categories of extra-divine things that God knows. For example, he knows all merely possible things; he also knows everything that is real and those things that are conditionally future. By the latter is meant those things that would have happened if I had made different choices in the past. Thus, we often say, "If I had stayed home, such and such would not have happened." God knows all those possibilities too.

It is a teaching of the Catholic faith that God is "limitless in intellect" and in every perfection. We read in the book of Esther that God knows all things (4:17). Because God comprehends his own nature and his own infinite power, he thereby knows every possible way in which it could be imitated by some creature. It follows then that God knows everything that is possible.

In addition to his knowledge of the possibles, God also knows everything that is real. This includes everything past, present and future. Actually, for God there is no such thing as past, present and future. For him, everything is present. The reason for this is that he does not exist in time. Time results from material bodies in motion and God is wholly immaterial. Also, time involves successive moments; in God there are no successive moments. He exists in eternity where all reality is simultaneously present.

The Bible asserts the universality of God's knowledge in many places. "All things were known to him before they were created, and are still, now that they are finished" (Sir 23:29). God's providence, which extends to every detail, presupposes infinite knowledge: "He decides the number of the stars and gives each of them a name" (Ps 147:4). "I know all the birds of the air" (Ps 50:11). His knowledge extends also to men's hearts: "God . . . can read everyone's heart" (Acts 15:8).

By our personal observation we know that some things happen in nature by necessity, while other things are the result of free choices on the part of persons. Both the Bible and the Church tell us that God knows with absolute certainty the future free actions of his rational creatures. The reason is that there is no such thing as the future to God: all choices and actions are present. Accordingly, we read in Hebrews 4:13, "No created thing can hide from him; everything is uncovered and open to the eyes of the one to whom we must give account of ourselves." And Jesus is described in the Gospels as knowing the thoughts of others and also what they were going to do. "Jesus knew from the beginning who they were that did not believe and who he was that would betray him" (Jn 6:65).

To some it has seemed that God's knowledge of future free acts is contrary to human freedom. One might ask: "If God knows what I am going to do, doesn't that mean that I am determined to do it?" Again, the answer is that nothing is future to God; he sees everything, the whole course of history, as present. Just because God knows what I am going to do tomorrow it does not follow that I am forced to do it.

Some people, when they reflect on God's certain knowledge of the future, worry about the value of prayer. "Why should I pray," one might ask, "if God already knows what is going to happen?" It is true that God knows what is going to happen, but choices flow from the human will and God can influence the will by his grace. Also, there is the possibility of miracles and cures. The Lord has told us to pray—to ask God for what we need. A good example is the *Our Father*. God deals with us as free beings. St. Thomas Aquinas gives the best answer to this problem when he says that God, in his providence, grants us his gifts and his grace on condition that we ask him. If we ask, he may grant our request. Jesus himself said, "Ask and you shall receive; seek and you shall find; knock and it shall be opened to you." So there is no conflict between prayer and God's certain knowledge of the future.

## 17

## GOD'S WILL AND THE PROBLEM OF EVIL

Wherever there is knowing there is also willing. The reason is that the knower tends towards or desires the known. That tendency towards the known good is what we mean by the power of "will".

Since God knows all things, it follows that he also wills them, at least in some way. So there is in God what we mean by "will". Frequently we acknowledge the fact of God's holy will in everyday speech, as when we say "God willing" or "please God". Each time we pray the *Our Father* we say, "Thy will be done on earth as it is in heaven."

The First Vatican Council teaches that God's will is

infinite. When talking about God's will we must be careful not to think of it in purely human terms. Our will is finite, weak and changeable. God's will is infinite, all-good and immutable. Since will is a perfection of God, it is actually identified with the divine essence, just like his intellect. For, in God everything is one except for the relations which constitute the three divine Persons.

What does God will? First of all, he wills and loves himself, because he knows himself as absolute and perfect goodness. And goodness is the object of will. Vatican Council I teaches that God loves himself necessarily. This has been the common teaching of Catholic theologians at least since the time of St. Thomas Aquinas.

The secondary objects of God's will and love are all those things that are external to him, that is, all creatures. It is an article of Catholic faith that God created all of them from nothing by a free act of his will. God was under no coercion or necessity to create anything. We read in the book of Wisdom, "You love all that exists, you hold nothing of what you have made in abhorrence, for had you hated anything, you would not have formed it" (Wis 11:25).

God loves creatures insofar as they participate in a finite manner in his perfections and have their final end in him. Also, God's love for creatures is benevolent, that is, God loves them not with a receiving, but with a bestowing and, therefore, with a most unselfish love. This means that God's love is not motivated by the creature's goodness, but is itself the cause of that goodness. As St. John puts it, "In this is charity, not as though we had loved God but because he first loved us" (1 Jn 4:10).

Granted the goodness of the divine will, a serious problem arises as soon as we try to understand and explain the reality of evil in the world. For, if God is the Creator of all things, and there is so much evil in the world, it seems to follow that God wills evil along with the good. I do not pretend to be able to solve all the difficulties involved in this important question, but I can give some indications of how the Church and great Catholic thinkers approach it.

First, it is important to make a distinction between physical evil and moral evil. By physical evil I mean all forms of suffering, illness and death. The Bible tells us that God did not make death: "God did not make death; neither does he take pleasure in the destruction of the living. For he created all things that they might be" (Wis 1:13). According to Genesis death, at least for men and women, is the result of sin. However, God does will certain physical evils at least indirectly, that is, as a means to a higher end of the physical order. Thus, plants absorb minerals; animals eat plants in order to live; higher animals eat lower forms; man uses all of them to further his own good and perfection.

By "moral evil" I mean sin which is a deliberate offense against the will of God. According to the Bible and the constant teaching of the Church, one cannot say that God wills moral evil or sin either directly or indirectly. In the sixteenth century the Council of Trent condemned the doctrine of John Calvin who said that "God performs the evil works just as he performs the good" (*Denzinger* 816). And the Psalmist sings: "You are not a God who is pleased with wickedness, you have no room for the wicked. . . . You hate all evil men, liars you destroy" (Ps 5:4–6).

There is no doubt that the total explanation of evil remains hidden from us; there is something very mysterious about it. Christian tradition says that God does not will evil but *merely permits it*. The reason is that God created man free and respects his freedom. Could God eliminate all sin from the world? Yes he could, but to accomplish that he would have to take man's freedom away from him. In God's providence it is a greater good to have freedom with some sin than to have no freedom and no sin. Faced with this problem, St. Augustine said that God is so wise and so powerful that he can bring good out of evil. Sometimes we see evidence of that in our own lives when sinners, suddenly afflicted with cancer or faced with death, turn to God and place themselves entirely in his hands.

18

# FOR GOD EVERYTHING IS POSSIBLE

There are sharp differences between the Catholic view of the world and the many non-Christian or pagan views. The one I wish to concentrate on here is the relationship of God's will, or his freedom, to the world. The immediate question is this: Did God freely create the world? or would it be more accurate to say that the universe is a necessary emanation from the divine abundant goodness?

You can easily find many evolutionists and materialists who say that matter has always existed and that God, however you want to think of him, is identified with the material world. For them, everything happens necessarily; there is no such thing as freedom or free will either in man or in God. Connected with these views you often find attitudes of *fatalism* and *despair*. For them, man is a plaything of fate, so the only thing he can do is suffer and die and pass into nothingness. For those who cannot take it any longer, suicide is considered a good way out.

Such views are directly opposed to the truly Christian view of God, man and the world, as expressed in the Bible and as taught by the Catholic Church for almost 2000 years. Because God is infinite being, as we have seen, he is totally sufficient to himself. Since he is also perfectly one, it follows that his knowing and willing are identified with his being. We may ask here: Does God love himself? The answer is Yes, he loves himself infinitely and necessarily. Because his will and his being are the same, he must love himself.

With regard to extra-divine things, however, God is perfectly free. We are all familiar with the account of creation in the book of Genesis. When we say that God is free with regard to his creatures, we mean that he was under no necessity whatsoever to create the world. Since he is absolutely sufficient to himself, he has no need of creatures. Then why did he create them? In order to manifest his goodness and to communicate it to others. For this reason the First Vatican Council said in 1870 that God created the world "by a completely free decision". Thus we read in Psalm 135:6, "Whatsoever the Lord pleased he has done, in heaven, on earth, in the sea, and in all the depths." St. Paul also says on this point, while writing to the Ephesians, "And it is in him (Christ) that we were claimed as God's own, chosen from the beginning, under the predetermined plan of the one who guides all things as he decides by his own will" (1:11).

As in all other things, God's will is not exactly like our human wills. He does not lack anything; we lack almost everything. Thus, since evil is contrary to his very being, God is not free to choose between good and evil. We can choose between good and evil because of our limitation and our ignorance. The possibility of choosing evil is not the essence of freedom; it is merely a sign of freedom, but it indicates an imperfect kind of freedom. God is free either to act or not to act, and he is free to choose between various goods. Thus he is free to create this world or that world, to create this person or that person, and so forth.

Closely related to God's freedom is his omnipotence. In proclaiming our Christian faith in the Creed we say, "We believe in one God, the Father, the Almighty. . . ." The words "almighty" and "omnipotent" mean the same thing. Power is the active principle which carries into effect what the mind knows and the will commands. When we say that God is almighty or omnipotent, we mean that he has the power to do everything he may wish to do, that is, all that is real and possible.

The Bible often asserts the omnipotence of God. Thus the angel Gabriel said to Mary, "nothing is impossible to God" (Lk 1:37). And Jesus said to his disciples, "for God everything is possible" (Mt 19:26).

The power of any thing is determined by the level of its being. A horse is more powerful than a worm, and a man through his intelligence is more powerful than an animal (we lock them up in zoos so we can go and look at them). God's omnipotence flows from his infinite being. Since God's power is identical with his essence, it does not extend to anything that contradicts the essence and attributes of God. Thus God cannot change; he cannot lie; he can make nothing that has happened not to have happened; he cannot do anything that is contradictory in itself. Accordingly, God cannot square a circle; he cannot create man free and then take his freedom away from him; he cannot make two and two equal five. So God can do everything that is intrinsically possible. We do not know positively all that that implies, but we can say with the angel Gabriel, "nothing is impossible to God."

19

## GOD IS INFINITELY JUST

In our day there is intense concern about the virtue of justice. We hear much more about that virtue than we do about the corresponding virtue of mercy. The Bible and our Christian faith tell us that God is infinitely just and infinitely merciful. Perhaps in certain concrete instances we do not know how to reconcile God's justice and mercy, but still we know by faith that God possesses both of these virtues perfectly. In this essay I will discuss God's justice; there will follow a consideration of his infinite mercy.

One of the problems in this age of instant communications is that words are used rapidly, often with no clear definition of their meaning. For example, the word "justice" can be understood in many different ways. When the Church says that God is infinitely just, she understands that in a very precise way. Let us try to see what that is.

What is justice? It is defined by philosophers and theologians as *the constant will to give to each person what is due to him*. This means that justice is a virtue—and a virtue that inheres in the will. So acts of justice in the concrete world flow from the virtue of justice in the will.

It is an article of Catholic faith that God is infinitely just. His justice is frequently extolled in Holy Scripture. Thus we read in Psalm 11:7, "The Lord is just and has loved justice," and in Psalm 119:137, "You are just, O Lord, and your judgment is just."

Justice is always related to some law or norm to which a person is bound in some way. Thus, God commands us to love our neighbor. Lying, stealing, killing and adultery, for example, are opposed to the love of neighbor and so are unjust. Since God is the Creator and Lord of the universe, there is no norm of justice which transcends him; he is himself the supreme norm, since he is the first origin of everything.

The justice which regulates the proper relationship between one individual and another is called "commutative justice". This type of justice governs the relationships between buyers and sellers, husbands and wives, and so forth. It implies a certain equality. Because the creature is totally dependent on the Creator, he cannot impose any obligation on God by performing some kind of service. Hence, in the proper sense this kind of justice cannot be applied to God.

The justice which regulates the legal relationship of the community to the individual is called "distributive justice". This type of justice can be applied to God in the proper sense. The reason is that God, having freely decided to create the world, by his wisdom and goodness must give to his creatures everything that they need in order to achieve the goals he has set for them. For, it would be contrary to his own nature, which is infinite goodness, to ordain creatures to a certain end and then not give them the means to attain that end.

As the supreme judge who is no respecter of persons (see Rom 2:11), God manifests his distributive justice by rewarding the good (remunerative justice) and punishing the wicked (vindictive justice).

The punishment ordained by God for the sinner is not merely a means of improvement and warning, but is also retribution for the insult offered to God and reparation for the moral order disturbed by sin. Thus the Lord says in Deuteronomy 32:41, "I will take up the cause of Right, I will give my foes as good again, I will repay those who hate me." St. Paul refers to the same truth when he writes, "For it is written 'revenge is mine, I will repay,' says the Lord" (Rom 12:19).

Suffering in this life often brings the sinner to repentance and so to eternal life. The punishment of hell, however, on account of its eternal duration for the damned, is vindictive only. In this regard, the somber words of Our Lord deserve long meditation: "Go away from me, with your curse upon you, to the eternal fire prepared for the devil and his angels" (Mt 25:41). For the sinners who deliberately choose hell there is no escape, no turning back.

We should not stress the vindictive character of God's justice to the point of saying that he owes it to himself to require full atonement for every sin. Since he is the

Supreme Lord who is not subject to any higher authority, he also has the right to pardon sinners. Thus, God is free to forgive the sins of the repentant sinner without requiring a corresponding atonement, and even without any atonement.

Because of our ignorance and weakness we cannot always see how God's infinite justice can be reconciled with his mercy. It is not easy for us to see how God's infinite mercy can be reconciled with the eternal damnation of a mortal sinner. But as Catholic Christians we believe that God is both just and merciful. Next we will consider his mercy and try to relate it to his justice.

20

# HIS MERCY IS EVERLASTING

Having considered God's justice, we will now reflect on his mercy. The Bible praises God more often for his mercy and love than it does for any other attribute. And it is the official teaching of the Catholic Church that God is infinite in his mercy.

What do we mean by "mercy"? Mercy is the readiness to relieve the defect or misery of another out of a sense of loving good will. God's mercy is his benevolent goodness insofar as it removes the tribulation of creatures, especially the tribulation of sin. In human beings mercy is usually accompanied by feelings of sympathy and compassion. God, as infinite being, cannot suffer and so is not subject to any passions as we are, but he exercises mercy by removing some of the defects of his creatures. He does this by coming to their aid, by healing their infirmities, by offering his grace.

The best current example of mercy that I know of is Mother Teresa of Calcutta and her Missionary Sisters of Charity. With little consideration for themselves, they spend their whole lives relieving the miseries of others. That is mercy. What Mother Teresa does is a faint reflected image of the mercy of God. We might say it is God's mercy shining through her and her Sisters.

The Psalmist sings that the mercy of God is manifest in all of his works. The reason for this is the insight that the totality of goodness in every creature is the result of a free gift from God. Even God's justice is based on his mercy, for nothing is due to any creature except insofar as it has been credited to that creature in advance by God himself. And Psalm 136 sings over and over again that the mercy or love of God is "everlasting".

The Psalmist constantly cries out, "Have pity on me, O Lord!" (Ps 4:2; 6:3; 9:14; 25:16). The liberation of Israel from Egypt is described as an act of divine mercy (Ex 3:7ff.). Out of his mercy God chastises his people (Jer 31:20) so that they will abandon their evil ways and be converted (Is 55:7). In short, both the Psalms and the Prophets abound in passages that praise the mercy of the Lord.

Mercy is the constant readiness to come to the aid of those in distress. In Jesus of Nazareth, as a result of the Incarnation, God himself assumed our mortal flesh and took to himself our infirmities. So he knows from his own experience about our weakness and misery. (See Lk 1:78; Jn 3:16; Heb 2:17).

Just as mercy is an essential quality of God—both as Creator and Savior of sinful mankind, so also is mercy necessary for all those who follow the way of God and strive to imitate Jesus Christ. He said in the Sermon on the Mount: "Blessed are the merciful, for they shall receive mercy" (Mt 5:7). So there is a special blessing attached to the practice of mercy toward others. In the "Our Father" we ask God to "forgive us our trespasses as we forgive those who trespass against us." Thus every time we pray the "Our Father" we beg God to be merciful to us to the same degree as we show mercy toward others.

We should remember those words of St. John: the love of God is found only in those who show mercy to others (1 Jn 3:17). According to Luke 6:36 we are to be merciful as our "Father is merciful". Simply stated, this is an essential condition for entering the kingdom of heaven.

In God mercy and justice are wonderfully interrelated. In one sense his justice is based on his mercy or love, because giving each person his due presupposes that the person already exists in a certain way. And whatever each one of us is to begin with is the result of God's infinite goodness. The Psalmist reflects this idea when he says, "All the ways of the Lord are mercy and truth for those who keep his covenant and his decrees" (25:10).

God's distributive justice, that is, the way he deals with each individual, is rooted in his mercy. The ultimate reason why God gives his creatures gifts and supernatural grace, and then rewards their good works, is his love and mercy. The rewarding of the good and the punishing of the wicked is not merely a work of divine justice; it is also a work of divine mercy, since he rewards beyond merits (see Mt 19:29) and punishes less than is deserved.

On the other hand, the forgiveness of sin is not merely a work of mercy; it is also a work of justice, since God demands from the sinner both repentance and atonement. The harmoniously beautiful association of God's mercy and justice is brilliantly shown in the sacrificial death of Jesus Christ on the Cross. St. John expresses this truth in 3:16, "God loved the world so much that he gave his only Son, so that everyone who believes in him may not be lost but may have eternal life."

# PART II

# TRINITY

I

# THE MOST HOLY TRINITY

There is an immense difference between God and any creature, no matter how noble and elevated. When we ponder over the infinity, power and majesty of God Almighty we are tempted to say that, in comparison with him, man is nothing. In one sense that is true, but at the same time we must not forget that creatures, even though weak and changeable, have an inherent goodness and dignity conferred on them by a beautiful, loving God.

For Catholic Christians who want to know more about God it is not sufficient to stop the investigation once the existence and nature of the divinity have been established. The reason for this is that we know, through the revelation of Jesus Christ, that in God there is a loving community of Persons—Father, Son and Holy Spirit. Thus, we must next consider the mystery of the Holy Trinity which is the central or basic mystery of the Christian faith.

The Catholic faith can be summarized as faith in the Trinity—Father, Son and Holy Spirit. Entrance into the Church is brought about for all of us by our Baptism "in the name of the Father, and of the Son, and of the Holy Spirit". Each Mass is started by invoking the three divine Persons. When we walk into any Catholic church we bless ourselves with holy water in the name of the Father, Son and Holy Spirit.

Most adult Catholics will have noted that the prayers of the liturgy are, for the most part, directed to the Father, through the intercession of the Son, and in the unity of the Holy Spirit.

When the Church speaks about the Holy Trinity she uses precise words whose meaning has been determined by various Councils and documents in the course of history. What I propose to do now is to explain the fundamentals, as clearly as I can, of the Catholic belief and doctrine relative to the Most Holy Trinity. I will try to clarify for the reader some of the basic words which always recur in discussions about the Trinity, such as Person, nature, procession, relation and mission.

It has been a source of surprise to me for many years that so few sermons are preached on the Trinity and that so little is written about it in Catholic publications. (The only sermons on the subject that I can recall are the ones I have preached.) This is certainly odd, especially if one considers that belief in the Trinity is absolutely fundamental to the whole Christian religion. Why do preachers and writers shy away from the subject? I am not sure of the answer to that question. It may be due to the complexity of the subject and to the fact that speculative theology over the centuries used some difficult philosophical concepts and arguments in the attempt to clarify the mystery. Of course, what we are dealing with here is the revelation given by Jesus to his Church (and stated in the New Testament) that there are three Persons in God—Father, Son and Holy Spirit.

We all know that there are a number of mysteries at the heart of the Christian faith. The most basic of all mysteries is that of the Holy Trinity. By definition, a "mystery" is a reality or truth that is hidden. Hidden from what? It is hidden from the knowledge and understanding of the human mind.

In Catholic theology there are three absolute mysteries. They are the Trinity, the Incarnation and divine grace. By an "absolute mystery" is meant one that totally surpasses the capacity of the created mind. Thus, the Trinity is an absolute mystery in the sense that even the blessed in heaven, including the holy angels, do not completely understand it. Nor will they ever totally grasp it for all eternity. It simply exceeds the power of the created intelligence.

Just because the Trinity is an absolute mystery, it does not follow that we cannot know *anything* about it. As a matter of fact, we know quite a bit about the Trinity. It is a mystery, however, that can be known only as the result of revelation. The human mind, reflecting on the beauty and power of nature, could never arrive at the tri-personal inner life of God. Thus, it is only through the revelation of Jesus Christ that we know about the intimate relations between Father, Son and Holy Spirit. In the Old Testament there are a few hints about this truth; in the New Testament it is fully revealed by God's only begotten Son, our Lord and Savior Jesus Christ. In the course of these essays I will attempt to spell out this truth more in detail.

Most Catholics have heard about the great theological writings of St. Thomas Aquinas. Someone has said that his major work, the *Summa Theologica*, is a meditation on the Holy Trinity—how all things proceed from the Father and return to him.

2

# GOD IS BOTH ONE AND THREE

Belief in the Trinity is central and crucial to our Catholic faith. Since it is so important, we should try to achieve a better understanding of it.

What the Church believes and proclaims is that in God there are three distinct Persons—the Father, the Son and the Holy Spirit. Each of the three Persons possesses the one same divine essence or being. So we can say that there is one God in three distinct Persons.

The terms "essence, nature, substance" refer to the divine "being", which is the same for the Father, the Son and the Holy Spirit. The word "Person" refers to the three owners or bearers of the divine being. Thus, what is one in God is the divine being, while what is three in God is the divine Persons. You will note that we are not contradicting ourselves by saying that one is three, since "one" refers to the substance of God, while "three" refers to the Persons. In a future essay I will give a more detailed explanation of the precise meaning of these theological terms.

For now let it suffice to say that we Catholics believe in the Most Holy Trinity, that is, we believe that there are three Persons in only one God. This profound truth was hinted at in the Old Testament and clearly revealed by Jesus in the New Testament. Before his Ascension into heaven, Jesus sent out his disciples into the whole world and told them to baptize all nations "in the name of the Father, and of the Son, and of the Holy Spirit" (Mt 28:19). The oldest doctrinal formulation of the Church's belief in the Trinity is the Apostle's Creed which served as the basis of catechetical instruction and as a baptismal confession of faith since the second century. It is based on the trinitarian formula of Baptism which was just quoted.

The best guide to the Church's belief in the Trinity is found in the Creed. In addition to the Apostle's Creed, there is also the Creed that we say together at each Sunday Mass. This Creed comes from the fourth century and is an excellent summary of our faith: "We believe in one God, the Father, the Almighty, maker of heaven and earth. . . . We believe in one Lord, Jesus Christ, the only Son of God, eternally begotten of the Father, God from God, Light from Light, true God from true God, begotten, not made, one in Being with the Father. . . . We believe in the Holy Spirit, the Lord, the giver of life, who proceeds from the Father and the Son." This profession of faith proclaims that there is only one God, but also that there are three Persons in the one God.

According to Catholic belief God is both one and three. If we ask, "What is one in God?", the answer is that he is one in being or substance. If we ask, "What is three in God?", the answer is that there are three "Persons" subsisting in one God.

Some Christian thinkers of the past, confusing what is meant by substance and person, have held that the three divine Persons are distinct individuals like three human beings; thus, they concluded that there are really three gods who work together in some sort of moral unity. Many contemporary Christians apparently have similar views about God. This opinion has often been condemned by the Church Councils of the past.

Others have held that God is one Person and one Being, only that he is given three different names in Scripture. These thinkers said that the names, "Father, Son, Holy Spirit", refer to just one Person in the Godhead, namely, the Father. Thus, in their view, the names "Jesus" and "Holy Spirit" are merely other ways of speaking of God the Father. This view has also been condemned as heretical often by the Church. If it were true, it would mean that the Father is Jesus and that the Father died on the Cross on Calvary; it would mean that the Father did not send his Son to redeem us, but "sent" himself; it would make many of Jesus' statements about the Father and the Holy Spirit either false or unintelligible.

The Fourth Lateran Council in 1215 enunciated the Catholic belief in the Trinity very clearly:

> We firmly believe and profess without qualification that there is only one true God, eternal, immense, unchangeable, incomprehensible, omnipotent, and indescribable, the Father, the Son, and the Holy Spirit: three persons but one essence and a substance or nature that is wholly simple. The Father is from no one; the Son is from the Father only; and the Holy Spirit is from both the Father and the Son equally. God has no beginning; he always is and always will be; the Father is the progenitor, the Son is the begotten, the Holy Spirit is proceeding; they are all one substance, equally great, equally all-powerful, equally eter-

nal; they are the one and only principle of all things—Creator of all things visible and invisible.

Some of these statements are difficult to understand. As we proceed I will try to explain them one by one.

# 3

# THE FATHERHOOD OF GOD

God's revelation to man about himself and his own inner life proceeded in stages. There is a steady progression through the Old Testament until the fullness of revelation is made by Jesus, the only-begotten Son of the Father, in the New Testament.

There are some hints about the inner trinitarian life of God in the Old Testament. For example, there is the remarkable passage in Genesis 1:26 where God says, "Let us make man in our own image and likeness." This is most likely the magisterial "we", such as the Pope uses in some of his talks, but still many of the Fathers of the Church considered it a hint.

In the wisdom books, especially Proverbs 8 and Wisdom 7 and 8, divine wisdom is personified; it has proceeded from God from all eternity and cooperates in the creation of the world. In the light of the full revelation of the New Testament, one may well see in these passages a pointer to the divine personality of the Word of God who is God's image or wisdom.

The Old Testament frequently mentions the "spirit of God". What is meant is not a divine Person but a power proceeding from God which gives life, bestows strength and illuminates. In the light of the New Testament many of these passages (see Ps 104:30; Is 11:2; Wis 1:7) were referred by the liturgy and the Fathers of the Church to the Person of the Holy Spirit.

In human language the word "father" designates a relationship that exists between a man and his offspring. A father is one who has begotten a child; he is an originator, a transmitter or a source of life. The term can be used in its proper sense of the relationship of father to son; it can also be used in an improper, derived or metaphorical sense of someone who causes or produces something else. Thus, inventors are often called the fathers of their inventions.

The Bible often speaks of the fatherhood of God in the metaphorical sense. For example, we read in Deuteronomy 32:6, "Is this the return you make to Yahweh? O foolish, unwise people! Is not this your father, who gave you being, who made you, by whom you subsist?" God is the "father" of created things, especially of man, by reason of his creation, preservation in being and providence. Through our redemption and elevation to the state of grace, God is our Father in the spiritual and supernatural order. Thus, Jesus says, "Your light must shine in the sight of men, so that, seeing your good works, they may give the praise to your Father in heaven" (Mt 5:16). And again, "You must therefore be perfect just as your heavenly Father is perfect" (Mt 5:48). God is our Father, yes, but not in the proper sense of generating us so that we are of the same nature as he. In that sense, God has only one Son, the eternally only-begotten Son who is Jesus, our Lord and Savior.

New Testament revelation teaches that there is in God a fatherhood in the proper sense which belongs to the first Person only. Jesus' relation to the Father is unique and exclusive. When he speaks of the Father in heaven he says either "my Father" or "your Father", but never "our Father". The reason is that his relationship to the Father is very different from that of the disciples or of us. When Jesus teaches the disciples to pray the "Our Father", he tells them how to talk to God. But this is not Jesus' prayer for himself; when he prays he says simply "Father" or "My Father".

Other statements of Jesus, which assert his identity with the Father, prove also that his sonship and the fatherhood of God are to be understood in the proper sense of originator or principle. This identity is brought out in terms of knowledge in the important passage in Matthew 11:27: "Everything has been entrusted to me by my Father; and no one knows the Son except the Father, just as no one knows the Father except the Son and those to whom the Son chooses to reveal him." The same idea is expressed even more clearly in John 10:30: "I and the Father are one", and in John 5:26: "For the Father, who is the source of life, has made the Son the source of life."

St. John calls Jesus the only-begotten Son of God: "And we saw his glory, the glory as it were of the only-begotten of the Father" (1:14). St. Paul says that "God did not spare his own Son" (Rom 8:32). Jesus' enemies clearly understood that he claimed equality with

God because God is his Father; for this reason they plotted to put him to death. St. John says that the Jews were "even more intent on killing him, because, not content with breaking the sabbath, he spoke of God as his own Father, and so made himself God's equal" (5:18).

Since Jesus is the Son of the Father, he has the same divine nature that the Father has. So he is equal to the Father in all things, except in the very special characteristic of being Father.

4

# THE SON AND THE HOLY SPIRIT

We have already considered the fatherhood of God. For most of us it is not difficult to think of God the Father in personal terms. Over the centuries a number of heresies have denied or questioned that the Son and the Holy Spirit are distinct Persons. Others have asserted that they are indeed distinct persons, but that they are not divine Persons. According to these heretics the Son and the Holy Spirit are creatures of the Father.

What do you think about this? Are the Son (Jesus) and the Holy Spirit really divine Persons, distinct from the Father, but subsisting in the same divine essence? Are you able to pray convincingly to all three Persons, Father, Son and Holy Spirit, and to be always aware that you are praying to the one God?

What is the teaching of the Catholic Church on this matter? The Church teaches that there are three Persons in one God. This means that the Son and the Holy Spirit are Persons distinct from the Father, but that they are God just as he is God, since they are united in the same divine essence or being.

For Scriptural confirmation of this belief we turn first to St. John's Gospel. In the Prologue (1:1–18), John writes about the Word of God: "In the beginning was the Word: the Word was with God and the Word was God." According to John, the Word is not an attribute or power of God; the Word is a Person. This is indicated by stating that "the Word was *with* God." He also says that the Word "came to his own domain" (v. 11) and that "the Word became flesh." Both of these expressions can refer only to a Person, not to some divine attribute.

The Word is not only God, but is also a different Person from God the Father. This follows from the fact that the Word was "with God", and also from the identification of the Word with the only-begotten Son of the Father in verse 14: "We saw his glory, the glory that is his as the only Son of the Father."

John also says, "And the Word was God." This means that the Word is *divine*. The true deity of the Word is also implied by certain divine attributes given to him. John ascribes creation to him: "Through him all things came to be" (v. 3), and eternity: "In the beginning was the Word." In addition to St. John's Prologue, many other passages from the Bible could be cited to prove the personality and divinity of the Son of God, who is Jesus the Lord.

It is also an essential part of Catholic belief that the Holy Spirit is a real Person and not just another name for some of the activities of God the Father. This is shown by the trinitarian formula of Baptism, ". . . in the name of the Father, and of the Son and of the Holy Spirit" (Mt 28:19). In this very important text the Holy Spirit is ranked on the same level with the Father and the Son. The Holy Spirit is also given the personal title of "Paraclete", which means helper, or representative or advocate (Jn 14:16, 26; 15:26). In addition, personal qualities are ascribed to the Holy Spirit, such as teaching the truth (Jn 16:13) and installing bishops (Acts 20:28).

The Holy Spirit is not just a real Person; he is also *distinct* from the Father and the Son. This is proved by the trinitarian formula of Baptism cited above. It is also indicated by the appearance of the Holy Spirit at the Baptism of Jesus in the Jordan under the special symbol of a dove (Mt 3:16–17). Moreover, in his discourse at the Last Supper Jesus distinguishes between the Holy Spirit, as one who is sent, and the Father and the Son who send him (Jn 14:16,26; 15:26).

The Holy Spirit is also a *divine* Person, co-equal with God the Father and God the Son. For proof of this we again turn to the trinitarian formula of Baptism in which the Holy Spirit is mentioned as equal to the Father and to the Son who are truly God. Another proof of the divinity of the Holy Spirit is the fact that the New Testament ascribed divine attributes to him. The Holy Spirit possesses the fullness of knowledge: he teaches all truth (Jn 16:13) and searches the innermost secrets of God (1 Cor 2:10). The divine power of the Holy Spirit is revealed in the Incarnation of the Son of God (Lk 1:35; Mt 1:20) and in the miracle of Pentecost (Acts 2:2–4).

The biblical teaching of three Persons in God can be reconciled with the same biblical doctrine of the oneness of the divine nature only if the three divine Persons subsist in one single nature or being. The numerical unity of the divine being is indicated in the trinitarian formulas (esp. Mt 28:19). Jesus explicitly declared the numerical unity of his divine nature with that of the Father when he said in John 10:30, "The Father and I are one."

In order to express the numerical unity of the essence of God, the Church says that the Son and the Holy Spirit are "one in being with the Father" or "consubstantial with the Father".

A final word. I realize that some of the ideas and expressions connected with the Catholic doctrine of the Holy Trinity are difficult to understand. As a help, I would suggest that my readers slowly recite and pray the Creed we profess at Sunday Mass. It would also help to look up the passages in Scripture mentioned and meditate on them.

5

# THE ORIGIN OF THE SON AND THE HOLY SPIRIT

We know from the New Testament, from the Creed and from the teaching of the Church that there are three Persons in one God, Father, Son and Holy Spirit. Two questions that naturally occur to a Christian who begins to reflect on the mystery of the Holy Trinity are: 1) Where did the three Persons come from? and 2) How are the three related to each other?

The first question touches on the *origin* of the three Persons. According to the Bible, the Father is the source or the originator of all things. All things outside of God, that is, the world and the universe and all finite things were created by the Father. We profess our belief in that every Sunday when we pray the Nicene Creed. But what about the internal divine life? Can we say that the Father created the Son and the Holy Spirit? No, we cannot say that, for we have already seen in a previous essay that the Son and the Holy Spirit are co-equal to the Father in divinity.

If the Father did not *create* the Son and the Holy Spirit, then where did they come from? The answer to this most difficult question is to be sought in Holy Scripture, Tradition and the faith of the Church. The Church teaches in this matter that in God there are two internal divine *processions*. By "procession" is meant the origin of one from another. A procession can be either external or internal, depending on whether the term of the procession goes outside the principle from which it proceeds or remains within it. Thus, creatures proceed from God by external procession, but the Son and the Holy Spirit proceed by an immanent act of the Most Holy Trinity, since they belong to the internal life of God. An "internal divine procession", therefore, refers to the origin of one divine Person from another through the communication of the numerically one divine essence.

The Catholic Creeds teach us that there are two internal divine processions: the generation of the Son and the procession of the Holy Spirit. Consider, for example, what we profess in the Creed at Sunday Mass: "We believe in one Lord, Jesus Christ, the only Son of God, eternally *begotten* of the Father"; and, "We believe in the Holy Spirit . . . who *proceeds* from the Father and the Son." What does this mean? It means that from all eternity the Father generates the Son, and the Father and the Son "breathe forth" the Holy Spirit. Thus there are two internal divine processions which give rise to three divine Persons.

Why is the word "procession" (= "coming forth") used for the internal divine activity? The reason is that Jesus himself used this expression according to St. John's Gospel. Thus, in 8:42 Jesus says, "I *proceeded* from God." In 15:26 he says that he is going to send to the Church the Holy Spirit, "the Spirit of Truth who *proceeds* from the Father". Accordingly, we learn from these and similar passages that there are two internal processions in God.

It is a dogma of Catholic faith that the second divine Person proceeds from the first divine Person by an act of generation and therefore is related to him as Son to a Father. The Nicene Creed says that Jesus Christ is "the only-begotten Son of God, born of the Father before all time". The Athanasian Creed of the fifth century says: "The Son is not made or created, but he is generated by the Father alone."

According to the New Testament the first and second Persons stand to each other in the relationship of a true fatherhood and sonship. The characteristic biblical name for the first Person is "Father", while that of the second Person is "Son". Jesus refers to the Father as "my own Father" (Jn 5:18). Jesus is spoken of as God's "own Son" (Rom 8:32), as "the only Son of the Father" (Jn 1:14), as "my beloved Son" (Mt 3:17). Thus, God's only-begotten Son is distinguished from the adopted children of God, which is what we are. Jesus, however, is the natural Son of God. The eternal generation of the Son from the Father is clearly expressed in Psalm 2:7 and Hebrews 1:5, "You are my Son; this day I have begotten you."

From the Creed at Mass we know that the Holy Spirit "proceeds from the Father and the Son". The Athanasian Creed states: "The Holy Spirit is not made nor created nor generated, but proceeds from the Father and the Son." It is also a matter of Catholic faith that the Holy Spirit proceeds from the Father and the Son "as from one principle". Thus, there are not two principles of the Holy Spirit, but only one. Thus, the Second Council of Lyons in 1274 proclaimed: "We confess that the Holy Spirit proceeds eternally from the Father and the Son, not as from two principles, but as from one."

By divine revelation and the explicit teaching of the Church, therefore, we know that in the inner life of God there are two processions and three divine Persons.

# 6

# JESUS IS THE PERFECT IMAGE OF THE FATHER

It is clear from the New Testament and from the Creed of the Church that the first Person in the Trinity is the Father, and that the second Person is the Son. Since God is a pure spirit, that is, since he does not have a body and is completely independent of matter, it should be obvious that there is no sexuality in God. But if there is no sex in God, we might ask, then why are the first two Persons in the Trinity called "Father" and "Son"? Among human beings, the father-son relationship is based on the sexual act of procreation.

The first two Persons are called "Father" and "Son" because there is a generative activity in God which has some similarities to generation among human beings and animals. "Generation" is defined as the origin of a living being from another living being, both having the same nature. Thus, oak trees produce oak trees, monkeys produce monkeys, and men produce men. You will note that the relationship in these examples is between material beings. But in all true generation there is a similarity between the origin or source and what is produced.

In the preceding chapter we considered the two "processions" in God—that of the Son and that of the Holy Spirit. At present we will confine our attention to the procession of the Son from the Father. We said that the Father "generates" the Son. How does the Father generate the Son if there is no sex in God? The Church, aided by her best theologians, teaches that *the Father generates the Son by an act of intellect*. I know that this is a hard point to grasp, so I will try my best to explain what is meant simply and clearly.

We all know that Jesus—the Son of God, the second Person of the Blessed Trinity—is called the "Word" in the New Testament. For example, we read in John 1:1, "In the beginning was the Word, and the Word was with God, and the Word was God." Now a word is produced only by an intellect or a mind. The external word, whether vocal or written, is a symbol of an idea in the mind, or what is called a "mental word". If there were no mental word, there would be no vocal word. Thus, animals utter grunts, groans, cries, and so forth, but they do not produce words. The reason is that, since they do not have a mind or intellect, they cannot produce an internal idea to which the word refers.

We have already seen that there are two processions in God. In a spiritual being like God there are only two internal activities—knowing and willing. If there is to be a difference between the two processions, and there is, then one must be according to intellect and the other according to will. Basing its teaching on the Bible and Tradition, the Church says that the Son is generated by the Father by an act of intellect.

It is possible to use the word "generation" for this activity because generation means the production of one living being from another, both having the same nature. Intellectual activity is similar to generation because the mind produces an idea which is the image or representation of the thing known. Thus, in order to know an oak tree some representation of the oak tree must be in my mind; if it were not, then I could not know an oak tree.

As we have seen, God is simple—he has no parts. This means that he is identified with his knowing and willing. God therefore knows himself perfectly, that is, he has a perfect idea or image of himself. That perfect idea or image is the second Person of the Blessed Trinity. He has the same nature as the Father and is equal to the Father. On this point the *Roman Catechism* (III, 9) teaches: "For just as our spirit, knowing itself, produces a picture of itself which theologians have called a 'word', so God also, insofar as the human can be compared with the divine, knowing himself, generates the Eternal Word. Thus the generation of the Son from the Father is to be conceived purely as an intellectual generation or as an act of intellect."

Generation and intellection both involve likeness. Since the Son of God is the perfect image of the Father, we are entitled to say that he is generated by an act of intellect. In the New Testament the second Person of the Trinity is called the "Word of God" (see Jn 1). Since a word is produced by an intellect, this name indicates that the Son is the product of the knowledge of the Father. Also, the second Person is called "the wisdom of God" (1 Cor 1:24). The personal name "Wisdom" indicates that the Son is generated by an act of cognition of the Father. The expressions "image of the invisible God" (Col 1:15) and "perfect copy of the substance of God" (Heb 1:3) indicate that the generation of the Son takes place through that activity of the Father which tends to produce a likeness of himself, namely, through the activity of knowing.

Therefore, since the Bible refers to the Son by using "Word", "Wisdom" and "Image", and since these terms are related to cognition, we are justified in saying that the Father generates the Son by an act of knowledge.

# 7

# THE ORIGIN OF THE HOLY SPIRIT

We have been considering the origin of the Son and the Holy Spirit from the Father. We reflected on the profound truth that the Father generates the Son by an act of intellect. When we know something there is a likeness of it in our mind. So also the Father, knowing himself perfectly, produces a perfect image of himself. That perfect Image is the Son of God, the second Person of the Blessed Trinity.

We know by faith—the Church tells us, the Bible tells us and we profess it in our Creed—that there is a third Person in the Blessed Trinity whom we call the "Holy Spirit". Today most of us are aware of the activity of the Holy Spirit in our lives and in the life of the Church. Many people now pray regularly to the Holy Spirit. Twenty years ago that was not so common. At that time he was often referred to as "the forgotten Person" in the Trinity.

Let's admit it: it is difficult for us to get a mental grasp on the Holy Spirit. We can imagine the Father and the Son, Jesus Christ. How do we imagine the Holy Spirit? About the best we can do is to picture to ourselves a dove descending on Jesus as St. John baptized him in the Jordan River. Or we might imagine the tongues of flame descending on the Apostles in the upper room on Pentecost. But it is difficult for us to attach the meanings of personality and divinity to a dove or a flame. The latter, however, are visible signs or symbols of the third Person of the Blessed Trinity.

We have already seen that there are two processions or internal activities in God—knowing and willing. The New Testament and the Teaching Authority of the Church say that the Son proceeds from the Father by an act of intellect. The Holy Spirit also proceeds from the Father (and the Son) but the New Testament does not specify precisely how or in what way he proceeds. The common teaching of the great theologians like Augustine and Thomas Aquinas is that the Holy Spirit proceeds from the *will* or from the *mutual love* of the Father and of the Son. Accordingly, there is a special relationship between the Holy Spirit and acts of the will, especially the act of love which proceeds from the will and not from the intellect.

The *Roman Catechism* teaches that the Holy Spirit "proceeds from the divine will inflamed, as it were, with love" (1.9.7). The biblical name of the third Person, "Holy Spirit" (pneuma = wind, breath, principle of life), designates a principle of activity. An act of will is an inclination to some known good.

The word "holy" in the personal name of the third Person indicates a relationship to the will, since holiness resides in the will. Also, works of love are attributed to the Holy Spirit. Thus, St. Paul says, "The charity of God is poured forth into our hearts by the Holy Spirit who is given to us" (Rom 5:5). The attribution of the works of love to the Holy Spirit is based on his origin from the will of the Father and the Son. We infer therefore that the Holy Spirit proceeds from the Father and the Son by an act of love. Thus, the Fathers of the Church, relying on Scripture, call the Holy Spirit: love, charity, gift, living fountain, bond of love, kiss of love. A gift, for example, is directly related to love since a gift is a visible sign of love. Thus, St. Peter uses the word "gift" in his sermon on the first Pentecost: "You will receive the gift of the Holy Spirit" (Acts 2:38).

Since the Holy Spirit proceeds by an act of will of the Father and the Son, it should be clear that he does not proceed as a perfect image through generation. So the Holy Spirit is not a Son of God; only the second Person of the Blessed Trinity can be called "Son", as we have already explained. Appropriately, then, the fifth century Athanasian Creed says: "The Holy Spirit is not made nor created *nor generated*, but proceeds from the Father and the Son."

The theologians have put a name on that type of proceeding, calling it "spiration", from the noun "spirit". It designates the loving activity between the Father and the Son which results in the term of their love, namely, the Holy Spirit. So they say that the Holy Spirit proceeds from the Father and the Son through spiration. This doctrine was taught clearly by the Second Council of Lyons in 1274.

There are three distinct Persons but only one God. So there is only one divine nature or essence which is common to all three. They are co-equal in power, majesty, wisdom and everything else. The distinction between them is to be found in their origin. The Father has no origin. The Son proceeds from the Father by intellectual generation. The Holy Spirit proceeds from the Father and the Son as from one principle because of their intense mutual love. The Father loves the Son and the Son loves the Father so intensely that their mutual love terminates in the third Person of the Blessed Trinity. Accordingly, we are justified in referring to him as the love of God, the power of God, the Spirit of truth, a river of living water and the kiss of the Father and the Son.

8

## THREE DIVINE PERSONS—ONE GOD

We believe that there are three Persons in one God—Father, Son and Holy Spirit. It is important to recall that there is only one God and that God is *absolutely simple*, as we saw earlier. Simplicity means that there is no composition of parts. An automobile is composed of parts; my idea of a car is simple.

If God is absolutely simple—having no parts or principles or elements whatsoever—how can there be *three Persons* in him? How can God be three and one at the same time and still be absolutely simple? Does not the Christian doctrine of the Trinity involve a contradiction?

Obviously three is not one and one is not three. The only way we can get out of this seeming contradiction of three Persons and one God is by showing that "three" is meant in one way, and "one" in another. That is exactly what the Fathers and theologians did centuries ago. By reflecting carefully on Holy Scripture and employing the most advanced philosophical concepts, they came to the conclusion that the "three" in God are Persons and that the "one" in God is the divine essence ( = nature or substance).

At this point the theologian must be able to show that the three Persons in one God, while retaining their distinctness in the divinity, are not three separate entities. For, if they were three separate individuals, like three human beings, we would have a *multiplicity of beings* in the Godhead, and there would be more than one God. Inevitably, we must ask: what constitutes the three Persons? The only suitable answer to this most difficult question is that they are *relations* within the divinity or Godhead.

We all know what a *relation* is, but very few are able to explain what it is, because it is one of the most difficult realities to grasp. Members of a family are related. There is a real relation between father and son. The father is related to the son by reason of generating him; the son is related to his father because he was generated by him. Thus, we define a relation as an ordination or reference of one thing to another. In every real relation there are three elements: 1) the subject (father), 2) the term (son), 3) the basis of the relation (activity of generating). The essence of the relation consists in *being ordered to another*.

Please note that a relation always exists in something else—it is not a new, separate individual. John and Jane get married and have a son. At the birth of their son they are now called "father" and "mother". Why? Because a new relationship has entered into their lives by reason of having a son. But they are still John and Jane.

Something similar takes place in God. The two internal divine processions of the Son and the Holy Spirit (which we have already considered) establish in God two pairs of real mutual relationships. Accordingly, there exist in God four real relations: 1) Father to Son; 2) Son to Father; 3) Father and Son to the Holy Spirit; 4) Holy Spirit to Father and Son.

The teaching of the Bible concerning the divine relations is found in the personal names Father, Son and Holy Spirit. The doctrine was developed by the Fathers of the Church, especially by St. Basil, the two Gregories and Augustine. St. Gregory Nazianzen said: "Father is not the name of the essence or activity but indicates the relation the Father has to the Son and the Son to the Father." The official teaching of the Church embodies this doctrine of the relations. It was taught by the Eleventh Synod of Toledo, Spain, in 675 and defined by the Council of Florence in 1442. Thus, the personal names in the Trinity are relative—Father, Son and Holy Spirit.

From a proper understanding of revelation and its development in the tradition it follows that the mutual relations in God are not just logical, that is, they are not just in our minds; rather, they are real relations in God which exist independently of our thinking about them. Otherwise the Trinity of Persons would be just different names that we give to God—and that is the condemned heresy of Sabellianism. Since there is only one God, and he is absolutely simple, it must follow that the difference between the three Persons cannot be based on the divine essence (which is common to all three) but on the mutual relations of the Persons to one another.

Of the four real internal divine relations, three stand in opposition to one another and, therefore, are really distinct, i.e., fatherhood, sonship and passive spiration ( = Holy Spirit). The active spiration stands in opposition to the passive spiration only; it is not opposed to fatherhood and sonship and, therefore, is not really distinct from them. So there are only three really distinct relations in God which constitute the three Persons.

It is very important to remember that the relations in God which constitute the Persons are really identical with the divine nature. Whatever is in God is God. The only difference in God is in the opposition of relations. Thus, the Council of Florence officially declared that in God "everything is one where there is no distinction by relative opposition" (*Denzinger* 703).


9

## WHAT IS A DIVINE PERSON?

Most of the prayers in the liturgy of the Church are offered to God the Father, through his Son, Jesus Christ, in the unity of the Holy Spirit. As we have seen in previous essays, there is only one God, but in God there are three distinct Persons. These remarkable truths about God were revealed to the Apostles by Jesus and eventually were written down in the collection of twenty-seven books that we call the New Testament.

Because of modern psychology, we tend to think of "person" as a center of consciousness—thinking and willing. That is true, but it does not exhaust the reality of what is meant in theology by a divine Person.

In the last essay we considered the difficult truth that the personal names in the Trinity are relative—Father, Son and Holy Spirit. Thus, when we say "God" we are referring to the divine essence (nature, substance) which is common to all three Persons. When we say "God the Father" we are referring to a relationship in the divinity which is personal. The same holds for the Son and the Holy Spirit.

According to the famous definition of the sixth century philosopher Boethius, "a person is the individual, incommunicable substance of a rational nature." It is an individual substance that exists completely in itself. Person and nature are related to each other in such a way that the person is the possessor of the nature and the ultimate subject of all being and activity, while the nature is that *through which* the person is and acts.

If you reflect on yourself for a few moments you will see what I mean. When you say "I think" or "my hand" to what reality do the words "I" and "my" refer? They refer to the owner or possessor of all your activities, namely to YOU or your person.

Through such a reflection we can come to see that there is a distinction between what we mean by "person" and what we mean by "nature". This distinction is now common, but it was discovered by the early Fathers of the Church who tried to get a better understanding of the Blessed Trinity.

As I pointed out previously, in God there are two processions—thinking and loving—which give rise to the three mutually opposed relations of fatherhood, sonship and passive spiration: these relations are the three divine Persons.

The fatherhood constitutes the Person of the Father, the sonship constitutes the Person of the Son, and the passive spiration constitutes the Person of the Holy Spirit. But in God "everything is one where there is no distinction by relative opposition." Consequently, even though in God there are three Persons, there is only one consciousness, one thinking and one loving. The three Persons share equally in the internal divine activity because they are all identified with the divine essence. For, if each divine Person possessed his own distinct and different consciousness, there would be three gods, not the one God of Christian revelation. So you will see that in this regard there is an immense difference between a divine Person and a human person.

A person is an individual, incommunicable substance. This definition applies to human beings and angels. In God, the internal divine relations are substantial because they are really identical with the divine essence. Because they are mutually opposed, incommunicability belongs to the three relations of fatherhood, sonship and passive spiration (active spiration is common to the Father and the Son). Therefore, only these three relations in God are divine Persons. Thus, St. Thomas Aquinas says that each divine Person is a subsistent, incommunicable, internal divine relation (see *Summa Theologica*, I, q. 29, art. 4).

By "subsistent" is meant a reality that exists of itself. Since the three divine personal relations are identified with the divine essence, they are subsistent. They are "incommunicable" in the sense that they are not shared by another.

We have been trying to answer the question: What are the "three" in God that the New Testament tells us about—Father, Son and Holy Spirit? or, How can we talk about them? The Church replies that the three are *Persons*. Then, if one asks: What is a divine Person? the answer is that it is a subsistent relation.

Obviously, it is not necessary to know the theology of the Trinity in order to be saved or to live as a devout Catholic. The heart of the Catholic religion is the love and worship of the Father, through the Son, in the Holy Spirit. Jesus said, "This is eternal life—to know you, the one true God, and Jesus Christ whom you have sent" (Jn 17:3). But it can be helpful for many Catholics to know that the Church possesses a highly developed rational explanation of the data of Scripture with regard to the Holy Trinity. For, in having us profess faith in the tri-personal One God, the Church is not asking us to believe in something that is contradictory or opposed to human reason. While the Trinity is an absolute mystery, that is, always beyond our grasp and intellectual reach, it is not opposed to reason.

## 10

# "THE FATHER AND I ARE ONE"

I have tried to sketch briefly and clearly the principal dogmas of the Church with regard to the three divine Persons. We have seen that there are two internal activities or "processions" in God, thinking and willing, which give rise to three Persons. In the last essay we saw that the three Persons are subsistent relations, that is, relations that are really identified with the divine substance.

When we reflect on our faith it is extremely important to realize that there is only one God, but that *in* God there are three distinct Persons. There is a question, then, obviously of both unity and multiplicity in God. We must retain both of them.

Many Christians, while verbally professing belief in the Trinity, in reality seem to think of God as just one Person. Thus, in their prayers they "pray to God", but they do not direct their attention to the Father or the Son or the Holy Spirit. When they neglect the three Persons and deal with God as if he were one Person, they are in effect functioning like Moslems or Jews who deny the Trinity. As instructed Catholics we must be on our guard against this all-too-common tendency.

Another common misunderstanding of the Trinity is

based on the multiplicity of the three Persons. Some Catholics think that the three Persons are separate, independent beings. In this view each of the three is thought of as having his own thinking, willing and separate consciousness. In other words, they are considered to be similar to three human persons, but only on a higher level and endowed with "divine" power. That view is false and is equivalent to affirming three gods. For, in God everything is one where there is not an opposition of relation. Thus, in him there is only one thinking, one willing and one "consciousness". The three Persons share equally in all the divine actions and operations that are proper to the divine nature.

In order to stress the divine unity the Fathers of the Church emphasized the mutual or reciprocal penetration and indwelling of the three divine Persons in one another. We note among human lovers the drive toward union. Kisses and embraces are manifestations of this drive. The highest form among human beings is marital union. The impulse of love towards mutual penetration which we witness among human beings is a faint reflection of the mutual indwelling of the three divine Persons.

St. Thomas Aquinas says that by reason of the undivided divine essence, each Person is in each other Person in the Trinity. Our Lord says in this regard, "I am in the Father and the Father is in me" (Jn 14:10). He also says, "I and the Father are one" (Jn 10:30; see also 10:38). The indwelling of the Holy Spirit in the Father and in the Son is indicated in 1 Corinthians 2:10, "The Spirit reaches the depths of everything, even the depths of God."

The doctrine of mutual penetration or indwelling of the three divine Persons was officially taught by the

Council of Florence in the fifteenth century. The Council Fathers declared: "Because of this unity the Father is entirely in the Son and entirely in the Holy Spirit; the Son is entirely in the Father and entirely in the Holy Spirit; the Holy Spirit is entirely in the Father and entirely in the Son" (*Denzinger* 704). In theology this mutual indwelling has been called, since the eighth century, "circumincession" which comes from the Latin *circum-incedere* and means "to go or move around". The point of the teaching is to stress that the three divine Persons are perfectly one in being, knowing and willing.

I have already mentioned the impulse of love towards union. In the Trinity each divine Person is irresistibly drawn, by the very constitution of his being, to the other two. Branded in the very depths of each one of them is a necessary outward impulse urging him to give himself fully to the other two, to pour himself out into the divine receptacle of the other two. Here we find an unceasing circulation of life and love. Thus, since each Person is necessarily in the other two, unity is achieved because of this irresistible impulse in each Person, which mightily draws them to one another.

In the Beatific Vision the blessed see and taste the divine unity and beauty. In this regard Pope Pius XII said in his letter on the Mystical Body of Christ (# 80): "It will be granted to the eyes of the human mind, strengthened by the light of glory, to contemplate the Father, the Son, and the Holy Spirit in an utterly ineffable manner, to assist throughout eternity at the processions of the divine Persons, and to rejoice with a happiness like to that with which the holy and undivided Trinity is happy."

11

# THE WORKS OF THE TRINITY

After explaining what is meant by the mutual penetration of the Father, the Son and the Holy Spirit, the next point to consider is the external activities of the three divine Persons. In this regard the Church, basing herself on the testimony of the Bible and the writings of the Fathers of the Church, teaches that *all the external activities of God* are common to the three Persons. In other words, no one of the three divine Persons can act separately and independently of the others on the created world that they produced acting as a single principle.

In support of the above let me point out briefly that the Fourth Lateran Council in 1215 said that the three divine Persons are the sole principle of all things. In 1441 the Council of Florence declared that Father, Son and Holy Spirit are not three principles but one principle of all things.

A careful reading of the Bible will reveal the same truth. For Scripture often attributes the same activity in the created world now to the Father, now to the Son and now to the Holy Spirit. For example, the Incarnation of the second Person is attributed to the Father (Heb 10:5), to the Son (Phil 2:7) and to the Holy Spirit (Lk 1:35; Mt 1:20). The same can be said for a number of other divine activities in the world such as creation, redemption, sanctification and the forgiveness of sins. One reason for these statements is to bring out that all three Persons are equally active in the creation and salvation of the world.

The basic reason for saying all external activities of God are common to the three Persons is that God acts through his substance or essence and the three Persons possess that essence equally. The only distinction in God, as I pointed out before, is in the internal life of the Trinity where there is an opposition of relationship that arises from the eternal origin of the Son and the Holy Spirit. But all three Persons are equally identified with the divine Substance and, therefore, equally God. Accordingly, when God acts externally all three Persons are acting.

Holy Scripture, however, very often attributes certain activities to the different Persons. Thus, works of power are attributed to the Father, the work of redemption to the Son and the work of sanctification to the Holy Spirit. These statements of the Bible do not mean that the Person in question acts alone and independently of the other two. Accordingly, even though certain "gifts" are attributed to the Holy Spirit, the actual production of those gifts in the faithful is common to all three Persons.

Why do the Bible and the Church speak in this way? Is it not confusing? It is not confusing if you reflect for a moment on what is meant. The purpose of these statements is to make manifest the differences between the Persons. That is, common attributes such as power, wisdom and goodness, and certain activities such as sanctification and creation, are attributed to a definite Person because they have a special relationship to the personal origin and property of that Person.

When we consider the divine perfections in their personal representative, they are more concrete than when we regard them in themselves or in reference to the divine substance. Thus, if I say, "God the Father, the source of the divine being, created and gives existence to the world and everything in it", that is clearer and more sublime than if I merely say, "God created the world." Likewise, do we not get a more vivid idea of the truth when we are told: "The Spirit of God moved over the waters, the Spirit of God animates everything that lives, the Holy Spirit sanctifies and purifies the creature", than when it is affirmed: "God moved over the waters, God gave us life, sanctification and grace"?

It is to be noted that just as the divine nature is transmitted from the Father through the Son to the Holy Spirit, so also the external activity of the divinity is transmitted from the Father through the Son to the Holy Spirit. This does not imply that the three Persons act externally in different ways. Rather, it means that all three Persons have the same activity, but that they come into possession of it in different ways. Therefore, the external activities of the Trinity do not manifest to us the inner distinctions of the three Persons. We can know about that only through positive divine revelation.

12

# FATHER, SON AND HOLY SPIRIT DWELL IN US

Now that we have come to some basic understanding of the teaching of Scripture and the Church about the Holy Trinity, it might be worthwhile to ask ourselves: So what? What does the doctrine of the Trinity have to do with me and the practical problems I must face every day? It has very much to do with you since, if you are in the state of sanctifying grace, the Holy Trinity dwells in you in a very special and personal way.

God is an intense and eternal lover. It was because of his love that he created you, and it is because of his love that he wishes to be united with you, to be present in you in a very special way. It is most important for us to realize that God's grace is more than merely some created thing that God imprints on us as a sign of his ownership—it is not just a brand mark or a tag of ownership signed "God". The full meaning of sanctifying grace is that *God himself*, that is, the Holy Trinity —Father, Son and Holy Spirit, is personally present in me in a way that he is not present in the rest of the material universe.

The Bible says that God, through his grace, dwells in

me, makes his home in me. For example, Jesus says in John 14:23: "If anyone loves me he will keep my word, and my Father will love him, and we shall come to him and make our home with him."

When the three divine Persons come to the sanctified believer, they come to him according to the special characteristics of their origin and procession. These are truths about the Trinity that I have already explained. The New Testament uses the word "sending" or mission in this regard. The point is that, because of the divine processions, the Father sends the Son, and the Father and the Son send the Holy Spirit. Thus, St. Paul says in Galatians 4:4, "God sent his Son." Both the Father and the Son are described as sending the Holy Spirit: "But the Advocate, the Holy Spirit, whom the Father will send in my name, will teach you everything and remind you of all I have said to you" (Jn 14:26). In the following chapter of John Jesus says that he will send the Spirit: "When the Advocate comes, whom I shall send to you from the Father . . . he will be my witness" (15:26).

The Blessed Trinity is the source or cause of all creation. The final end or purpose of the universe is also the Trinity. By reason of his creative power God is present in all creation, sustaining all things in existence. Irrational creatures, that is, all things beneath man, glorify God necessarily by their very existence. The glory of God from rational creatures requires free worship, praise and honor. Through the sin of our first parents, Adam and Eve, we lost the grace that God had intended for us to have. That situation was abundantly restored by the Incarnation of the second Person of the Blessed Trinity in Jesus Christ. God's will is that through faith in Jesus

Christ, the acceptance of Baptism and incorporation into his Church, we should be made temples of the Holy Spirit, children of God and heirs of heaven. This is all accomplished through the indwelling of the Holy Trinity in the souls of the just.

The "indwelling" means that Father, Son and Holy Spirit become personally present to us through grace in a unique way. Their presence in the soul affects both our knowledge and our love. When the Bible speaks about "sending" or "mission" of the Son and the Holy Spirit it is referring to the special way in which they proceed in the Trinity itself. The temporal missions, therefore, reflect the individual characteristics of the divine Persons: The Father sends, but is not sent; the Son is sent and sends. The Holy Spirit is sent, but does not send.

In the course of salvation history, or God's dealing with mankind, we discover both external and internal divine missions. They could also be called visible and invisible missions. Thus, the Word of God became man in Jesus of Nazareth. That is what is meant by a visible mission. The Holy Spirit appeared under the form of a dove at the Baptism of Jesus (Mt 3:16), under the form of a brilliant cloud at the Transfiguration (Mt 17:5) and under the form of tongues of fire in the upper room on Pentecost (Acts 2:3–4).

The visible missions are external signs of the invisible missions, namely, the Trinity dwelling in the souls of the just. This means that the Son and the Holy Spirit are present in a new manner in creatures. It is a new, interior and invisible presence, which sanctifies the soul and imparts to it a new supernatural life. The Father is also present in the sanctified soul because, as we have seen, where the Son and the Spirit are personally present, the

Father, who is one with them, is present. So when we pray to God within us we should pray to the Father, through the Son, in the Holy Spirit.

13

# THE TRINITY IS AN ABSOLUTE MYSTERY

A final point to consider with regard to the Holy Trinity, before moving on to another subject, is that it is a *mystery* of the Faith. By a "mystery" is meant something that is hidden, veiled, unknown. In this sense, there are many mysteries of nature, since there are aspects of atoms, molecules and living beings that are not yet known. Thus, science is constantly trying to unravel the "mysteries" of nature. This is not what is meant by mystery in the theological sense since human science by experiments and perseverance can finally unlock the secrets of nature. In other words, natural truths are not beyond the power of human reason.

In Catholic theology a "mystery" of faith is a truth revealed by God which totally surpasses the power of the human mind. Once it has been revealed by God we can know something about it, such as the Holy Trinity, the Incarnation and divine grace, but we could never come to any knowledge of it from our observation or experience. Fr. John A. Hardon, S.J., gives the following definition of mystery in his book *Modern Catholic Dictionary* (Doubleday, 1980): "MYSTERY. A divinely revealed truth whose very possibility cannot be rationally conceived before it is revealed and, after revelation, whose inner essence cannot be fully understood by the finite mind."

Mysteries in this sense are truths that concern God himself, since he is infinite and absolutely incomprehensible to the created mind. Theologians usually list three mysteries in this category: the Trinity, the Incarnation and divine grace. For, these three have to do with the very being of God. According to Catholic teaching these truths are *absolute mysteries*. By an absolute mystery is meant a truth that not only surpasses the power of the human intellect in this life, but also will surpass it in the next life in heaven. Thus, it follows that the blessed in heaven do not comprehend the Holy Trinity, that is, they do not fully understand it; for all eternity they can learn more and more about it and never exhaust its knowability. Such a consideration gives a hint of the activity connected with the lives of the saints who see God face to face.

The Catholic Church teaches that

> there are two orders of knowledge, distinct not only in origin but also in object. They are distinct in origin, because in one we know by means of natural reason; in the other, by means of divine faith. And they are distinct in object, because in addition to what natural reason can attain, we have proposed to us as objects of belief mysteries that are hidden in God and which, unless divinely revealed, can never be known (*Denzinger* 1795).

By natural reason we can come to a knowledge of God as the origin and source of created beings (cf. Rom 1). But the various perfections of God which are revealed through the contemplation of created things, such as his power, wisdom and goodness, are common to the three divine Persons, as we have seen previously. Therefore, natural reason can know God only in his unity of substance, but not in his Trinity of Persons.

Our knowledge of the inner life of God—the life of Father, Son and Holy Spirit—must come through revelation by God in history. That took place primarily in Jesus Christ and through his Apostles.

Jesus revealed to us the absolute mysteries of the Holy Trinity, his Incarnation and divine grace. In order to receive this revelation we must be able to understand something about these mysteries. They are revealed to us through human words and human actions. We understand something about them when we accept them in faith, but we do not completely grasp them. In theological language, we do not "comprehend" them because "comprehend" means to understand something completely. By reading the Bible, by prayer and by meditation we can come to a deeper understanding of these mysteries, but we will never exhaust them because they have to do with God himself and he is infinitely exalted above us.

Once we know about the inner life of God we can learn more about it by comparing it with the created things we know. In fact, we have already done that in this series when we considered how the Son proceeds from the Father by way of intellectual generation. But the truth about God always remains obscure because, as St. Paul says, in this life "we walk by faith and not by sight" (2 Cor 5:6f.).

Finally, it is important to note that the dogma of the Trinity is *beyond reason*, but *not contrary to reason*. St. Thomas Aquinas says that human reason of itself cannot show the possibility of the Trinity, but it can show that it is not contradictory, and so it can refute all counter-arguments. The Church in Vatican I said that, even though faith is above reason, "yet there can never be any real disagreement between faith and reason, because it is the same God who reveals mysteries and infuses faith and has put the light of reason into the human soul" (*Denzinger* 1797). Therefore, it is reasonable to believe in the Trinity and to adore the Trinity because God has revealed it "who can neither deceive nor be deceived".

# PART III

# CREATION

I

# GOD CREATED THE HEAVENS AND THE EARTH

I have sketched the basic outlines of the Church's teaching on the Holy Trinity—Father, Son and Holy Spirit. We have been considering the being of God and his tri-personal nature. It is now appropriate to move on to a series of reflections on the origin, nature, multiplicity and kinds of beings that are distinct from God. So we come to the question of creatures, both spiritual and material.

As soon as a person reaches the stage of reflective consciousness he feels the urge within himself to ask: Where did I come from? Have I always existed? Or did I just begin to exist when my parents conceived me? Where did the world and the sun and the moon and the stars come from? Have they existed for all eternity? Or did they have a beginning? If they had a beginning in time, where did they come from? Who made them?

In the course of history many different answers have been given to these questions. Some have said that matter is eternal—it has always existed and always will exist. Others have claimed that there are two principles or sources of all things: a good God who made man's soul and an evil principle or Satan who made matter and the material world. Still others, called "pantheists" and very common today, say that everything is God. In this view the world and everything in it emanate from the divine being and so are various manifestations of God.

What are we to think about the origin of ourselves and this material universe in which we live? Where did we—where did all of it come from? Divine revelation, transmitted and infallibly guaranteed by the living Teaching Authority of the Catholic Church, instructs us that everything outside of God was *created* by him. Even those who know very little about the Bible can cite the first sentence of the book of Genesis: "In the beginning God created the heavens and the earth" (1:1).

Let us reflect for a few moments on the meaning of the word "creation". In Catholic theology and teaching it means the production of something out of nothing. When we say "out of nothing", what is meant is that there is no pre-existing material which is used or shaped in the formation of the new being. For, "nothing" is the same as "no being". St. Thomas Aquinas says that creation is the production of something according to its whole substance, without presupposing any previous material either created or uncreated (*Summa Theologica*, I, q. 65, art. 3). Vatican Council I in 1870 decreed the following: "If anyone does not admit that the world and everything in it, both spiritual and material, have been produced in their entire substance by God out of nothing . . . let him be anathema" (*Denzinger* 1805).

The same truth is given utterance in the Profession of Faith that we make each Sunday at Mass: "We believe in one God, the Father, the Almighty, *maker of heaven and earth, of all that is seen and unseen.*"

Under divine inspiration the idea of creation from nothing developed among the Israelites during the time of the Old Testament. We find it in Genesis; we find it in the Psalms: "Our help is in the name of the Lord, who made heaven and earth" (124:8; see also 146:6 and 33:9); we find it in Isaiah 48:13.

The belief of the Jewish people in creation is found in a remarkable passage in 2 Maccabees 7:27–28 in which the mother adjures her youngest son to accept martyrdom: "My son, have pity on me; I carried you nine months in my womb and suckled you three years, fed you and reared you to the age you are now. I implore you, my child, observe heaven and earth, consider all that is in them, and acknowledge that God made them out of what did not exist, and that mankind comes into being in the same way."

The New Testament bears witness to the same belief among Christians. Thus, St. John says of Jesus, the Word of God: "Through him all things came to be, not one being had its being but through him" (1:3). And St. Paul says of God: "All that exists comes from him; all is by him and for him. To him be glory forever" (Rom 11:36). In Colossians 1:16 Paul writes: "He is the image of the unseen God and the first-born of all creation, for in him were created all things in heaven and on earth: everything visible and everything invisible . . . all things were created through him and for him."

The Fathers of the Church considered the creation of the world out of nothing a basic truth of the Christian faith and defended it against the false dualism of some of the pagan philosophers. Today many of our contemporaries hold that matter is the only thing that exists, that it is eternal, and that there is no such thing as God or anything spiritual like a human soul. Belief in the first article of the Creed, that God created all things out of nothing, is a basic truth of the Catholic religion. Anyone who denies that truth is certainly not a Catholic and not even a Christian.

2

# WHY DID GOD CREATE THE WORLD?

In the last essay we saw that God created all things, both visible and invisible, out of nothing, that is, he did not make use of any pre-existing material since there was absolutely nothing but God himself before he produced creatures. That is an article of faith which we profess each Sunday in the Creed.

Once we have come to the realization that God created everything that is, we naturally move on to the next question: Why did God create the world? Since we live in a pleasure-seeking culture that flees from such questions, many of our contemporaries may think it a waste of time to inquire into the purpose of creation. The tendency is to concentrate on the here and now, to solve urgent problems, and to ignore philosophical and theological questions that probe into the meaning of reality.

In reality, however, the answer to the question about why God created the world concerns all of us most intimately. That answer is found in God's revelation as it is expressed both in the Bible and in the official teaching of the Church.

In the Psalms we are urged to praise and glorify the Lord because of his great goodness in making the sun, moon, stars, earth, man and all the various aspects of the world. All creatures are said to glorify God. Thus, in Psalm 19:1 we pray, "The heavens declare the glory of God, the vault of heaven proclaims his handiwork." Similar sentiments are expressed at length in Psalms 146, 148, 150 and also in Daniel 3:52ff.

The First Vatican Council declared that God created the world "in order to manifest his perfection through the benefits which he bestows on creatures, not to intensify his happiness nor to acquire any perfection". In another decree the Council went on to reject any theory which "denies that the world was made for the glory of God" (*Denzinger* 1783, 1805).

It is important to note that God does not get anything out of creation. As a matter of fact he cannot acquire anything from creation because he is infinitely perfect and happy, as we have seen in a previous essay. So the praise and glory given to God by the whole universe does not add one iota to the dignity and goodness of God.

Why did God create the world? The answer is twofold: 1) the revelation or manifestation of the divine perfections and the glorification of God which flows from this; 2) the communication of good to creatures, especially to those endowed with intelligence.

As we see in the great Psalms of praise, all creatures,

both rational and irrational, glorify God by their very existence. In this context the word "glory" or "glorify" means an acknowledgement of God's goodness in some way; in rational creatures it has the further meaning of consciously praising God because of his goodness. Thus, when men glorify God they praise him, acknowledge his goodness, follow his commandments.

When we were in school, many of us learned from the Sisters to write A.M.D.G. at the top of each sheet of paper. Those four letters also adorn many of our churches and altars. They mean "for the greater glory of God". It is a fine motto, the purpose of which is to direct our thoughts, words and actions to the praise and glory of God.

So God created everything for his own glory. This should not be understood in the sense that God is the supreme egotist who produced men and women so that he could have billions of people to tell him how great he is. Such an explanation is a complete travesty of the Judaeo-Christian idea of the glory of God and flows from an attitude of either agnosticism or atheism.

There is a saying in philosophy that "good is diffusive of itself", that is, it is of the very nature of goodness that it seeks to communicate itself to others. While this is true of creatures, it is even more true of the Creator. God gets nothing out of creation. Moreover, he derives no profit from our good deeds, from our observance of his commandments, from our acts of virtue. From our good acts we are the ones who profit, not God. The great paradox in all of this is that creatures, by knowing and loving and serving God, achieve the purpose for which they were made and so attain happiness. Happiness, therefore, is to be found in glorifying God and not in glorifying the self.

This is the message of the Bible and the constant teaching of the Church.

No one can outdo God in generosity. He is the one tremendous lover. The more generous we show ourselves toward him by striving to know him and selflessly to do his will, the more lavishly he bestows his blessings on us.

3

## THE BEST POSSIBLE WORLD?

The question I now pose for your consideration is: Was God totally *free* in creating the world? Or must we say that God was not free and that the world flows with necessity from the infinite goodness of God? Perhaps you have not thought seriously about this question, but it has exercised many minds in the course of history.

Just reflect a moment, for example, on the pervasive influence of evolutionary thought. Millions of our contemporaries believe in evolution with a faith that is as strong as the faith of many Christians. Evolutionists hold that the higher forms of life, like man and the higher animals, evolved from lower forms of life and ultimately from inanimate matter. Many of them also, rejecting creation, maintain either that matter always existed or that it developed from nothing. In any event, they deny creation, and, therefore, they must deny any role to freedom in the origin of the universe.

The Catholic faith teaches that God created the world free from any necessity, either external or internal. The First Vatican Council affirmed this teaching against certain nineteenth century philosophers and theologians who maintained that God's infinite goodness imposed on him a necessity to create and so to communicate his goodness to others. External or internal necessity, however, are incompatible with God's infinite being and the absolute self-sufficiency which this implies. Also, God's goodness cannot force him to produce creatures, because the desire for self-communication inherent in the nature of goodness is satisfied perfectly in God's case through the internal divine communications among the three Persons in the Trinity. God's goodness is certainly the reason for his communication of being to creatures, but it does not compel him to do so.

Thus, by his freedom of decision, God was at liberty either to create the world or not to create it. The Bible supports this in many places: "The Lord's will is sovereign" (Ps 135:6), and "You are our Lord and our God . . . because you made all the universe, and it was only by your will that everything was made and exists" (Rev 4:11).

If we admit that God was free either to create or not to create, once he decided to create did he have to create the world we now know? Another way of asking the same question is: Was God obliged to create the best possible of all worlds? In the history of Christian thought there have been those, sometimes called "optimists", who have claimed that the world we live in is the best of all possible worlds. That position, however, runs counter to the experience of most people who are regularly confronted with suffering and death. Moreover, Catholic teaching asserts that God did not have to create the best possible world because his perfections and happiness cannot be increased even by the best world. A denial of God's freedom in the choice between this or that world would imply a limitation on his omnipotence. One does not have to be a saint or a genius to imagine a better world than the one we now live in.

To deny that this is the best possible world is not the same thing as saying that the world is evil. God created a good world, as we know from the Bible and the teaching of the Church, no matter how difficult it might be to explain the presence of evil. We have already touched on the problem of evil, and we will do so again; for now let it suffice to say that evil flows from the misuse of free will in the rational creature—whether angel or man. In the very first chapter of the Bible we read: "God saw all he had made, and indeed it was very good" (Gen 1:31). And St. Paul writes to Timothy that "Everything God has created is good" (1 Tim 4:4).

Another aspect of the same truth is that God could not create a world that was morally evil, since by virtue of his absolute holiness he cannot be the source of moral evil. Thus, God is free to confer his blessings on creatures or not to confer them, but he does not have the freedom of choice between good and evil. Everything God is and does is good. Only a free creature can be the source of moral evil, because only a creature, who is by nature limited and changeable, can choose that which is not appropriate.

In the last century there were a few philosophers, unduly influenced by Buddhism, who said that our world is the worst imaginable. Arthur Schopenhauer (1788–1860) was one of them. Steering a middle course between the extremes of optimism and pessimism, the Catholic Church professes a world view that can be termed "relative optimism". While admitting the reality of sin and the evil that flows from it, the Christian view considers the present world to be relatively best since, being a product of divine wisdom, it corresponds to the end pre-determined for it by God and is uniquely suited to achieve it. Also, our world brings together in beautiful harmony the various stages of the perfections of the natural and supernatural orders.

4

## THE BEGINNING OF THE WORLD

Time is an essential part of our daily lives. We live "in time" and "in space". We all know what time is, since we experience it every moment of our lives. In fact, our whole life is measured in terms of seconds, minutes, hours, days, weeks, months and years. Our life begins at a certain moment on a particular day—our birthday—and it ends at a precise moment on a given day known only to God. That is our death. Between these two extremes we live out our life, as the expression goes.

While a beginning and an end are common to the living beings we are familiar with, what are we to say about the world itself and the whole material universe? Did the world have a beginning in time? Or has it existed for all eternity? That is a question that many people have pondered over in the past. Scientists and philosophers today still ask the same question and offer various answers.

What does the Catholic Church say on this point? As a matter of fact, the dogmatic teaching of the Church is that the world had a beginning in time, that is, the world has not existed from all eternity, but began to be. According to the Fourth Lateran Council (1215) and Vatican I (1870) God is the "Creator of all things visible and invisible, spiritual and corporeal, who, by his almighty power, from the very beginning of time has created both orders of creatures in the same way out of nothing, the spiritual or angelic world and the corporeal or visible universe" (*Denzinger* 428). What this means is that time began when the world was created by God. So before creation there was no time because there were no changeable beings whose change could be measured by time until the unchangeable God willed to bring creatures into existence by his almighty power.

The same truth is frequently stated in Holy Scripture. "In the beginning God created the heavens and the earth" (Gen 1:1). "Now, Father, it is time for you to glorify me with that glory I had with you before ever the world was" (Jn 17:5). "Before the world was made, he chose us, he chose us in Christ" (Eph 1:4). You can find many more texts in the Bible that bear witness to the same truth.

In the course of history the pope and bishops have been somewhat reluctant to make dogmatic pronouncements. Most often they have been prodded into doing so by the propositions of various thinkers—either Christian or pagan—that are opposed to the divine revelation that they have sworn to defend and hand on to future generations.

As early as the second century after Christ there were heretics who said that the world was eternal. Some claimed that the material world was produced by an evil god and that spiritual beings such as angels and the human soul were produced by the good god. But we do not have to go back that far in history in order to find those who say that the world is eternal or always existed. Most materialists of our day and those who do not believe in a personal God say that the matter of the universe always existed. During trillions of years, they say, it has gone through various transformations, but the material building blocks—whether atoms or whatever—have always existed. Recent progress in atomic physics, however, has raised some doubts about that position.

The Fathers of the Church rejected the idea of the eternity of the world in their battle against the error of dualism. Their arguments were derived both from revelation and from philosophy, since there are no convincing philosophical arguments to prove that the world is eternal.

St. Thomas Aquinas held that there is no compelling proof, on merely rational grounds and independently of divine revelation, against an eternal creation of the world. St. Athanasius, however, was sure that a creature without a beginning is impossible. His basic reason is that an unchangeable creature is impossible, since changeability necessarily exists in all finite creatures. And the world is a finite creature.

Eternal creation involves an intrinsic contradiction because creation out of nothing means: first not to be and then to be. Athanasius says: "Even if God can always create, still the created things could not always be, for they are out of non-being, and were not before they came to be."

So when the Bible says, "In the beginning God created the heavens and the earth", it means that the material universe and time began simultaneously. They go together. They cannot be separated. Thus, it is a truth of divine revelation and the official teaching of the Church that the world had a beginning in time.

5

# GOD KEEPS THE WORLD IN EXISTENCE

If you ask a believing Catholic where the world came from, he will tell you that it was created by God, understanding "creation" as the production of something out of nothing. But once God created the whole universe, perhaps billions of years ago, what role has he played in the continuing existence of his creatures? May we think that God, with one mighty act of creation, produced everything and then stepped into the background, so to speak, and watched his universe proceed on its own?

Maybe you never thought about these questions, or thought of them and were not able to come up with a satisfactory answer. A group of thinkers in the eighteenth century called "Deists" admitted that God created the world at the beginning but then more or less lost interest in his creation. He allowed it to go forth on its own, they said, and has not been personally involved in it since the beginning. That position of the Deists has been strongly rejected by the teaching authority of the Catholic Church.

The Catholic position is not only that God created absolutely everything out of nothing, but also that he keeps all created things in existence at every single moment. In other words, God was active not only at the beginning of each creature, but he constantly sustains in existence all things. Another way to grasp this truth is to think that the act of creation continues from the first moment, billions of years ago, right down to the present and will continue until "the end of time" and for all eternity for those creatures—saved and damned—that continue to exist. Thus, the constant application of divine power to created things is essential for their survival. If God did not preserve all things with the same power with which they were created in the beginning they would fall back into nothingness immediately. If God were to forget or not will some object for a moment it would be annihilated.

God's conserving activity is a constant causal intervention by which he keeps all things in existence. Also, in order to preserve his creation God does not act mediately through secondary causes, but he immediately provides for the existence of all creatures. Thus, God is intimately involved in the moment by moment existence of the world and every creature in it.

The Bible bears witness in many places to God's activity in conserving the world. Thus, we read in Wisdom 11:26, "And how, had you not willed it, could a thing persist, how be conserved if not called forth by you?" Jesus says in John 5:17, "My Father goes on working, and so do I." St. Paul attributes both the creation and the preservation of the world to Christ: "Before anything was created he existed, and he holds all things in unity" (Col 1:17).

St. Thomas Aquinas wrote penetratingly about the question of the conservation of the world by God. He bases his position on the argument that God is not merely the cause of the *becoming* of all creatures but also the source of their *being*. Therefore, the creature depends on God not just in its coming into being but in every moment of its existence.

What about the activities of creatures? What about my actions? Do they also depend on the divine cooperation? Yes, they do. And this means that God is active in me in a way that is most intimate. He is more intimate to me than I am to myself.

In the past many philosophers have erred either by making God too distant from man, or by identifying man with God and so eliminating the distinction between the two. The Catholic faith holds the delicate middle against both extremes: God is both infinitely distant from us in his essence and intimately close to us by his presence. St. Paul told the haughty Athenians that God "in fact is not far from any of us, since it is in him that we live, and move, and exist" (Acts 17:28). Thus, God is intimately involved in our lives; he sustains us in existence every moment; nothing escapes his eyes. He knows when we sit and when we stand, what we eat and what we drink, what we think and what we desire. He is more intimate to us than we are to ourselves.

Saints and spiritual writers, following Holy Scripture, urge us to think often about God's many gifts to us and of his constant presence. For example, St. Ignatius Loyola in his *Spiritual Exercises* suggests the following reflection: "God dwells in creatures: in the elements giving them existence, in man bestowing understanding. So he dwells in me and gives me being, life, sensation, intelligence, and makes a temple of me." Great spiritual peace and consolation can be attained by reflecting on the nearness of our good Creator and God.

6

# THE DIVINE PLAN FOR CREATION

Where is the world headed? Is it possible to make any sense out of the wars and disasters that flood our television screens almost every day? Does everything happen just by chance? Or is there a plan in the lives of individuals and in world events that makes them ultimately intelligible? These and similar questions perplex the minds of many of our contemporaries.

In the course of history different answers have been given to these questions by philosophers and religious thinkers. Some have said that everything happens by chance. Such a view excludes all hope and so ends in despair. The eighteenth century Deists said that God created the world but then let it go its own way and has no concern for it. Materialistic determinists say that everything is predetermined by physical necessity. According to the Marxian view, the world is headed toward utopian communism and the classless society.

The Christian view of the world is very different. According to that view almighty God, who created everything that is, has a plan for each creature and for the totality of creation. He carries out his plan by his loving rule or governance. His fulfillment of both plan and governance we call *divine providence*. This means that, from God's point of view, nothing happens by chance.

The First Vatican Council in 1870, basing itself solidly on the Bible and the constant teaching of the Church, made this view official Catholic teaching. The Council declared: "By his providence God watches over and governs all the things that he made, reaching from end to end with might and disposing all things with gentleness (see Wis 8:1). For 'all things are naked and open to his eyes' (Heb 4:13), even those things that are going to occur by the free action of creatures."

Holy Scripture bears witness to the operation of divine providence on almost every page. The Old Testament stresses the providence of God for the people of Israel and for certain individuals, such as Abraham, Joseph, Moses. In praise of Wisdom we read: "She deploys her strength from one end of the earth to the other, ordering all things for good" (Wis 8:1). In the Sermon on the Mount Jesus teaches that the providence of the heavenly Father extends to the birds of the air, the lilies of the field, and to each hair on our heads.

In theological language, providence (Latin: *providere* = to see in advance) is the plan in the mind of God according to which he directs all creatures to their proper end. Providence belongs to the divine mind, but it also presupposes that he wills the goal or end. Since it pertains to

God himself, providence is universal, infallible and immutable.

God's providence is *universal* because it extends to everything that happens in the universe. Thus everything serves a purpose, mysteriously foreseen and foreordained by God. Providence is *infallible* because God's plan cannot fail; his infinite knowledge and will embrace everything. What God has intended for the world will eventually come about. Finally, divine providence is *immutable* because God himself cannot change. Since he sees everything at once from beginning to end, nothing can change his mind. God is not like us—fickle and changeable.

Reflection on divine providence raises a number of serious problems. For example, how does human freedom fit into the picture if God has planned everything? The answer is that human freedom is part of the divine plan. God wills the end to be achieved by two different kinds of created agents: necessary causes (like gravity, chemical reactions) and free causes (like love, obedience, repentance). This of course does not explain *how* our actions can be free if they are eternally willed by God. But we do know that they are free from our own experience and from divine revelation.

The doctrine of providence also raises a question with regard to the prayer of petition. If God knows and orders all things, then why should we pray? If providence is immutable, why pray? Since God sees everything from all eternity, his plan is established in that light. Thus, what happens may depend on whether or not you pray. St. Thomas Aquinas said that God grants some gifts only on condition that we ask for them. The fact that he foresees our free prayer does not make that prayer any less free.

Perhaps the most difficult fact to reconcile with divine providence is the manifest existence of evil. No matter what we say here, evil remains a mystery. But it proceeds ultimately from the misuse of freedom: that was the case with the angels, and it is also the case with men. God has such a high regard for our freedom that he will not interfere with our use of it even if we use it against him. Greater than evil is the existence of free acts of love, hope, faith, obedience, mercy and humility. On a very broad scale we can say that God permits evils so that he can bring good out of them. In order to eliminate all evil God would also have to eliminate freedom. Thus, the patience and heroism of the martyrs presupposes unjust persecution. In general, in order to overcome evils many virtues are brought into play.

There is no way to understand completely the divine plan—either for ourselves or for the world. We have a glimpse of it in the life, death, passion and Resurrection of Jesus Christ. Faithful following of him is the surest way for each of us to fit into divine providence according to the will of God.

# 7

# THE ORIGIN OF MAN

Each one of us has a father and a mother. We know their names, and we know that they each had their own father and mother. If we could trace this sequence back to the beginning, we would come to the first man and the first woman. Who were they? Where did they come from?

The Bible, which is God's revealed Word, tells us in its very first chapters in the book of Genesis that the first man was called Adam and the first woman was called Eve. Where did they come from? The Bible says that they were created by God. "God created man in the image of himself, in the image of God he created him, male and female he created them" (Gen 1:27). In chapter 2:7 we also find: "The Lord God fashioned man of dust from the soil. Then he breathed into his nostrils a breath of life, and thus man became a living being."

In the thirteenth century at the Fourth Lateran Council the Church taught that God created all things visible and invisible, spiritual and corporeal, and afterwards "he formed the creature man, who in a way belongs to both orders, as he is composed of spirit and body."

As everyone knows, modern theories of evolution, which are now commonly taught even in our grade schools, in effect often contradict and deny the teaching of the Bible and the teaching of the Catholic Church. The most radical form of evolution says that all living things, including man, evolved by chance from inanimate matter. They go on to say that man, in both body and soul, evolved after millions of years from brute beasts. This theory must be categorically rejected by all Catholics, since it denies the direct creation of the human soul by God. For, it is a dogma of the Catholic faith that each human soul is created immediately by God. So it is impossible for the whole man to evolve from inanimate matter though brute beasts.

With regard to the creation of man's body, both the Bible and the Church allow for a broader interpretation.

Its immediate formation from inorganic matter by God cannot be maintained with absolute certainty. A number of interpretations are possible of the statement in Genesis that God "fashioned man of dust from the soil" or "from the slime of the earth" as another translation has it. In addition to the literal interpretation, the passage might also mean that God breathed the spiritual soul of man into organic matter, that is, into an originally animal body. Thus, a Catholic may hold a limited type of evolution; he may hold that the human body evolved up to a certain point. But he must hold that a special intervention of God in the evolutionary process was required for the production of the human spiritual soul, no matter what explanation is used for the origin of the human body.

According to the literal sense of Genesis, God created the body of the first man out of inorganic material ("dust from the soil") and breathed into it a spiritual soul. The idea that man's soul was infused into an animal body is foreign to the literal meaning of the Bible. The notion of the descent of the human body from the animal kingdom first appeared under the influence of the modern theory of evolution. It is important to note that the biblical text does not completely exclude an interpretation in support of evolution. While the fact of the creation of man by God in the literal sense must be closely adhered to, with regard to how the human body was formed an interpretation which diverges from the strict literal sense is still allowed by the Church, provided that solid reasons for the position are advanced.

There is disagreement, of course, about what is meant by "solid reasons". Many scientists hold that evolution is an established fact; others, equally distinguished, deny it is a "fact" and say that it is only a theory. When scientists stick to facts they are on solid ground. A major problem with the whole question of evolutionism, however, is that often unstated philosophical presuppositions creep into the argument—presuppositions that amount to a denial of the existence of a supreme being. When that happens it is predetermined that the conclusion will conflict with the Catholic faith.

Many Catholics hold what is known as "moderate evolutionism", that is, the theory that the human body evolved to a certain point from animals, and then God intervened directly and breathed into this living, animal body a human soul and so produced the first man and the first woman. Such a theory does not seem to be contrary to Catholic teaching, and Catholics are free to hold it.

The whole matter of evolution is highly speculative. The affirmation that man descended from the apes has not been proven. We know for sure that God created man—when and how he did it we do not know.

8

# ALL THE CHILDREN OF ADAM AND EVE

We have considered the Catholic teaching that the first man, called "Adam" in the Bible, was created by God. Granting a certain latitude about *how* God created Adam's body, that is, whether directly from the dust of the earth or indirectly through some process of evolution, the

Church insists that the spiritual soul of Adam and of each human person is immediately created by God.

So much for Adam. But where did Eve, the first woman, come from? According to Genesis 2:21–22 the body of the first woman was formed from the body of the first man: "The Lord God made the man fall into a deep sleep. And while he slept, he took one of his ribs and enclosed it in flesh. The Lord God built the rib he had taken from the man into a woman, and brought her to the man." Most of the Fathers of the Church understood this passage in the literal sense, but some interpreted it allegorically or symbolically. According to a decision of the Pontifical Biblical Commission in 1909 the literal historical sense is to be adhered to in regard to the formation of the first woman out of the first man. St. Paul says in 1 Corinthians 11:8 that "the woman is of the man". We must admit though that the saying is and remains quite mysterious.

The account of Eve's creation from the rib of Adam says a great deal about the relationship of the sexes. Upon first seeing Eve, Adam exclaims: "This at last is bone from my bones, and flesh from my flesh! This is to be called woman, for this was taken from man." Here we find the essential equality of man and woman. Thus, according to the Bible, woman is not meant to be just a slave of man, as was common in the Middle East of the time. Here we also find the divine institution of marriage: "This is why a man leaves his father and mother and joins himself to his wife, and they become one body" (Gen 2:24). Moreover, in the manner of Eve's creation from Adam, the Fathers saw a symbol of the origin of the Church and the sacraments from the gaping wound in the side and heart of Christ, the second Adam.

Do the biblical names "Adam" and "Eve" stand for

one man and one woman who were the first human pair? Or does "Adam" stand for a multiplicity of first men and "Eve" for all the first women? Although it is not a dogma of the faith, the Church does teach that the whole human race stems from one single human pair. The reason for this is that it is a necessary presupposition of the dogma of original sin and the Redemption of all men by Jesus Christ.

Under the influence of materialistic evolutionism some scientists and theologians have maintained that, about the same time, nature gave rise to many primitive men and women. They mated and so gave rise to the various races. This theory is often called "polygenism" (many stems). The Church teaches that the first couple, Adam and Eve, are the progenitors of the whole human race. This view is usually called "monogenism" (one stem).

If polygenism were true, there would be serious theological and religious consequences. For example, it would mean that all men and women are not related since they do not all derive from one single human pair, Adam and Eve. It would raise serious difficulties about original sin: how it happened and how it is transmitted from one generation to the next. The Biblical Commission in 1909 said that the unity of the human race is to be reckoned among the facts which affect the foundations of the Christian religion, and which, therefore, are to be understood in their literal, historical sense.

In 1950 Pope Pius XII strongly rejected the theory of polygenism:

> Christians cannot lend their support to a theory which involves the existence, after Adam's time, of some earthly race of men, truly so called, who were not descended ultimately from him,

or else supposes that Adam was the name given to some group of our primordial ancestors. It does not appear how such views can be reconciled with the doctrine of original sin, as this is guaranteed to us by Scripture and tradition, and proposed to us by the Church. Original sin is the result of a sin committed, in actual historical fact, by an individual man named Adam, and it is a quality native to all of us, only because it has been handed down by descent from him (see Rom 5:12–19) (*Humani Generis, Denzinger* 2328).

As Catholics, then, we must hold that all men on the face of the earth today descended from Adam and Eve. If there ever were any so-called "Pre-Adamites", they all perished before the creation of Adam.

According to the Bible, Adam and Eve were the very first man and woman. Thus, we read in Genesis 2:5 that before Adam "there was not a man to till the earth." Also, Adam "named his wife 'Eve' because she was the mother of all those who live" (Gen 3:20). St. Paul teaches the same truth in Acts 17:26, "From one single stock he created the whole human race so that they could occupy the entire earth."

Jesus Christ is a descendant of Adam; he is the second Adam. Therefore, he is a member of the one human race. As such he has redeemed us and established us as the adopted sons of God and heirs of heaven. If he were not our brother in the flesh, this would not be so. Thus, we are all children of one single human pair, Adam and Eve.

9

# BODY AND SOUL

A correct understanding of the Catholic faith is closely connected with a correct understanding of the nature of man. If a person has false ideas about human nature, such as thinking that there is no basic difference between a man and an animal, then that person cannot embrace the Catholic faith until those false ideas have been abandoned.

A convincing and consoling aspect of Catholicism is its concern for the truth about human nature. In America we are surrounded by materialists and atheists who say that man is no more than a complex combination of atoms and molecules. They deny therefore that there is anything truly spiritual about man. Others claim and often have claimed in the past that the true man is a spirit and that the body is only a shadow or an appearance. The Greek philosopher Plato, for example, said that man is a soul and that the body is just a shadow.

In opposition to both exaggerated spiritualism and materialism the Catholic Church teaches that man consists of two essential parts or principles—a material body and a spiritual soul. The rational soul is the principle of life and unity for the human person; it is the basic source of all vital activities—vegetative, sensitive and intellectual.

According to the teaching of the Bible, man is composed of body and spirit and will be resolved again into both at death. Thus, we read in Genesis 2:7, "And the Lord God fashioned man of dust from the soil. Then he breathed into his nostrils a breath of life, and thus man became a living being."

It is important to note that *body and soul are not two complete things* set side by side like two blocks of wood. They are *two principles* of the one being, man. We should not think of the soul in the body as a driver in his car. Rather, the two principles form an intrinsic natural unity so that the spiritual soul gives being and life to the body. Thus, death results in the corruption and disintegration of the body. This means that the material elements that go to make up the body, once they have been abandoned by the soul, lose their principle of unity (namely, the soul) and fall back into their former multiplicity.

According to Genesis 2:7, by virtue of the creation of the soul, the dust from the soil becomes a living human body and thus an essential part of human nature. According to the vision of Ezekiel in chapter thirty-seven the dead and dry bones are awakened to life by the spiritual soul.

In the course of the centuries various thinkers have denied the individuality and immortality of the human soul. Such a denial is an obvious consequence of atheism and materialism. But in the Middle Ages there were some theories, derived from Arab philosophers, that there is only one world soul for all human beings. One might say that it was a form of pantheism. In any event, the Church reacted strongly and rejected these theories and asserted both the individuality and the immortality of each human soul.

The above consideration might appear abstruse, and it might seem to have little to do with belief in Christ. But that is not so. For, if the human soul is not individual and not immortal, then there is no theological basis for responsibility for our moral actions. The warning of Jesus about divine judgment, his promise of eternal life for those who believe and follow his commandments, his warning about eternal death for obstinate sinners—these truths and many others in the Bible lose their urgency and are turned into some kind of poetic imagery if the human soul is not immortal.

The firm belief in the next world expressed in the New Testament rests on the conviction of personal immortality. Thus, Jesus says, "Do not be afraid of those who kill the body but cannot kill the soul; fear him rather who can destroy both body and soul in hell" (Mt 10:28). And again in Matthew 25:46 he says, "And they will go away to eternal punishment, and the virtuous to eternal life." St. Paul believes that he will be united with Christ immediately after his death, and not only after the resurrection: "I am caught in this dilemma: I want to be gone and be with Christ" (Phil 1:23).

There are some good philosophical arguments for the spirituality and immortality of the human soul. Personally, I think they are quite convincing. However, we have a much more certain source for our certainty about the immortality of the human soul. That is the teaching of the Bible and the Magisterium of the Church. The Church teaches that man is one being, composed of a rational soul and a body. She also teaches that each soul is unique, individual and endowed with personal immortality.

10

# WHERE DOES THE HUMAN SOUL COME FROM?

Man is composed of two essential principles—a material body and a spiritual soul. It is obvious that our bodies come from our parents as a result of the act of generation. But where do our souls come from?

In the course of history there have been a number of conflicting answers to this perplexing question. One theory, probably influenced by the Eastern pantheistic religions, said that human souls pre-existed from all eternity. This means that they existed long before their infusion into the body. Some early Christian thinkers held this view, of whom Origen (185–254) was the most noteworthy. Some claimed that our souls are imprisoned in our bodies for a sin committed long ago. This view, in effect, denies that man is composed of both a soul and a body as a substantial unity; it says that the soul is the true man and that the body is a temporary and unnecessary addition. The theory of the pre-existence of souls was rejected by the Church in the sixth century.

A second position on the origin of the soul is called "emanationism" or the theory of "flowing out from" the divine substance. This view was taught by the ancient Gnostics and Manichees. The idea is that individual souls proceed by emanation from the essence of God and therefore are part of God. This theory contradicts the absolute simplicity of God who is not composed in any sense. The First Vatican Council in the last century declared this opinion to be heretical. With regard to this view, St. Augustine said: "The soul is not a part of God; for if it were then it would be in every respect unchangeable", which it most certainly is not.

Another theory about the origin of the soul is called "generationism". It traces the origin of the human soul back to the act of generation performed by the parents. It is obvious that our bodies come from our parents. So why not our souls too? In its crude form this theory is called "traducianism" (from *tradux*, a cutting or slip). It holds that the soul is produced immediately from the male sperm and that children are, in a sense, "cuttings" from the souls of their parents. A more sophisticated form of generationism, recognizing the immaterial nature of the soul, postulates a type of "spiritual seed" by which parents communicate their souls to their children. It is as if the parents transmit a part of their own souls to their children.

The theory of generationism contradicts the simplicity and the spirituality of the soul. An immaterial substance like the soul cannot be cut up into parts. In the fourteenth century Pope Benedict XII condemned generationism and rejected the proposition that "the human soul of a son is propagated from the soul of his father, as his body is from the body of his father".

Where does the human soul come from? The Catholic Church teaches that each and every human soul is immediately created by God. When does God create the soul? Today, as a result of advances in biology, many scientists and philosophers hold that the soul is created at the moment of conception. The constant teaching of the Church on the evil of abortion lends much support to this view, although outstanding thinkers of the past, like St. Thomas Aquinas, have left open the possibility that the soul is created at some point after conception (forty or eighty days).

Even though creationism has never been formally defined by the Church, the fact of a direct creation of each individual soul belongs to the deposit of the Christian faith. Thus, the Fifth Lateran Council in 1513 said that the soul "is immortal and, corresponding to the number of bodies into which it is infused, is capable of being multiplied in individuals, is actually multiplied, and must be multiplied. . . ." In his 1950 Encyclical *Humani Generis* in which he rejected certain deviations from Catholic orthodoxy on the question of human origins, Pope Pius XII said: "The Catholic faith obliges us to hold that the human soul is immediately created by God."

Indications of the doctrine of creationism are found in the Bible. Thus, in Genesis 2:7 God "breathed into his nostrils a breath of life, and man became a living being." In the book of Wisdom 15:11 we read that God "breathed an active soul into him and inspired a living spirit."

So far the Church has not defined the exact moment when the soul is created and infused into the body. Different views have been permitted, but the Church has always insisted that the fetus must be treated as a human being at every stage of its development. Thus the Church has always prohibited abortion at any stage of pregnancy. Given the finalized direction of the conceptus, zygote, embryo and fetus to the fully formed human being who is made in the image and likeness of God, it has become clear to more and more philosophers, theologians and scientists that the creation of the soul and its infusion take place at the moment of conception.

11

# THE IDEA OF THE SUPERNATURAL

When was the last time you heard someone say that God has conferred on man a *supernatural* destiny? When was the last time you heard a sermon on grace as the *supernatural* life of the soul? If I am reading the situation correctly, I suspect that you have heard very little about the supernatural during the past ten or more years.

Not so very long ago almost every instruction in the Catholic faith would include at least some reference to divine grace as the "supernatural life" of the soul. At the present time, I am not aware of many open denials of the Catholic teaching on the supernatural. Rather, what has happened is that the word and, to a great extent, the idea of the supernatural has just dropped out of the Catholic vocabulary. This is unfortunate because the reality behind the word "supernatural" is central and essential to the Catholic faith.

In order to understand what is meant by the supernatural it is first necessary to understand what is meant by "natural". The natural is that which is either a part of nature or proceeds from nature as its effect or that to which nature has a claim. Thus, it is natural for man to breathe, eat, walk, talk, and so forth. By the "natural order" we mean the ordination of all creatures to their particular ends in accordance with their nature. Thus, it is natural for fish to swim, birds to fly and rabbits to hop.

In theological language and in contrast to the "natural", the "supernatural" is that which is neither a part of nature nor proceeds from nature as its effect nor can be claimed by nature. The supernatural, therefore, simply transcends the being, the powers and the claims of nature. The supernatural is super-added by God over the claims and endowments of nature to the natural gifts of the creature.

The Church applies this notion of the supernatural to the life of grace that is communicated to us by faith and Baptism in Christ Jesus. Thus, through the grace of Christ we are elevated to a new level of being and given an end or destiny that totally surpasses the powers and claims of nature, namely, the face to face vision of God himself in ecstatic bliss for all eternity. The Church proclaims as a dogma of the Catholic religion that this end of man is *supernatural*, that is, it is not required by man's nature. Another aspect of this same teaching is the truth that God could have created man and ordained him to a purely natural end—that would make sense and would be no injustice to man. But as a matter of historical fact, after creating man and giving him all that his spiritual nature required (that was the first gift), God added a second and wholly gratuitous gift—possession of himself in knowledge and love as the final end of man.

We might aptly call the supernatural "a gift added to a

gift", since both the natural and supernatural are gifts, but on different levels.

Because of man's spiritual nature and because of his transcendence toward the infinite, he has a certain receptivity for the supernatural. In this regard he is similar to the angels, who also share in the same supernatural destiny.

It is important to note that the supernatural is not some existing being or thing; it does not exist in itself, but in something else, namely, in the human soul. Thus, the supernatural first presupposes an already-existing created nature which receives it and in which it operates. For example, as a result of faith in Jesus and Baptism, God pours divine grace into the soul.

The supernatural is not added merely externally to human nature; it affects nature intrinsically. It permeates the being and powers of man's nature and elevates him to the divine order of being and activity. Therefore, many theologians of the past have said that "the supernatural perfects nature." The reason is that man not only acquires a supernatural end, but also he receives the infused theological virtues of faith, hope and charity and receives the gifts of the Holy Spirit. In order to bring this out, it has been said that the supernatural is to the natural life of the soul similar to the fire that makes iron glow a bright red: red hot iron remains iron, but it has taken on a new mode of existence.

The First Vatican Council in 1870 defined as a dogma of Faith that "God, out of his infinite goodness, destined man to a supernatural end, that is, to a participation in the good things of God, which altogether exceed the human mental grasp" (*Denzinger* 3005). In other words, God freely elevated man to the face to face vision of himself—an end that man's nature in itself does not require, for no creature can claim a right to the personal knowledge and love of the infinite Creator. The attainment of this end by men gives glory to God and fills men with ecstatic, permanent happiness.

Finally, it should be noted that there is no other happy final end for man. Either he attains his supernatural destiny by meriting the Beatific Vision of God, or else he is lost forever. There is no third alternative; there is no eternal "waiting room" for those who have not yet decided which way they want to go.

## 12

## ADAM AND EVE BEFORE THE FALL

Most Catholics know something about the sin of our first parents, Adam and Eve. Most know that they sinned grievously against God and transmitted to us the graceless state called "original sin". One reason for this is the popularity of the account in Genesis, chapters one to three. In the present and following essays I will try to explain the basics of the Catholic teaching on original sin.

We all know from the book of Genesis that God created the world and man, that he placed Adam and Eve in the Garden of Paradise, that, being tempted by the devil, they sinned against God and were cast out of the

Garden. As a result of their sin they lost their state of sanctifying grace; they also became subject to suffering and death.

Today I would ask you to reflect for a few moments on the condition of Adam and Eve before they sinned or *before the Fall*. In previous essays I have explained what is meant by sanctifying grace as the divine life of the soul. It is this grace that makes us "new creatures"; it is this grace that makes us "born again"; it is absolutely essential to possess this grace in order to be able to enter the Kingdom of Heaven. Now the Church teaches that our first parents, before the Fall, were endowed by God with sanctifying grace. Thus, they were in truth children of God and heirs of heaven.

As I explained before, sanctifying grace is a supernatural gift, that is, it is a gift superadded to the gift of nature. It is wholly gratuitous and cannot be the right of any creature. What the Church teaches in this matter, basing herself on the Bible and the writings of the Fathers of the Church, is that Adam and Eve were elevated to the state of sanctifying grace. This is indicated by the intimacy that exists in Paradise between our first parents and God himself (see Gen 1, 2, and 3). St. Paul offers a scriptural proof of the same thing. He teaches that Christ, the second Adam, restored to us what the first Adam had lost—the state of holiness and justice. But if Adam lost it, he must previously have possessed it (see Rom 5:12–21). So it follows that our first parents were endowed with sanctifying grace before the Fall.

It is a disputed point among theologians whether Adam was created in grace or whether he was created and lived for some time before he was raised to the state of sanctifying grace. St. Thomas Aquinas and many of the Fathers of the Church taught that Adam was created in grace, but since other theologians questioned the matter it was left open by the official decree of the Council of Trent in the sixteenth century.

In addition to their original justice or sanctifying grace, our first parents also possessed other wonderful gifts that were lost, both for themselves and for us, when they sinned. They are called the "preternatural gifts". A consideration of these gifts helps us to understand better the blessed life our first parents had before the Fall. When we contrast these gifts with our own present situation, we can perhaps come to a better understanding of the gravity of original sin and how much we have lost as a result of it.

First of all, Adam and Eve, before the Fall, did not have concupiscence, that is, they were free from all irregular desire that is contrary to the law of God. They had perfect control of their passions, which were subject to reason and will at all times. This means that Adam could not get angry unless he freely willed to be angry. The Bible attests to the perfect harmony that existed between reason and sensuality in Genesis 2:25: "Now both of them were naked . . . but they felt no shame in front of each other." After they sinned they began to feel shame (Gen 3:7, 10).

Secondly, our first parents were not subject to the law of death; they had the gift of bodily immortality. Holy Scripture records that God threatened and imposed death as punishment for the violation of his commandment (Gen 2:17; 3:19). And St. Paul says that "by one man sin entered into the world and by sin death" (Rom 5:12).

Thirdly, they had the gift of freedom from suffering; this gift was closely associated with their bodily immortality. The Bible describes suffering as the consequence of sin (Gen 3:16ff.). Before they sinned, our first parents lived in a condition of relatively perfect happiness.

Fourthly, our first parents had an infused gift of knowledge of both natural and supernatural truths. Since they entered into existence in the adult state (they were never babies or children) and since they were the first teachers of humanity, God equipped them with all the knowledge they needed. The profound knowledge of Adam is indicated by his naming of the animals (Gen 2:20).

The Council of Trent, relying on St. Paul, teaches that Adam lost sanctifying grace not merely for himself but also for us. He also lost "the gifts of integrity" both for himself and for us. It is important to note that Adam received the gifts of the original state, not as an individual person, but as head of the human race and so *for* the whole human race. They were an additional enhancing gift to human nature and, according to the will of God, were to be transmitted with that nature to all of us. So original grace, in all its dimensions, was intended to be hereditary grace, passed down from one generation to another.

## 13

# THE SIN OF OUR FIRST PARENTS

In the previous essay we considered the condition of Adam and Eve before the Fall or before original sin. We saw that God created them and placed them in a garden of delight. Having ordained them to the face to face vision of himself, he endowed them with sanctifying grace and with the special "gifts of integrity" which included bodily immortality, freedom from disordered desire, freedom from suffering and infused knowledge.

From our own experience of suffering, ignorance, temptation and the constant threat of death it is obvious that our situation is very different from that of our first parents. How did that come about? What happened? We long for happiness and a permanent grasp on life, but they always seem to elude us.

The answer to this perplexing problem is to be found in the first three chapters of the book of Genesis, in the writings of the Fathers of the Church (esp. in St. Augustine) and in the official teaching of the Catholic Church. In the past many heretics have separated themselves from the unity of the Catholic Church because they have denied one or more aspects of the Catholic teaching on original sin.

According to revelation and the authoritative interpretation of it by the Magisterium of the Church, our first parents, Adam and Eve, sinned grievously in the Garden of Eden by transgressing a divine commandment. Their love for God was tested, and they failed the test, that is, they sinned seriously against God. This doctrine is clearly taught in chapters two and three of Genesis.

In the sixteenth century the Council of Trent declared as infallibly true:

> If anyone does not profess that the first man Adam immediately lost the justice and holiness in which he was constituted when he disobeyed the command of God in the Garden of Paradise; and that, through the offense of this sin, he incurred the wrath and indignation of God, and consequently incurred the death with which God had previously threatened him and, together with death, bondage in the power of him who from that time had the empire of death (see Heb 2:14), that is, of the devil; 'and that it was the whole Adam, both body and soul, who was changed for the worse through the offense of this sin': let him be anathema (*Denzinger* 788).

According to our Catholic faith, therefore, we must hold that our first parents sinned grievously against God. Their sin was a sin of disobedience of some kind, represented in the Bible by the tree of "knowledge of good and evil".

The consequences of their sin were disastrous both for them and for us. They lost sanctifying grace; that meant that they were forever excluded from the possibility of attaining heaven and the Beatific Vision of God—something that their whole nature longed for. They were expelled from the Garden of Paradise. They became immediately subject to suffering and death. They lost the gifts of integrity and thus became subject to concupiscence or irregular desire; the passions could confuse and overcome the mind.

Christian tradition has called the sin of Adam and Eve "original sin". Unfortunately, there is a certain ambiguity in the expression. For, original sin was a personal sin on the part of our first parents; for that sin they paid a terrible price in suffering and death. The effects of that sin have tormented the human race from the beginning. As a result of their sin, they lost both sanctifying grace and the gifts of integrity.

Please note that Adam was deputed by God as the moral head of the human race. That means that in a certain sense he acted in our place. So our possession or non-possession of grace and the special gifts depended on whether or not Adam was faithful to God. If he had been faithful and had not sinned, we would have come into this world with the same gifts that he possessed; since he sinned, we now come into this world lacking those gifts. But the point is that we still need divine grace in order to attain the end to which God has ordained us.

Original sin, therefore, was a personal sin of Adam, but it is not our personal sin. As a result of that first sin we come into this world lacking something we need in order to attain God, namely, divine grace. We also lack the gifts of integrity, but they are not as important for us as divine grace is.

It is precisely at this point that the Incarnation of the Word, the coming of Jesus into the world, is so crucial. Without Christ all was lost; no one could reach eternal life. Through Christ now all can attain eternal life, provided that they have faith in him and lead a good life. What was lost for us by Adam has been superabundantly restored to us by Christ, the "second Adam". For more on this please read and meditate on what St. Paul says in Romans 5:12–21.

14

# THE TRANSMISSION OF ORIGINAL SIN

At the present time in this series of essays we are trying to get a grasp of the Church's teaching on original sin. I pointed out already that our first parents sinned grievously against God and as a result lost not only sanctifying grace but also the extra "gifts of integrity". It is very important to note that Adam was the head of the human race—not only the physical head but also the moral head. This means that in some sense we were included in him, that he acted as our representative. Thus, our possession or non-possession of grace and the preternatural gifts depended on the fidelity of Adam. If he were faithful, we would have the same gifts he had; if he sinned, we would be deprived of the gifts that he was deprived of.

All of us are confronted with the problem of evil—moral evil and the physical evils of suffering and death. We sense intuitively that something is wrong with human nature and the human family. Why is there so much killing, lying, selfishness, infidelity and hatred? There is no doubt that it is all around us. Where does so much evil come from? The Bible and the Church say that the source of all these evils is the sin of Adam and Eve, original sin, and the personal sins of all the human beings who have ever lived on the face of this planet. Just imagine what kind of world this would be if every person did the minimum by observing the Ten Commandments. We would have a veritable paradise on earth.

As you know, there have been many attempts to explain the origin of evil. Some of the early heretics, especially the Gnostics and the Manichaeans, said that the moral corruption of mankind comes from a god of evil who is engaged in an eternal struggle with a good god. Others, influenced by the philosophy of Plato, said that man's inclination to evil comes from a sin committed by the soul before it was imprisoned in the body.

The great St. Augustine spent a good part of his life fighting errors concerning original sin. His chief opponents were Pelagians, followers of the English monk Pelagius (355-425 A.D.), who taught: a) the sin of Adam is transmitted to posterity not by inheritance but through imitation of bad example; b) death, suffering and concupiscence are not punishment for sin but are the natural condition of man; c) the Baptism of children is administered, not for the remission of sin, but as a sign of acceptance by the Church and to enable men to reach the Kingdom of Heaven.

These errors are far from dead today. They live on in contemporary secular humanism, in modern atheism and in the writings of some liberal Protestant and Catholic theologians.

What does the Catholic Church say about the transmission of original sin? She teaches infallibly in the decrees of the Council of Trent in the sixteenth century that the sin of Adam is "communicated to all men by propagation" and "not by imitation". Trent says explicitly that Adam lost grace not just for himself but also for all of us, his descendants. It positively teaches that sin, which is the death of the soul, is inherited by all his posterity by descent, not by imitation of his bad example, and that it resides in every single human being. Sin can be removed only by the merits of Jesus Christ; normally those merits are conferred on both adults and children through the Sacrament of Baptism. Therefore, children are also baptized for the forgiveness of sins (*Denzinger* 789-791).

Although there are some hints of the doctrine of original sin in the Old Testament (see Ps 51:7; Job 14:4; Sir 25:33; Wis 2:24), the main proof is found in Romans 5:12–21, where St. Paul establishes a parallel between the first Adam, who transmitted sin and death to all of us, and Jesus Christ, the second Adam, who merited for us divine grace and eternal life. Let us consider what Paul says:

> Well then, sin entered the world through one man, and through sin death, and thus death has spread through the whole human race because everyone has sinned. . . . Again, as one man's fall brought condemnation on everyone, so the good act of one man brings everyone life and makes them justified. As by one man's disobedience many were made sinners, so by one man's obedience many will be made righteous (Rom 5:12, 18–19).

Belief in original sin is not a late addition to Catholic faith, as is evidenced by the words of St. Paul. Also, the fact that the primitive Church baptized children "for the remission of sin" is solid proof that the first Christians believed in the reality of original sin. Otherwise, they would not have baptized children who are not yet capable of committing any personal sins.

In summary, the main points I wish to make here are that the sin of Adam alone is the principal cause of original sin and that it is transmitted to us by natural generation and descent from Adam.

## 15

## WHAT IS ORIGINAL SIN?

One of the most difficult truths in the Catholic faith to understand properly is the doctrine of original sin. The sixteenth century Protestant dissenters rejected the traditional Catholic understanding of original sin and gave it a new meaning.

What do we mean when we say that a child is born with original sin? A new-born infant or a very young child is a beautiful creation of God. When we look at a baby we might ask ourselves or others: How can that child, who does not yet have the full use of its mind and free will, be guilty of sin? Something seems to be wrong here since we know from the book of Genesis that everything God creates is good.

This problem can be solved by coming to a proper understanding of what the Church means by "original sin". First of all, it is important to note that original sin is very different from what we call "personal sin", that is, the free, deliberate sins that adults commit. A personal sin is a willful violation of one of God's commandments.

It is not just breaking one of God's commandments; it is the *willful*, *deliberate* violation of God's law. Now, only a person who has the use of reason can do that. Personal sins can be either venial or mortal, depending on the gravity of the case and the degree of freedom. The main consequence of a mortal sin is that the sinner loses sanctifying grace; he becomes an enemy of God and loses the right to enter heaven.

Let us return to a consideration of sin in the baby. Since he does not have the use of reason and free will, he cannot commit a personal sin. But the Church teaches, relying on the Bible and on the constant testimony of tradition, that all babies are born into this world with original sin on their souls. It follows, therefore, that the "sin" in "original sin" does not mean the same thing as it does in "personal sin". That is true and that is precisely the point I want to make in this essay.

The word "sin" in the expression "original sin" does not mean that the child has personally offended God by a willful and deliberate violation of one of the commandments. It means that the child is born into this world lacking something that it needs in order to attain the end for which God has destined it, namely, the face to face vision of God in the Beatific Vision. In a previous essay I explained that God has destined man for a *supernatural end*, that is, the beatifying vision of himself in eternal love. In order to attain that end he must possess sanctifying grace.

Adam was given sanctifying grace, but through his sin he lost it both for himself and for all his posterity. So infants today are born into this world lacking what they need in order to attain their end, that is, they are born without sanctifying grace. That is what the Church means by the expression "original sin". In no sense does it imply that infants are personally guilty of any sin. The personal guilt involved in original sin is the guilt of Adam, not the guilt of the child.

One might protest: "Why should the child be punished for something that Adam did?" That is a good question. The solution lies in the mysterious will of God who established Adam as the moral head of the human race and made our possession or non-possession of divine grace dependent on whether or not Adam remained faithful to God. He sinned and fell, and so did we, in him. Thus we lost the special gift of grace, but we did not lose something we had a right to.

The story of the fall of Adam and its dire consequences on the human race is spelled out in the whole Bible. That is what the Bible is all about. Let us face it: Adam made a mess of things. In order to get man back on the right track and to bring him to heaven and his eternal destiny, God chose Israel as the vehicle of his promises and grace. He sent the Patriarchs, the prophets and, finally, his only Son, Jesus Christ our Lord. So the grace that was lost by Adam has been superabundantly restored by Jesus Christ. That is the message of the Bible, and it is stated explicitly by St. Paul in the famous passage in Romans 5:12–21. It is for this reason that Jesus is often referred to as the "second Adam".

In the course of history there have been many false explanations of original sin; many of those are still circulating today. The Catholic Church rejects the notion that original sin is to be identified with concupiscence or sexual desire. She also rejects the Lutheran and Calvinistic idea that by original sin man was corrupted in his very nature so that he cannot think or do anything good.

Catholic teaching insists that man is born without grace, which he needs but which he can acquire through faith in Jesus Christ and Baptism. Original sin has left him "wounded", for he is burdened with concupiscence which comes from sin and can lead to sin. But his nature is good, and with the grace of God he can overcome all obstacles and attain the supernatural end for which he was created.

## 16

## NEVER MAKE LIGHT OF SIN

In previous essays we have considered that God destined all men for a supernatural end, that the possession of sanctifying grace at the moment of death is necessary in order to attain that end, that Adam was established in grace at the very beginning and that Adam, through his own personal sin, lost that grace both for himself and for all of his posterity. God had created Adam as the physical and moral head of the human race, and he made our possession/non-possession of sanctifying grace dependent on whether or not Adam remained faithful to him. Adam fell and so did we, in him. That is the message of the Bible and that is the constant teaching of the Catholic Church (see Rom 5:12–21).

It is very sobering to reflect on what our lives might be like if Adam had not sinned. It is not possible to know exactly what life would be like, but we do have a few indications from Holy Scripture, especially in the accounts of Adam and Eve in the Garden of Paradise before the Fall. Just think for a moment: if Adam and Eve had not sinned there would be no suffering, no death as we know it, no lying, stealing and killing, no passions out of control; we would have infused knowledge so there would probably be no need to go to school; there would be no war, no oppression, no exploitation of one group by another. Sounds like utopia or paradise, doesn't it? If Adam had not sinned, the many evils recorded in human history would never have taken place.

Many of our contemporaries, mostly those who have lost all faith in God, deny the reality of original sin and say that man is naturally good. Since they cannot deny the many evils in the world, they try to explain them as the result of social structures and social conditioning. Just change the structures of society, they say, and all these evils will be eliminated. All communists and most socialists view man in this light. They do not locate the source of evil in man's heart, as the Bible does; they locate it in social structures.

The Catholic Church, relying on the Bible and the divine revelation committed to her by the Lord Jesus, proposes a very realistic view of man, his strengths and his weaknesses. As a result of original sin, she says, when men and women come into this world they are deprived of sanctifying grace and the preternatural gifts of integrity. The lack of sanctifying grace, as a result of man's turning away from God, has a certain character of guilt; the turning of God away from man has the character of punishment. The lack of gifts of integrity has the result of man being subject to concupiscence, ignorance, suffering and death. These results remain even after the removal of original sin by faith in Jesus Christ and Baptism.

Thus, by Adam's sin man is deprived of the supernatural gifts, and he is wounded in his nature.

The wounding of human nature must not be conceived, with the Protestant reformers and the Jansenists, as the complete corruption of human nature. Man's nature remains basically good. In the state of original sin man still has the ability to know natural religious truths, such as the existence of God, and to perform natural morally good actions. Thus, the Council of Trent in the sixteenth century taught that free will was not lost by the fall of Adam; Vatican I in the nineteenth century taught that man, with his natural power of cognition, can know with certainty the existence of God.

The Church taught officially at the Council of Orange in 529 A.D. that the wounding of nature extends to the body as well as to the soul. There are two wounds of the body: openness to suffering and openness to death.

St. Thomas Aquinas, and many theologians since his time, list four wounds of the soul, which are opposed to the four cardinal virtues: 1) *ignorance* = the difficulty of knowing the truth (opposed to prudence); 2) *malice* = the weakening of the will in embracing the good (opposed to justice); 3) *weakness* = recoiling before difficulties in the struggle for the good (opposed to fortitude); 4) *concupiscence* = the persistent desire for satisfaction of the senses against the judgment of reason (opposed to temperance). The wounds of the body have been caused by the loss of the preternatural gifts of impassibility and immortality; the wounds of the soul have been caused by the loss of the preternatural gifts of knowledge and freedom from concupiscence.

The human lot is to suffer and to die. There are moments of joy, but there is much suffering and unhappiness. We rebel against this state and instinctively feel that something is wrong; we feel that our lot should be better. God intended that it should be better, much better, but sin has changed all that. The person who knows what sin is can never make light of it.

17

## DO INFANTS DYING WITHOUT BAPTISM GO TO LIMBO?

We have seen that as a consequence of original sin the sons and daughters of Adam are born into this world deprived of sanctifying grace and the preternatural gifts of integrity. The question I would like to consider here is: What is the situation in the next life of the person who dies in the state of original sin alone, that is, without Baptism but also without personal mortal sin? A closely related question is: What happens to unbaptized infants who die before reaching the use of reason? (One may immediately add: What is the eternal destiny of the millions of aborted babies who die without Baptism?)

In this consideration it is absolutely essential to remember the necessity of Baptism for eternal salvation. For, our Lord says clearly, "Unless a man is born again of water and the Holy Spirit he cannot enter into the

Kingdom of God" (Jn 3:5). Relying on this revelation and the constant practice of the Church, the Magisterium teaches that those who depart this life in the state of original sin are excluded from the Beatific Vision of God.

The Second Council of Lyons (1274) and the Council of Florence (1438–45) declared: "The souls of those who die in mortal sin *or with only original sin* soon go down into hell, but there they receive different punishments" (*Denzinger* 464, 693). It is very important here to understand precisely how the Church understands the phrase "different punishments". The Church does not say that unbaptized infants who die are punished forever in hell like mortal sinners.

With regard to the punishment of hell theologians distinguish between the "pain of loss", which means exclusion from the Beatific Vision of God, and the "pain of sense", which is caused by external means and which will be felt by the senses even after the resurrection of the body.

St. Augustine and many of his followers thought that infants dying in original sin must suffer both the pain of loss and the pain of sense. The Greek Fathers and the scholastics from the time of St. Thomas Aquinas favor the teaching of Pope Innocent III (1201) that "the punishment for original sin is the loss of the vision of God, but the punishment for actual sin is the torment of an everlasting hell." Now a state of natural bliss or perfect natural happiness is compatible with the "pain of loss".

If infants dying in original sin are in a state of natural bliss, then they are not in heaven; also, they are not in hell in the usual sense of that term, that is, a place of everlasting punishment. Therefore, they must be in some third state or place. It was as a result of this consideration that theologians postulated a place called "limbo". It is not known who first used the term in this sense or when it occurred; the term and the idea have been known to Catholic theologians since the thirteenth century.

Limbo is defined as "the place or state of infants dying without the Sacrament of Baptism who suffer the pain of loss but not the pain of sense". It may come to you as a surprise to learn that the Church does not affirm the existence of limbo. Its existence is a postulate of theologians. The last time limbo was mentioned in a papal document was by Pius VI in 1794. In that bull he did not teach the existence of limbo, but rejected the arguments of the Jansenists against it.

Since about 1900 a number of theologians have defended the thesis that infants dying without Baptism can attain heaven and the Beatific Vision. We know that this is the case for those infants who, like the Holy Innocents in Bethlehem, die for the Faith and so receive a baptism of blood. Different theologians have proposed substitutes for Baptism, such as the prayer and desire of their parents or the Church, or the attainment of the use of reason at the moment of death (by a divine illumination) so that the dying child can decide for God, or the suffering and death of the child as a quasi-sacrament. These means of salvation are possible, but their reality cannot be proven from the sources of revelation.

There is no doubt that many theologians today reject the notion of limbo and teach one or other salvation theory for infants dying without Baptism. But I believe that the common opinion still among the majority of Catholics is that they go to limbo. This does not mean, however, that the teaching of limbo has been embraced by the Church as a certain and definite solution. The question of limbo is still an unsettled question in Catholic theology. The Church does not officially endorse the existence of limbo.

Since we would like to see everyone saved, there is a natural tendency to want to place all the infants dying without Baptism in heaven. This is definitely the present tendency, but it is not without its dangers. One consequence of this theory is to tend to neglect the Sacrament of Baptism for infants. For, some say, "Why baptize them since they are saved anyway." That is not what the Church says. In fact, in 1958 the Holy Office warned against this opinion, saying that it "lacked solid foundation".

In the present stage of our understanding of revelation, only limbo as a solution to the problem seems to preserve intact the doctrine and practice of the Church concerning the absolute necessity of Baptism for eternal salvation.

18

# ANGELS BY THE MILLIONS

We have been considering the divine work of creation. So far we have reflected on what revelation has to say about the world and man. Before we leave this area of

Catholic doctrine there is still one more part of God's creation to consider, namely, the angels.

We don't hear much about the angels these days, even though they are a part of God's revelation to us and also a part of our world. I suppose we could say that the angels are not popular today (unless they happen to be devils). An exception to this modern trend was the surprising success of Billy Graham's book, *Angels: God's Secret Agents* (Doubleday, 1975). The book was a Best Seller for many weeks and sold hundreds of thousands of copies, so there must be much interest in angels out there somewhere. The reason Billy Graham wrote the book was that one day he decided to preach a sermon on angels and he could not find much material on them. He decided to study the Bible carefully on the subject; he found so much material, over three hundred references to angels, that he produced the book from his research.

Many Catholic churches used to have angels in an adoring position on either side of the altar, facing the tabernacle. Unfortunately, most of them have been thrown out since Vatican II by liturgical "purists" who have a certain dislike for images of angels and saints. One Catholic church they have not been removed from, and could not be removed from without substantially changing its whole appearance, is St. Peter's Basilica in Rome. If the visitor looks for them, he will find angels everywhere in the Basilica. They are on the facade, the ceiling, the pillars, the Bernini columns; there is even one in marble on the floor. There is no doubt in my mind that the popes and artisans who built that magnificent edifice believed in the existence of angels, and strongly believed.

As a matter of fact, the existence of angels and their spiritual nature are doctrines of Faith that have been solemnly proclaimed by the Church. The Bible witnesses not only to what the Church formally teaches but also to many aspects of angelology that are part of historic and traditional Christianity.

Since biblical times there have always been skeptics about the existence of angels. St. Luke testifies in the Acts of the Apostles that "the Sadducees say there is neither resurrection, nor angel, nor spirit." Of course, materialists and rationalists in all ages deny that angels exist. If they have any regard for the Bible at all, then they interpret the passages in which angels are mentioned as a type of mythology. And there are many Catholics in the United States today—priests, nuns, theologians, lay people—who, influenced by the materialism and skepticism around them, firmly deny the existence of angels in opposition to the solemn teaching of the Church and the historic faith of those who have preceded us. It seems to me that a reasonable index of fidelity to supernatural revelation and to the Teaching Authority of the Church is the acceptance of angels as created by God.

The Fourth Lateran Council (1215) declared that God "by his almighty power, from the very beginning of time has created both orders of creatures in the same way out of nothing, the spiritual or angelic world and the corporeal or visible universe." These same words were repeated by Vatican I in 1870. The Church has not made a decision on whether or not the angels were created before the material universe or at the same time. The common opinion of theologians is that they were both created at the same time.

The name "angel" is the English word for the Greek *angelos* which means "messenger". So an angel is a messenger of God to men. The name "angel", therefore, describes the function or office, but not the nature of the being in question.

Usually we apply the name "angel" only to good spirits. The bad angels, or those that rebelled against God and were cast into hell, are called "devils" or "demons". An angel is a purely spiritual created substance who exists as an individual person with mind and will but, unlike man, has no body or bodily parts.

According to the Bible the number of angels is huge. Hebrews says that there are millions of them (12:22); other passages speak of "ten thousand times ten thousand" angels (Dan 7:10; Rev 5:11). The various biblical names seem to indicate a gradation and order among the angels. The names given, though not all in one passage are: Seraphim, Cherubim, Thrones, Dominations, Principalities, Powers, Highnesses, Archangels, Angels. They have different functions. The last two orders of angels, "Archangels and Angels", are the ones who, according to the Bible, carry messages from God to men.

## 19

## WHAT IS AN ANGEL?

We know from the Bible and the official teaching of the Church that angels, both good and evil, exist. Even though we cannot see them with our eyes or in any way perceive them with our senses, they are a part of our world. I have defined an angel as "a purely spiritual created substance who exists as an individual person with mind and will but, unlike man, has no body or bodily parts". In this essay I propose to develop more at length what the Church understands the nature of an angel to be.

The definition given above responds to the question, "What is an angel?" Both the Old and the New Testaments often refer to the angels as "spirits". And what is a spirit? In Catholic theology and in Church teaching "spirit" is contrasted to "matter". A spirit is a conscious person with a mind and will who does not have a body; it is a bodiless person. In Catholic teaching that is what an angel is. One should also note that angels are creatures; they were created by God at the beginning of time, just as the material universe was. So they are subject to God and in no sense his rivals.

In the Gospels Jesus often expels evil spirits by the power of his word (see Mt 8:16; Lk 6:18). Good spirits are before the throne of God: "Grace and peace to you from him who is, who was, and who is to come, from the seven spirits in his presence before his throne" (Rev 1:4).

Since the angels are pure spirits, with no admixture of matter, their mode of existence is very different from ours. Not having bodies, they are not tied to bodily necessities the way we are. Thus, they do not eat or sleep; they do not get thirsty; they do not have sexual differentiation into male and female angels.

Since an angel does not have a body, it can never die or lose its existence. Death is a process of disintegration, a falling into parts. Not having a body, an angel cannot be broken into parts. Therefore, it follows that angels are naturally immortal. Once an angel has been created by God, he continues to exist for all eternity. Our Lord alludes to this truth in at last three passages. "Neither can they (the resurrected) die any more for they are equal to the angels" (Lk 20:36). "I say to you that their angels in heaven always see the face of my Father, who is in heaven" (Mt 18:20). At the Last Judgment the Son of Man will say to those on his left hand, "Go away from me, with your curse upon you, to the eternal fire prepared for the devil and his angels" (Mt 25:41).

We see then that angels are naturally immortal. This means that the only way an angel could cease to exist would be if he were annihilated by God. That will not happen since it would imply that God, who is all-wise, had made a mistake in creating the angel in the first place. God is not like us. He does not make mistakes.

The angels are spiritual beings. Intelligence and free will are the two primary attributes of spirit. It follows, then, that the angels are endowed with understanding and free will. Because the angels are pure spiritual beings, their intellect and will are more perfect than those of men. This means that they are more intelligent than we are and also that their wills are stronger than ours, that is, they find less difficulty in adhering to the good than we do. The reason is that they do not encounter the material impediments that we do; their minds and wills cannot be obscured or confused by passion and ignorance as ours often are.

Of course, there is an infinite distance between the perfection of the angels and that of God. They are in no sense "mini-gods". Let us not forget that the Blessed Virgin Mary is above them in heaven since she is the Queen of Heaven.

The angels know only those things that pertain to them and to their functions. They do not know the secrets of God for only the Holy Spirit knows them (1 Cor 2:11); they do not know the thoughts in our minds, for Scripture says of the Lord, "you alone know the hearts of all mankind" (1 Kings 8:39); they do not have certain knowledge of future free actions. Thus, with regard to the coming of the Son of Man, Jesus says: "But as for that day and hour, nobody knows it, neither the angels of heaven, nor the Son, no one but the Father only" (Mt 24:36).

With regard to how the angels know, we can say that, since they do not have a body with senses, they do not receive their information from the outside as we do. It is commonly held by theologians that the angels received infused knowledge from God at the moment of their creation.

Since the angels are superior by nature to all other creatures, they are also more powerful than other creatures. According to 2 Peter 2:11 the angels are superior in strength and power to men. The angels, however, cannot create anything and they cannot work miracles. These powers belong to God alone.

## 20

# THE ANGELS WERE TESTED TOO

Even though there are some similarities between angels and men, there are also some significant differences. The human soul is spiritual (endowed with intellect and free will) and immortal; to that extent it is just like an angel. The main difference is that the human soul is essentially united to a body; being united to a material body it is confined to time and space. Angels are not limited by time and space.

Those similarities and differences are in the order of nature; the natures of the two beings are different. We know from revelation that man has been elevated to a supernatural end, namely, the face to face vision of God. In order to achieve that end he must have sanctifying grace, which is a gift of God, and he must die in the state of grace. The person who dies in the state of grace and is not burdened with any debt of sin goes immediately to God and enjoys the Beatific Vision for all eternity.

The point I want to bring out is that angels also need sanctifying grace. Did you ever think of that? Or have you more or less assumed that the angels were given the Beatific Vision from the moment of their creation? The Beatific Vision is natural only to God. It must therefore be a supernatural gift to any creature—whether angel or man.

Just as he did for mankind, God set a supernatural end for angels, that is, the immediate vision of God. In order to achieve this end he endowed them with sanctifying grace. Most of the Fathers of the Church, along with St. Augustine and St. Thomas Aquinas, taught that the angels were created in grace. The *Roman Catechism*, which was written in the sixteenth century after the Council of Trent, and most catechisms since that time have taught the same thing.

Having sanctifying grace is not, however, the same thing as enjoying the Beatific Vision. Thus, the Catholic who avoids all mortal sin is always living in the state of grace, but he or she does not yet enjoy the face to face vision of God; that comes only after death in the next life. Likewise, the angels were first created in grace. Before they were admitted to the Beatific Vision they were subjected to a trial or a moral testing of their love for God. The angels who remained faithful to God were rewarded with the blessedness of the face to face vision of God. The angels who failed the test and rebelled against God were punished with eternal damnation. The former are called good angels, while the latter are called bad angels or devils.

That the good angels see God face to face is clear in Holy Scripture. Thus we read in Matthew 18:10, "I tell you that their angels in heaven are continually in the presence of my Father in heaven." St. John says in Revelation 5:11, "In my vision, I heard the sound of an immense number of angels gathered round the throne. . . ."

God does not condemn anyone; those who are lost condemn themselves by their own evil choices. Thus the devils were not created devils; they were created good, but rebelled against God and therefore merited to be banned from heaven. With regard to the fallen angels, their moral testing can be deduced from the fact of their fall. Thus, we read in 2 Peter 2:4, "When angels sinned, God did not spare them: he sent them down to the underworld and consigned them to the dark underground caves to be held there till the day of Judgment." St. Jude is witness to the same point: "Next let me remind you of the angels who had supreme authority but did not keep it and left their appointed sphere" (Jude 6).

What we concluded from this is that in the beginning God created millions of angels and endowed them with sanctifying grace. Before they could be admitted to the Beatific Vision they had first to undergo a moral testing. Those who passed the test were admitted immediately into heaven; those who failed the test were cast into hell. In fact, in that moment hell was created.

Some have objected to what seems to be unfair: the angels got only one chance, while human beings get many chances to be saved. The answer to the objection can be found in the different natures of angels and men. Since they are pure spirits, angels choose with their whole being and irrevocably. That is why they could have only one chance and their reward followed immediately. Since men are burdened with passions, concupiscence and ignorance, they cannot put their whole being into one act. Therefore, it takes much time and practice to reach full moral and spiritual maturity. And, thankfully, the Lord is patient with us.

What was the nature of the test the angels were subjected to? Scripture does not give a direct answer to that question. Some theologians, however, both ancient and modern, speculate that the angels were confronted with some image of Jesus Christ the God-man and asked to adore him. They think that some of the angels refused to adore him because of his humanity, which is a nature inferior to theirs. Those who adored him are the good angels, while those who refused are now the devils.

There is a certain propriety about this argument since the resurrected Lord is the King of heaven and the center of the universe. But we do not know for certain what the test was. That is another one of the things we may find out in heaven.

21

# WHERE DID THE DEVIL COME FROM?

God created an immense number of angels in grace, but then they were subjected to some kind of test of their love, as we have seen. Through the centuries there have been those who, obsessed by the power and the extent of evil in the world and not being able to reconcile that with a good God, have said that the devils exist independently of God and are his rivals for domination in the world. They portray God and Satan as two mighty wrestlers in an eternal struggle, with the good God winning for a time and then the evil Satan getting the upper hand. Those who hold this view are often called "Manichaeans"; St. Augustine held this erroneous view for many years before his conversion.

There is no doubt that the devil is very powerful, but he is not a god; he is a creature of the one God of heaven and earth. Scripture says God created everything that is, visible and invisible, and it is all good. If that is so, then how does one explain the existence of the devil? The infallible teaching of the Church, based on Scripture and Tradition, is that the evil angels or devils were created good by God but became evil through their own fault. God tested them but they did not pass the test. Instead of choosing to serve God they chose to love themselves and to oppose God. Thus, in an official declaration on this point the Fourth Lateran Council (1215) said: "The devil and the other demons were created by God good according to their nature, but they made themselves evil by their own doing." So as far as their nature is concerned, the devils are good, just like the angels in heaven; what is evil in the devils is their perverted will which has turned against their God and Maker.

The Fourth Lateran Council did not say explicitly *when* the devils rebelled against God. It implied, however, that the sin of the angels occurred before the creation of man. Also, it should be recalled that in the Book of Genesis the devil is already lurking around when Adam and Eve find themselves in the Garden of Paradise.

Neither the Bible nor the Church says precisely what sin the angels committed. Many of the Fathers of the Church thought that it was a sexual sin. They based their opinion on the mysterious statement in Genesis 6:1–4 about the "sons of God" marrying the daughters of men. They also thought that the angels possessed very subtle or tenuous bodies, thus enabling them to have sexual relations. This view, however, was later rejected when Christian thinkers came to a clearer realization of the spiritual nature of the angels.

The sin of the angels, therefore, must be regarded as a sin of the spirit. According to St. Augustine and St. Gregory the Great it was a sin of pride. St. Thomas Aquinas also said that it was a sin of pride because Lucifer wanted to be like God. Many Fathers and theologians apply to the devil the words of the rebellious Israel to God, "I will not serve" (Jer 2:20). They also apply to the devil the prophecy of Isaiah against the king of Babylon: "How did you come to fall from the heavens, Daystar, Son of Dawn? . . . You used to think to yourself, 'I will climb up to the heavens; and higher than the stars of heaven I will set my throne . . . I will rival the Most High' " (Is 14:12–14). But some modern theologians, as I pointed out before, think that the sin of pride of the angels was in some way related to the Incarnation of the Word and their refusal to adore him.

The Council of Trent said that the devil rules the kingdom of death; this means that he is responsible for death—a teaching which is found in both the Old and New Testaments (Wis 2:24; Jn 8:44). There are those who, admitting the obvious existence of evil in the world, deny that it is related to personal beings or devils; they say that it is the result of impersonal forces. In 1950 Pope Pius XII listed as an error the view that angels are not "personal beings". From this it follows that not only the good angels but also the devils are indeed persons in the full sense of the term.

We have seen that the good angels enjoy the Beatific Vision for all eternity. Likewise, the punishment of the bad angels is without end. For, we read in Matthew 25:41, "Go away from me, with your curse upon you, to the eternal fire prepared for the devil and his angels."

Is it possible that after thousands or even millions of

years of punishment that God will eventually relent and take back into the joy of heaven all the devils and the men and women in hell? It would be comforting to think so. Origen and many of his followers thought so; they taught that damned angels and men, after a long period of purification, will be re-established in grace and will return to God. It is indeed a comforting thought, but it has been repeatedly condemned by the Church as false and heretical. It is a form of wishful thinking that we all can fall into.

22

# EACH PERSON HAS A GUARDIAN ANGEL

The good angels are intelligent spiritual creatures who do not have bodies and who are perpetually in the presence of God—they see him face to face in the Beatific Vision. One might ask, "What do the angels do?" The answer is that their primary task is the glorification and service of God. Gathered around the throne of God (Rev 5:8), they constantly cry out, "To the One who is sitting on the throne and to the Lamb, be all praise, honor, glory and power, for ever and ever", and "Holy, holy, holy is the Lord God, Almighty; he was, he is and he is to come" (Rev 4:8).

Not only do the angels worship and praise God, but they also serve him in various ways. As messengers of God the angels transmit revelations and directions to men and women on earth. Thus, the angel of the Lord appeared to Zechariah, the future father of John the Baptist, in the temple and conveyed a message to him (Lk 1:11ff.). The angel Gabriel appeared to Mary and announced to her that she was to be the mother of Jesus the Messiah (Lk 1:26ff.). Likewise, an angel appeared to St. Joseph in his sleep and told him to take Mary and Jesus to Egypt. An angel spoke to Philip, to Cornelius, and another one freed St. Peter from prison (Acts 8:26; 10:3; 12:7ff.). The angels, therefore, carry out God's commands with reference to human beings. St. Thomas Aquinas points out that the angels are an integral part of divine providence and God's governance of the world.

The secondary task of the good angels is protection of men and care for their eternal salvation. The Holy Bible testifies in many places that the angels are in the service of mankind. Thus we read in Hebrews 1:14, "The truth is that they (= angels) are all spirits whose work is service, sent to help those who will be the heirs of salvation." Psalm 91:10ff. describes the care that the angels have for the just: "No disaster can overtake you, no plague come near your tent: he will put you in his angels' charge to guard you wherever you go. They will support you on their hands in case you hurt your foot against a stone." Protecting angels make regular appearances in the Old Testament, for example, in Genesis, Exodus, Tobit and Daniel.

The guardian angels are honored in the liturgy of the Church on October 2. The traditional *Roman Catechism* teaches: "By God's Providence the task is given to the angels of protecting the human race and individual human beings, so that they may not suffer any serious harm."

Although the Church has no official teaching on the matter, it has been commonly taught for hundreds of years by theologians that every one of the faithful has his own special guardian angel from the moment of Baptism. In addition, many theologians, including St. Thomas Aquinas, teach that every human being, believer or unbeliever, has his own special guardian angel from birth. The biblical foundation for this belief is found in the words of our Lord in Matthew 18:10, "See that you never despise any of these little ones, for I tell you that their angels in heaven are continually in the presence of my Father in heaven." Commenting on this passage, St. Jerome wrote, "How great is the value of the human soul that every single person has from birth received an angel for his protection."

We know from the Bible and from the teaching of the Church that guardian angels really exist. It is fitting, therefore, that we should show veneration for them, for they not only see God but they are also a part of our world. They merit our respect because they continually worship in the presence of God and because they constantly watch out for our welfare. Thus, it is a good and holy practice to pray to one's guardian angel. This has been a common practice among Catholic Christians now for about a thousand years.

In the centuries between the fall of Jerusalem and the birth of Jesus Christ postexilic Judaism came to a deeper realization of how God governs the world and how he makes use of his angels. A good example of this is the divine tenderness exercised by the angel Raphael in the book of Tobit in the Old Testament.

Thus, the way was prepared for the Christian view of the angels as spelled out in the New Testament. Jesus'

Good News about the universality of God's love is the basis of the Catholic doctrine of guardian angels, especially since Jesus himself said that "their angels in heaven are continually in the presence of my Father in heaven." Devotion to a guardian angel is not just for children. We all have one, and we should pray to him. When was the last time you prayed to your guardian angel?

23

# THE POWER OF THE DEVIL

In the previous essay we considered the role of guardian angels in our lives. We saw that they work within God's providence to help protect us from physical and moral evils. The other side of the coin is that there are fallen angels or devils around. How do they fit into the complete picture of God's good creation? To what extent can they harm human beings? These are two points that I would now like to consider.

We have already seen that the bad angels became evil by their own fault. They were condemned to hell, but until the Last Judgment they retain a certain influence over the affairs of this world. There is something very mysterious about evil. It was even present in the Garden of Paradise in the form of the serpent who tempted Eve and, through Eve, Adam. The devil does have power over us, but that power is limited. He is like a dog on a leash. The Lord permits the devil to tempt us in order to purify our love for him. Also, we should never forget that God is infinitely more powerful than Satan—so much so that he is able to bring good out of evil. I make no claim that this explains the whole problem, but it does help to make some sense out of it.

It is simply a matter of Catholic faith that the devil possesses a certain dominion over all mankind as a result of Adam's sin. The Council of Trent solemnly declared that Adam "incurred the wrath and indignation of God, and consequently incurred the death with which God had previously threatened him and, together with death, *bondage in the power of him who from that time had the empire of death* (see Heb 2:14), *that is, of the devil*" (*Denzinger* 788). We can thank the devil for death, and since we are all destined to die we are all subject to his "kingdom of death".

We should not make light of the devil since he is mentioned repeatedly in the Gospels and in other New Testament writings. Jesus calls him "the prince of this world" (Jn 12:31 and 14:30). St. Paul refers to him as "the god of this world" (2 Cor 4:4). Before Christ's redemptive death and the birth of the Church, the devil seems to have had a pretty free hand. By his sacrificial death on Calvary, in principle Jesus destroyed the power of the devil; it remained only to apply the grace of Christ to all mankind through the preaching of the Good News and the administration of the sacraments. At the Last Supper Jesus said, "Now the prince of this world is to be overthrown", referring to the efficacy of his death (Jn 12:31).

The devils try to do us moral injury by tempting us to commit sin. Some of the devils' successes recounted in the Bible are: the fall of Adam and Eve, Cain's murder of his brother Abel, Judas' betrayal of Jesus. St. Peter himself warns us: "Be calm but vigilant, because your enemy the devil is prowling round like a roaring lion, looking for someone to devour" (1 Pet 5:8).

According to St. Peter we should have a healthy fear of the devil because he is dangerous; he is also much more clever than we are. Thus, it is very foolish—like playing with fire—to have anything whatsoever to do with Satanism and Satanic cults in any of their forms. The devil is evil; he is an envious liar who has nothing but hatred for human beings, especially for Christians who are in the state of grace.

We should not, however, have an exaggerated fear of the devil. We should always remember that he is also a creature and that he is totally under God's control. He can tempt a person only to the extent to which God in his wisdom permits him. Thus, Paul writes these consoling words: "You can trust God not to let you be tried beyond your strength, and with any trial he will give you a way out of it and the strength to bear it" (1 Cor 10:13). Man's will always remains free, so the devil, no matter how furious his temptations might be, cannot force a person to commit sin. Also, God's grace is always there to help us. Therefore, there is no such thing as an irresistible temptation to sin; it might be very, very appealing, but it is not irresistible.

The evil spirits also try to harm man physically, sometimes through demonic possession. We heard a lot about that some years ago when the film "The Exorcist" was making the rounds. Possession sometimes occurs when an evil spirit takes forceable possession of the human body, so that the bodily organs and the lower powers of the soul, but not the higher powers of mind and will, are dominated by him. The possibility and reality of possession are clearly established by the testimony of Jesus himself who drove out many devils (see Mk 1:23ff.; Mt 8:28ff. and passim).

When I was growing up I was told that everyone has his or her own guardian angel and tempting devil. You have seen the picture: the good angel at the right ear and the bad angel at the left ear. Many Christian authors of the past have taught this, and I believe it has been quite common in catechism classes. There is, however, no basis in the Bible and in the official teaching of the Church for the opinion that God appoints a bad angel for each person to tempt him or her throughout life. Such an opinion is not compatible with the goodness and mercy of God. Satan might assign a fallen angel to tempt a particular person, but God does not.

# PART IV

# CHRISTOLOGY

I

# JESUS CHRIST IS TRUE GOD

So far I have treated the Church's doctrine about the one God, the Holy Trinity, the divine act of creation and the Fall of Adam and Eve. We have concluded that area of consideration with a final essay on the angels.

Now I will move into another important part of Catholic theology, namely, God's revelation about the Person and Work of our Redeemer, Jesus Christ.

The belief of the Church about precisely who Jesus is and what he did during his earthly life and how he now relates to us from his place in heaven at the right hand of the Father is crucial for our own Christian existence. We are, it must never be forgotten, *Christians*. That means that we are followers of Jesus Christ. In order to understand properly what it means to be a Christian we must know clearly who Jesus is and what he expects of us.

The most basic belief of the Catholic Church about Jesus Christ is that he is truly God and truly the Son of God. I will now try to point out more in detail what that means.

The Church's belief in the divinity of Jesus Christ and in his divine sonship is clearly expressed in all the creeds that have been worked out in the course of history. The one most familiar to us is the Nicene-Constantinople

Creed of 381 A.D. which we pray each Sunday at Mass: "We believe in one Lord, Jesus Christ, the only Son of God, eternally begotten of the Father, God from God, Light from Light, true God from true God, begotten, not made, one in Being with the Father." The Athanasian Creed of the fifth century puts it this way: "The true Faith is: we believe and profess that our Lord Jesus Christ, the Son of God, is both God and man. As God he was begotten of the substance of the Father before time; as man he was born in time of the substance of his mother. He is perfect God; he is perfect man." What the Church believes, therefore, is that Jesus Christ possesses the infinite divine nature with all its perfections by virtue of his eternal generation from God the Father.

From the time of Jesus' earthly life there have always been those who opposed him and rejected his claim to be true God and the Son of God. The Pharisees accused him of blasphemy and had him put to death. The early heretics refused to accept either his divinity or his humanity. Modern liberal and process theologians will refer to Jesus as the "Son of God", but they do not understand the phrase in any metaphysical or real sense. They give the expression an ethical meaning in the sense that Jesus had a unique awareness of the fact that God is our Father. They say that Christ is the Redeemer of the world, not because he is the natural Son of God, but because he communicated to us the unique knowledge of God which he experienced. This view is quite common among Protestant liberal theologians; it is also the view of some contemporary Catholic dissidents, though it is often disguised under rather ambiguous terminology.

The Old Testament offers a few hints of the divinity

and divine sonship of the Messiah, but the full meaning of the relevant passages was not grasped until after Pentecost. Texts often adduced in this regard are Psalm 2:7, "The Lord said to me: 'You are my son, this day I have begotten you' "; and Isaiah 7:14 which calls him "Emmanuel" or "God is with us". There are many other passages from the Psalms and the Prophets that hint at the divinity of the Messiah, but they are not clear statements, and they were not understood in the full sense of divinity by the Jews of the time. It was not until after the Resurrection and Pentecost that the early Church came to the full realization that Jesus is God himself, the second Person of the Blessed Trinity.

The New Testament contains many passages—in the synoptic Gospels, in St. John, in St. Paul—that either affirm or at least point to the full divinity of Jesus Christ. Thus, at the beginning of Jesus' ministry he is baptized by St. John in the Jordan River. At that moment a voice from heaven said, "This is my Beloved Son in whom I am well pleased" (Mt 3:17). At the transfiguration of Jesus on Mount Tabor a voice came from the clouds and said the same thing (see Mt 17:5; Mk 9:7; Lk 9:35). Peter, James and John heard the voice; it was followed by the injunction, "Listen to him." The biblical expression "my Beloved Son" means the same thing as "only Son".

The testimony of the heavenly Father was understood at the time by John the Baptist and the disciples as an assertion of Jesus' messianic mission. Their minds were not yet ready for the idea that Jesus is one in being with the Father. In the early Church, however, under the influence of the Holy Spirit its true significance as an affirmation of Jesus' divine sonship was fully realized.

2

# JESUS' DIVINE KNOWLEDGE AND POWER

The constant belief of the Church has been that Jesus Christ is true God and the true Son of God. If one were to remove belief in the divinity of Christ from the Christian Creed it would make the lives of Christians and the bloody deaths of the martyrs basically unintelligible.

The Gospels of Matthew, Mark and Luke—often called the *synoptic* Gospels because they give a brief account of Jesus' life and death—present a Jesus who is aware of his unique relationship to God the Father. To anyone who has studied the Gospels or prayed with them for some time it is obvious that Jesus is no ordinary human being. There is something special and something different about him. That "something different" is his consciousness of being the true, consubstantial Son of God.

We must remember, however, that the Gospels were written, most probably, between twenty and fifty years after Jesus' death. They were written after Pentecost, after the early preaching of the Apostles and after the first Christian communities had been functioning for a number of years.

The Apostles themselves did not come to the full realization of who Jesus was until after his Resurrection and after the Holy Spirit had been poured out upon them on Pentecost Sunday. Once their minds had been enlightened by the Holy Spirit they were able to see implications in things that Jesus had said that were not clear to them at the time he said them. Their recollections of what Jesus had done and said were used in their preaching of the Gospel. Eventually that preaching crystallized into definite patterns and form. When the early Christians saw that the Apostles were dying off, they pleaded with them to commit their recollections to writing so that they would be preserved for Christians of future generations. Because of that request we now have the Gospels.

What do the synoptic Gospels tell us about Jesus? They tell us of a man who was aware of his superiority over all creatures, men and angels. He was greater than the prophet Jonah and king Solomon (Mt 12:41–42), greater than king David who regards him as his Lord (Mt 22:43ff.). Angels are his servants, for they appear and minister to him (Mt 4:11), and they will accompany him at his Second Coming (Mk 8:38).

In a number of New Testament passages Jesus makes himself equal to the Lord God of the Old Testament because he asserts of himself what the Old Testament says about the Lord. Thus, Jesus claims to be superior to the Old Testament Law; in his own name he completes and changes certain precepts of the Old Testament Law (Mt 5:21ff.). The Jews believed that Yahweh had established the Sabbath worship and rest; Jesus says that he is Lord of the Sabbath (Lk 6:5)—that is equivalent to claiming to be God.

Aware of his divinity, Jesus imposes obligations on his disciples that only God can require. Thus, he establishes himself as the content and object of faith: "If anyone is ashamed of me and of my words, of him the Son of Man will be ashamed when he comes in his own glory and in the glory of the Father and the holy angels" (Lk 9:26). Moreover, Jesus demands of his followers a love which surpasses all earthly love—something that only God can require: "Anyone who prefers father or mother to me is not worthy of me" (Mt 10:37).

Jesus is not like other men. He is fully conscious of his divine power. Who else but God could truly say, "All authority in heaven and on earth has been given to me. . . . And know that I am with you always—yes, to the end of time" (Mt 28:18–20). During his earthly life Jesus used his divine power to work many miracles, to drive out devils. He also communicated that same power to his disciples (Mt 10:1). Jesus claimed to have the power to forgive sins, which belongs to God alone (Mk 2:5), and showed by miracles that he really did possess that power (Mt 9:6).

We all know the beautiful prayer, "Our Father". Jesus clearly distinguishes his divine sonship from the adoptive sonship of the disciples. Thus, when he speaks of his relation to his heavenly Father he says, "My Father". When he speaks of the disciples' relation to the Father, he says, "Your Father".

The first revelation of Jesus' unique consciousness of being the Son of God was on the occasion of the Finding in the Temple when he was only twelve years old. He said to his sorrowing parents, "Why were you looking for me? Did you not know that I must be busy with my Father's affairs?" (Lk 2:49).

In a remarkable passage, Matthew 11:27, Jesus says

that "no one knows who the Son is but the Father; and who the Father is but the Son." In this statement Jesus made his knowledge equal to the divine knowledge. Jesus also claimed to be the Messiah and the Son of God before the Sanhedrin, an assembly of leading Jewish officials. To the question put to him by the high priest Caiphas, "I put you on oath by the living God to tell us if you are the Christ, the Son of God" (Mt 26:63), Jesus replied clearly, "The words are your own" (26:64). St. Mark gives an even more direct answer, "I am he" (Mk 14:62).

There is much evidence in the synoptic Gospels, therefore, that Jesus is and claimed to be true God and the true Son of God.

3

## THE DIVINITY OF JESUS IN ST. JOHN'S GOSPEL

The Catholic Church believes and proclaims that Jesus Christ, the Son of Mary according to the flesh, is truly God and the Son of God. This stupendous truth—the realization of which has changed millions of lives and continues to inspire hundreds of millions of people—is expressed in the New Testament, in the constant teaching of the Catholic Church throughout the world and in the sacred liturgy which is celebrated each day.

In the New Testament one of the witnesses who constantly emphasizes the divinity of Jesus is St. John in the Gospel that carries his name. From the Prologue in the first chapter to the end of the book the author affirms over and over again that Jesus of Nazareth is the only-begotten Son of God and therefore equal to the Father.

The Gospel of St. John was written to show that Jesus is the promised Messiah and the Son of God: "These are recorded so that you may believe that Jesus is the Christ, the Son of God, and that believing this you may have life through his name" (Jn 20:31). By "Son of God" John means that he is one in being with the Father, as we say in the Creed. In order to see this one need only read carefully the first eighteen verses of St. John's first chapter—commonly called the Prologue.

The Prologue begins with a description of the Word who exists from all eternity, who is an independent Person side by side with God, who is himself God, through whom all finite things were created, who is the source of eternal life (1:1–5). John says that the Word is "the only Son of the Father" (1:14) and that he entered into the world by becoming flesh. The Word made flesh is identical with the historical Jesus of Nazareth (1:17–18).

An important part of the proof of Jesus' divinity is what is known in theology as his "pre-existence". By this is meant a number of affirmations, not only in St. John's Gospel but also in the other Gospels and in other books of the New Testament, to the effect that Jesus always existed with the Father *before* he was conceived in the womb of the Virgin Mary. Thus, Jesus says that he was sent into the world by the Father (5:23), that he came "down from heaven" (3:13), that he came from the Father (16:27ff.). In these and other statements Jesus asserts his pre-existence with God, not in the sense of a created angel but in the sense of his sonship to God. This makes him equal to God the Father and, therefore, asserts his pre-existence from all eternity.

From the Creed and our Christian faith we believe and know that there are three Persons in one God. To say, therefore, that the Son and the Holy Spirit are identical with God or that they are "one in being with the Father" is to assert their full divinity. This truth of the Creed is based, in part, on a number of affirmations in the Gospel of St. John in which Jesus claims identity with the Father.

There is no doubt that Jesus claimed identity with the Father. Consider, for example, the following two texts: " 'My Father goes on working and so do I.' But that only made the Jews even more intent on killing him, because, not content with breaking the sabbath, he spoke of God as his own Father, and so made himself God's equal" (5:17–18). The Pharisees saw clearly that Jesus claimed identity with God; for that reason they wanted to put him to death. Likewise, on another occasion, Jesus said to his enemies, "the Father and I are one" (10:30). Here Jesus is speaking about substantial unity with the Father. The Pharisees understood him in that sense since they accused him of blasphemy and again tried to kill him: "We are not stoning you for doing a good work but for blasphemy: you are only a man and you claim to be God" (10:33).

We should also note that Jesus claimed divine qualities for himself. Thus, he said clearly that he is eternal: "Before Abraham ever was, I am" (8:58). He alone has full knowledge of the Father (7:29), equal power with the Father (5:17ff.) and the power to forgive sins (8:11).

Moreover, he calls himself "the light of the world" (8:12) and "the way, the truth and the life" (14:6). Only God himself can truthfully make such claims.

Jesus also makes divine demands on us by requiring faith in his Person: "You believe in God, believe also in me" (14:1). The reward of faith is to be loved by the Father and by Jesus; they will also come to dwell in the hearts of the faithful: "If anyone loves me he will keep my word, and my Father will love him, and we shall come to him and make our home with him" (14:23). Only God can do that.

St. John also records the solemn profession of Jesus' divinity by the Apostle Thomas. For, when Thomas sees Jesus for the first time after the Resurrection he exclaims, "My Lord and my God" (20:28). Jesus accepts that as the type of faith that Christians should have in him. In fact, the whole Gospel of St. John was written "so that you may believe that Jesus is the Christ, the Son of God, and that believing this you may have life through his name" (20:31).

## 4

## ST. PAUL ON THE DIVINITY OF JESUS

We have considered the testimony of the synoptic Gospels (i.e., Matthew, Mark, Luke) and the writings of St. John to the effect that Jesus is truly God, equal to the

Father. It might be helpful to point out next that St. Paul is also very strong in his writings in affirming the divinity of Jesus.

For those who have the eyes to see and to perceive, the Letters of St. Paul are shot through with his passionate belief that "Jesus is Lord." I will make reference to some of these passages with the hope that you will take out your New Testament and carefully read some of them for your own spiritual profit.

One of the clearest expressions of Paul's belief in the divinity of Jesus is contained in Philippians 2:5–11. In the first two verses we read: "His state was divine, yet he did not cling to his equality with God but emptied himself to assume the condition of a slave, and became as men are . . . ." Here the Apostle distinguishes three different levels of Jesus' existence. First, "his state was divine", that is, he possessed "equality with God"; then, he "became as men are"; finally, "God raised him high and gave him the name which is above all other names" (v. 9).

In the New Testament the Greek word for God (*ho theos*) is normally applied only to God the Father, but on a few occasions Paul also says that Jesus is God. Thus, while speaking of the many gifts conferred on the Israelites, Paul says: "They are descended from the patriarchs and from their flesh and blood came Christ who is above all, *God* for ever blessed" (Rom 9:5). In writing to Titus Paul says: "we must be self-restrained and live good and religious lives here in this present world, while we are waiting in hope for the blessing which will come with the Appearing of the glory of our great *God* and savior Christ Jesus" (2:13). In Colossians 2:9 Paul says the same thing in a different way: "For in him dwells all the fullness of the Godhead corporeally."

One of the most interesting and important titles given to Jesus in the New Testament is that of "Lord", the English translation of the Greek "Kyrios". Most Catholics are still familiar with this Greek word from the "*Kyrie* Eleison", of the Latin Mass. Paul constantly refers to Jesus as "the Lord". Thus, he frequently uses such expressions as "the Lord Jesus" or "the Lord Jesus Christ" or simply "the Lord".

Among the Greek-speaking Jews at the time of Jesus, Kyrios was the correct translation of the Hebrew God-names Adonai and Yahweh and, as such, was applied to the one true God. According to the witness of St. Paul and the Acts of the Apostles the early Christian communities applied this title to the glorified Jesus after his Resurrection.

In the usage of St. Paul the title "Lord" is equivalent to a confession of the divinity of Jesus Christ. Consider, for example, the following: "In the name of Jesus every knee should bow . . . and every tongue should acclaim Jesus Christ as Lord" (Phil 2:10–11).

One way to prove the divinity of Jesus is to show that the Bible ascribes to him certain qualities or attributes that properly belong to God alone. St. Paul does exactly that. Thus, St. Paul attributes divine omnipotence to Jesus: "All things were created by him and in him . . . and by him all things consist" (Col 1:15–17). He also ascribes to Jesus omniscience and eternity, qualities, as we have seen, that belong only to God: "In him are hidden all the treasures of wisdom and knowledge" (Col 2:3); he is "the firstborn of every creature" (Col 1:15). According to the first commandment, worship or adoration is due to God alone, but Paul says that Jesus should be adored: "In the name of Jesus every knee should bow" (Phil 2:10), and "Let all the angels of God adore him" (Heb 1:6).

So from the titles of "God" and "Lord" that St. Paul attributes to Jesus, and from the divine qualities that he attributes to him we can rightly conclude that Paul believed in and proclaimed the divinity of Jesus Christ.

When we consider the biblical data on the divinity of Father, Son and Holy Spirit we should not forget that the New Testament authors did not have all the concepts to work with that we have as the result of almost two thousand years of reflection on the life and words of Jesus. If all three are God, how are they related to each other? That was a difficult question. Paul defines the relationship of Jesus Christ to God as one of sonship. This sonship, however, is not adoptive, as ours is; it is a true and consubstantial sonship of God, as we profess in the Creed. Thus, Paul says, "God sent his own Son" (Rom 8:3); "God did not spare his own Son" (Rom 8:32); and, he has "created a place for us in the kingdom of the Son that he loves" (Col 1:13).

The above few quotes then offer ample evidence for the assertion that St. Paul believed in the full divinity of Jesus Christ the Lord. I suggest that you read one of Paul's Letters today and look for corroborating passages yourself.

5

# JESUS CHRIST IS TRULY HUMAN

Having considered Jesus' true divinity, we now move on to a reflection on his true humanity. It may seem strange to some of my readers that I stress the importance of the real humanity of Jesus Christ. Most Catholics just assume that Jesus of Nazareth, born in a stable of the Virgin Mary on Christmas day, is a man just like other men, sin only excepted.

In the course of Church history, however, there have been a number of heresies that directly concerned the full humanity of Jesus. In the first and second centuries there were heretics called "Gnostics" or "Docetists" who taught that Jesus Christ, the divine Son of God, was only *apparently* a man. They said that he *appeared* to be a man to his disciples and to the crowds as he taught them, but that he did not have a real body such as we have. The reason for this strange view was their belief that matter and the material world are basically evil. They said that God did not create matter; according to them, matter came from an evil principle.

Since Christ in their view is truly God, and since God cannot be touched by evil, it followed that God could not become a true man. Thus, in their view, God revealed himself to us through what appeared to be a man, namely Jesus Christ, but actually he was something like a ghost.

Needless to say, the Church reacted very strongly against this serious error. The Fathers of the Church were tireless in pointing out the many errors that this "Docetism" leads to. For, if Jesus was not truly a man, then he was not born, he did not suffer, he did not die on the Cross. He only *appeared* to do these things. Such a view of Christ would destroy all Christian striving for virtue and attempts to follow in the footsteps of Jesus as the way to the Father. It undermines all credibility in the historicity of the Bible since the Gospels recount many concrete details about the life and death of Jesus. The doctrine of Docetism also wipes out the Church's belief and doctrine of the seven sacraments since they use material things such as water, wine, bread, oil; it nullifies the Holy Sacrifice of the Mass and the real presence of Jesus in the Eucharist. In effect, it destroys the whole Christian faith.

For these and many other reasons the Church has always firmly condemned theories that lead to the denial of the true humanity of Jesus Christ.

The constant faith of the Church is that Jesus Christ assumed a real body, not just an apparent body. This is testified to by the most important facts of the earthly life of Jesus, that is, his conception, birth, public life, suffering, dying and resurrection.

By reflecting for a moment you will recall that we acknowledge these facts each time we pray the Creed. In the Apostle's Creed we say: "I believe in . . . Jesus Christ, his only Son our Lord, who was *conceived* by the Holy Spirit, *born* of the Virgin Mary, *suffered* under Pontius Pilate, was *crucified*, *died* and was *buried*; he *descended* into hell; the third day he *rose* again from the dead." These statements are all based on the experiences that the Apostles and early disciples had of Jesus during his earthly life; later they were written down and were treasured by succeeding generations of Christians. That is how they came to be part of the Bible as the Gospel according to Matthew, Mark, Luke and John.

Jesus did not merely appear to be a man; he truly became one of us. As St. John says in 1:14, "And the Word became flesh and dwelt among us." St. Paul says that he was "born of woman" (Gal 4:4) and experienced the weaknesses and frailties of human flesh.

Jesus did not just appear to be an infant and a child. He was nursed and cared for by his mother. He grew up into manhood and maturity just as we do: "And Jesus increased in wisdom and in stature, and in favor with God and man" (Lk 2:52).

The Gospels are full of references to the true humanity of Jesus. He was tired and sat down at Jacob's well in Samaria. He slept on the boat on the Sea of Galilee. He wept at the grave of Lazarus. On the way to Calvary, he carried his own cross and was thirsty in his agony. When he died, blood and water flowed from his opened side. After the Resurrection, Jesus assures his doubting disciples of the reality of his human body with the words, "Handle and see" (Lk 24:39).

As you can well imagine, the denial of Jesus' true humanity under the pretense of some "higher spirituality" is a dagger in the heart of the Christian faith. What it really means is that there was no Incarnation, no Redemption and no Salvation for mankind. It is a cruel attempt on the part of arrogant, proud and conceited intellectuals to remove Jesus Christ from the realm of historical reality and transfer him into the area of philosophical speculation. We may rightly apply to them the words of Mary Magdalene at the empty tomb on Easter morning: "They have taken away my Lord and I know not where they have laid him" (Jn 20:13).

# 6

# THE PERFECT MAN

In order to understand clearly who and what Jesus Christ is according to Catholic faith, it is not sufficient to say that Jesus had a truly human body just like ours. We must also affirm that he had a fully human *soul* just like ours. For, if Jesus had only a human body but not a human soul, then he would not really be like us and he would not be our brother.

To say that Jesus had a human soul means that he had a human, finite mind and will like ours. In other words, he possessed the fullness of humanity.

The reason for stressing this point arises because certain heretics, both ancient and modern, have claimed that Jesus did not have a human soul. The famous Arians of the fourth century said that Jesus did not have a human soul and that the Logos or the Word of God took the place of the soul in Jesus. If that were true it would mean that Jesus was not truly a man like us. The great St. Athanasius spent most of his life fighting the heresy of

Arianism which was condemned in the very first ecumenical council of Nicaea in 325 A.D.

A variation of Arianism was proposed by Bishop Apollinaris of Laodicea (about 390). Influenced by Platonic philosophy, he taught that the divine Logos had assumed a human body and an animal soul, but that the Logos itself had taken the place of the rational soul in Jesus. He falsely believed that only in this way could the unity of Person and the sinlessness of Christ be preserved. This theological theory was condemned at a particular synod at Alexandria in 362 under the presidency of St. Athanasius and was rejected as heretical at the First Council of Constantinople in 381.

The great Council of Chalcedon also condemned the view of Apollinaris in 451: "We declare that He (Jesus Christ) is perfect both in his divinity and in his humanity, truly God and truly man composed of body and rational soul; that He is . . . consubstantial with us in His humanity, like us in every respect except for sin" (see Heb 4:15). So it is an article of Catholic faith that Christ assumed not only a body but also a rational soul endowed with intellect and will.

There are many indications of this truth in the New Testament. In fact, Jesus speaks of his human soul. Consider, for example, the following: "My soul is sorrowful to the point of death" (Mt 26:38); "Father, into your hands I commend my spirit" (Lk 23:46). And all four evangelists affirm that at his death Jesus "yielded up his spirit" (Mt 27:50; Mk 15:37; Lk 23:46; Jn 19:30).

The human spirituality of Jesus' soul is manifested in his many prayers of petition and thanksgiving; it is shown very clearly in the subordination of his human will to the divine will: "Not my will but thine be done" (Lk 22:42).

The Fathers and theologians of the fourth and fifth centuries argued for the necessity of the assumption of a rational soul by Christ on the basis of two axioms: "That which has not been assumed has not been saved", and "The Word assumed the flesh through the medium of the soul." The first axiom refers to the redemptive purpose of the Incarnation of the Word; the second refers to the philosophical idea that the soul is the form of the body and that a human body must be informed by a human or rational soul. The problem of how Jesus Christ can be both human and divine at the same time, and how unity between the two is achieved, will be treated in a subsequent essay.

Another proof for the reality of Jesus' human nature is the fact that he was truly generated and born of a human mother. Through his descent from Mary, a daughter of Adam, he became a son of Adam according to his human nature. Thus, Jesus Christ is truly our brother, one of us.

In her various Creeds and professions of faith the Church teaches that Jesus was generated and born of the Virgin Mary. For example, we pray in the Apostles' Creed that he was "born of the Virgin Mary". The fifth century Athanasian Creed puts it this way: "We believe and profess that our Lord Jesus Christ . . . as man was born in time of the substance of His Mother. He is perfect God; and He is perfect man, with a rational soul and human flesh."

The New Testament explicitly stresses the true motherhood of Mary of whom "was born Jesus who is called Christ" (Mt 1:16). The angel Gabriel said to Mary, "Listen! You are to conceive and bear a son" (Lk 1:31). St. Paul says that when the appointed time came "God sent his Son, *born of a woman*" (Gal 4:4).

It is essential for the very survival of the Church that

the integral humanity of Jesus Christ be defended and preserved. For, he died for us on the Cross as our brother and Savior. He is also the model for all Christian virtue and living. We follow and imitate the man Jesus Christ on our way to the Father.

7

## JESUS IS A DIVINE PERSON

Having shown that Jesus Christ is both God and man, the next step is to explain the Church's teaching on how the human nature and the divine nature are joined together. When we consider this great mystery we are coming very near to the core or heart of the Christian religion. A small error in this matter can have serious consequences for the whole Church and for Christian living.

The clarity of the Church's teaching about the unity of the human and divine natures in Christ was occasioned by the false teaching of Nestorius, Patriarch of Constantinople (about 451). Nestorius said that Mary was not the Mother of God; according to him she was only the Mother of Christ. There are in Christ, he said, two natures and two persons, one divine and one human. According to him, the two persons are connected with each other in a moral unity. Thus, the man Christ is not God, but a very holy man who is the *bearer of God*. The Incarnation, therefore, does not mean that God the Son became man really but only that the Divine Logos resided in Jesus in the same way that God dwells in the just.

According to the Nestorians the human activities of Jesus (birth, suffering, death) may be asserted of the Man-Christ only; the divine activities (creation, omnipotence, eternity) may be asserted of the God-Logos only. This means that there are in Christ two natures and two persons, divine and human. According to this theory, Mary gave birth to the man Jesus and later the divine Logos came to dwell in him in a special way. That is why the Nestorians said that Mary is not the Mother of God.

The Church reacted strongly against this new teaching under the leadership of St. Cyril of Alexandria (444). In the General Councils of Ephesus (431) and Chalcedon (451) the Church taught officially that the divine and human natures are united in Jesus Christ in one Person—and that Person is the Logos or the second Person of the Blessed Trinity. Thus, in Jesus there is one Person but two natures—a human nature taken from Mary and the divine nature which is common to Father, Son and Holy Spirit. Since a mother gives birth not just to a human nature but to a person, it can be said with full truth that Mary is the Mother of God. For, Jesus is not a human person; he is a divine Person who has taken himself a human nature.

The New Testament offers many proofs that Jesus Christ is both God and man. It attributes to him both divine and human qualities or characteristics (omnipotence, eternity, birth, suffering, death). Since all of these attributes are affirmed of the one Jesus Christ, it follows that the two natures must belong to one and the same subject or person.

The oneness of Christ's personality is especially clear in those texts where the human qualities are predicated of his Person under the title of God, and his divine qualities of his Person referred to according to his human nature. Thus, we read in John 8:58, "I tell you most solemnly, before Abraham ever was, I Am." St. Luke reports that Peter said in Acts 3:15, ". . . you killed the prince of life." St. Paul says in Galatians 4:4, ". . . when the appointed time came, God sent his Son, born of a woman, born subject to the Law."

In this regard it helps to reflect on how Jesus uses the first personal pronoun, "I". On one occasion he would say, "I and the Father are one", or "I am the way and the truth and the life", or "I am the bread of life"; on another occasion he would say, "I am thirsty." Both human and divine predicates are affirmed of the same personal subject in Jesus. Thus, the New Testament witnesses to the fact that in Jesus there is only one Person, not two persons.

The Church in her doctrinal teaching has explained this mystery in the phrase, "Hypostatic Union". The word "hypostatic" comes from a Greek word which means the same thing as "personal". So what the Church says is that the two natures in Christ, divine and human, are joined together or united in the one Person of the divine Logos.

This is a statement of fact; it does not explain *how* it is possible for the divine and human natures to be united in the Person of the Logos or Word of God. That is the mystery of the Incarnation of God; that is what we celebrate on the feasts of the Annunciation and Christmas. The acceptance and affirmation of this great mystery requires faith, not philosophical or theological insight.

The more one reflects on this stupendous mystery, the more one comes to the realization of how much God loves us. He loves us so much that he became one of us in order to save us from sin and death. With the advent of Christ there is no reason for a Christian to be a pessimist; we should all be optimists. For, by becoming man God has raised us up to his level and destined us for eternal life.

8

## JESUS IS BOTH GOD AND MAN

We have just considered the Church's teaching about the union of Jesus' divine nature and his human nature in his Person, which is the second Person of the Blessed Trinity or the Word of God. We saw that those who, in one way or another, posit *two persons* in Jesus (both divine and human) are called "Nestorians". Their error was exposed and condemned by the Council of Ephesus in 431.

At the same time there were some Christians who reacted so strongly against the Nestorians that they fell into another error. Under the leadership of a monk in Constantinople by the name of Eutyches (378–454), a group began to stress the oneness or unity of Jesus. They affirmed not only that Jesus is one Person, but they also said that his two natures (divine and human) were fused together by some kind of mixture or composition in order to form one nature. In Greek one is *mono* and nature is *physis*. Thus, in theology these early thinkers are called "Monophysites" and their heresy is called "Monophysitism".

Once again, under the inspiration of the Holy Spirit and the leadership of the Pope in Rome, the Church reacted strongly and moved to reject this error. For, the witness of Scripture and the faith of the Fathers of the Church testified to a different understanding of who and what Jesus is. According to the traditional faith, Jesus Christ is both God and man. He is one divine Person in two natures—the divine nature and a human nature taken from his mother Mary. The understanding of the Church is that in the Hypostatic Union each of the two natures of Christ continues unimpaired, untransformed and unmixed with the other. Both natures remain fully intact and come together or are united in the one Person of the Word of God. It is for that reason that we can truthfully say that this man Jesus is God. We can also say with full truth that Mary is the Mother of God because she gives birth to the second Person of the Blessed Trinity, not of course in his divine nature, but in his created human nature.

In philosophical terms "nature" means the principle of operation of any being. Thus it follows that, if Jesus exists in two natures (divine and human), he must have two kinds of activities. And so it is. In his divine nature he creates, he performs miracles, he raises Lazarus from the dead, he calms the storm on the Sea of Galilee. In his human nature he walks, talks, eats, sleeps, suffers and dies. The same Person operates on two levels, but there is perfect unity of Person. This is the mystery of the Hypostatic Union and the Incarnation that we profess in faith each Sunday when we pray the ancient Creed of the Church.

It is very important to note that the two natures of

Christ are not mixed or confused or divided. Clarity on this matter was established for all time and all generations by the great Council of Chalcedon in 451. I would ask you to read carefully and prayerfully the following infallible pronouncement of that Council:

> Following the holy Father, we all with one accord teach the profession of faith in the one identical Son, our Lord Jesus Christ. We declare that he is perfect both in his divinity and in his humanity, truly God and truly man composed of body and rational soul; that he is consubstantial with the Father in his divinity, consubstantial with us in his humanity, like us in every respect except for sin (Heb. 4:15). We declare that in his divinity he was begotten of the Father before time, and in his humanity he was begotten in this last age of Mary the Virgin, the Mother of God, for us and for our salvation. We declare that the one selfsame Christ, the only-begotten Son and Lord, must be acknowledged *in two natures without any commingling or change or division or separation*; that the distinction between the natures is in no way removed by their union but rather that the specific character of each nature is preserved and they are united in one person and one hypostasis. We declare that he is not split or divided into two persons, but that there is one selfsame only begotten Son, God the Word, the Lord Jesus Christ. This the prophets have taught about him from the beginning; this Jesus Christ himself taught us; this the creed of the Fathers has handed down to us.

The above doctrine of Chalcedon contains the Church's classic expression of her faith in Jesus Christ. Many important truths of Faith are contained in the doctrine: that Christ assumed a real and not just an apparent body; that he had a rational soul with intellect and will like ours; that the two natures in Jesus are united to form one individual; that in Jesus each of the two natures remains unimpaired; that Jesus is both true God and true man; that Mary is the Mother of God.

It has often been pointed out that the Monophysite

doctrine of unification and fusion contradicts the absolute immutability of God. In fact, it means a denial of the true humanity of Jesus. We have already seen that such a denial logically leads to a denial of the Church, the sacraments and our redemption from sin.

# 9

# THE TWO WILLS IN CHRIST

We have already considered that Jesus Christ, according to the ancient Catholic faith as defended in the Councils and professed in the Creed, is one divine Person who possesses or exists in two natures—the divine nature and a human nature taken from his mother Mary. This mysterious union of the divine and the human in Jesus Christ is called the "Hypostatic Union". In this phrase the word "hypostatic" means "personal". Thus, the two natures come together or are united in the Person of the Word, the second Person of the Blessed Trinity.

There are many interesting and truly mysterious consequences of the Hypostatic Union. One of them has to do with the number of wills in Christ. In our experience each person has one will and one intellect. When we look at the beautiful figure of Jesus in the Gospels we see a fully integrated personality. Suppose I put the question to you: How many wills are there in Christ? What would your answer be?

When I teach a college course on Christ I always ask the students how many wills there are in him. In a class of thirty students it is very rare to find even one who will reply, "There are two wills in Christ, a divine will and a human will." The common answer is, "There is one will in Christ." Then I proceed to point out that they are in serious error with regard to the essential constitution of Jesus Christ our Savior.

A moment's reflection on the great truth of the Hypostatic Union will reveal that there must be two wills in Christ—one divine and one human. Christ is both God and man. That means that he has a divine nature and a human nature. But what is a "nature"? A nature is understood by philosophers and theologians to be a principle of operation. A nature then is active; it does something or a number of things.

Accordingly, since Jesus Christ possesses both a divine nature and a human nature, it follows that he must exercise both divine and human activities. What are the activities that are proper to divinity and humanity? They are precisely *thinking* and *willing* which proceed from the spiritual faculties of intellect and will.

No one doubts that Jesus, as a divine Person, possesses divine intellect and will. But he assumed a human nature when he was conceived in the womb of the Blessed Virgin Mary. The theological question here is whether or not he also assumed a human intellect and a human will. Some Christian thinkers of the past have thought that he did not, that the divine intellect and will took the place of the human intellect and will. But that is basically the error of Monophysitism which, as we have seen, was condemned by the Council of Chalcedon in 451. If that position were true it would follow that Jesus was not truly a human being like us in all things, sin alone excepted.

The infallible teaching of the Church in this matter is that each of the two natures in Christ possesses its own natural will and its own natural mode of operation. Thus there are in Christ two wills and two intellects, one human and one divine. This teaching was sanctioned for all time by the Third Council of Constantinople (680–81): "We promulgate, according to the teaching of the Holy Fathers, that in Him are also two natural wills and two natural modes of working, unseparated, untransformed, undivided, unmixed."

According to the New Testament Jesus explicitly distinguishes his human will from his divine will, which he possesses in common with the Father. At the same time, however, Jesus stresses the complete subordination of his human will to his divine will. Thus he prays in Luke 22:42, "Father, if you are willing, take this cup away from me. Nevertheless, let your will be done, not mine."

In a similar vein Jesus says in John 6:38, "I came down from heaven not to do my own will but the will of him that sent me." Also, Jesus' relation of obedience to the heavenly Father, often stressed in the Bible, presupposes a human will (see for example, Jn 4:34; Phil 2:8; Rom 5:19; Heb 10:9).

Commenting on Matthew 26:39 (parallel to Lk 22:42) St. Athanasius says: "He announces two wills here, the human, which is an affair of the flesh, and the Divine which is the affair of God. The human will, on account of the weakness of the flesh, prays for the aversion of suffering, but the Divine Will welcomes it."

The Fathers of the Church derive the doctrine of the two wills and modes of activity in Christ from the two natures, divine and human. Will and activity depend on the number of natures, not on the Person. Therefore, since Christ possesses two integral natures, he has two different modes of activity. This means that he has two wills and two intellects, both divine and human.

10

# HIS KINGDOM WILL HAVE NO END

The more we reflect on the incomparable mystery of the Incarnation of the second Person of the Blessed Trinity the more we become aware of the infinite mercy of God. Many, many questions can be asked about this amazing manifestation of God's love for man. In order to get a little better insight into the mystery it might be helpful to consider the following two questions: When did the Hypostatic Union begin and how long will it last?

With regard to the beginning of the Hypostatic Union (= union of God and man in the one Person of the Logos: Jesus Christ of Nazareth), two false opinions are worthy of notice. In the third century Origen, influenced by Platonism, said that Christ's human soul pre-existed its union with his body, and was, already before the Incarnation, united with the Logos or the second Person of the Trinity. This opinion was rejected in 543 by Pope Vigilius as false.

Another erroneous view in this matter is that of some of the Gnostics who said that the Logos first descended on the man Jesus on the occasion of his Baptism in the Jordan River by St. John the Baptist. This error has reappeared recently in the writings of some biblical scholars who maintain that Jesus did not know that he was the Son of God until the Holy Spirit descended on him at his Baptism.

The two theories just mentioned run counter to traditional Catholic faith as it is expressed in the Creed of the Church. The Creed asserts the conception as man of the Son of God. Mary did not conceive a human person who later became "Son of God". The latter would have to be correct if the Hypostatic Union of the two natures had occurred at a later point in time. Thus, the Apostles' Creed proclaims, "I believe . . . in Jesus Christ, his only Son our Lord, who was conceived by the Holy Spirit, born of the Virgin Mary. . . ."

The New Testament bears witness to the fact that the Son of God became man because he was conceived and born of a woman. Thus, St. Paul says, "But when the fullness of time had come God sent his Son made of a woman" (Gal 4:4; see Rom 1:3).

Another truth to consider is that Mary is the Mother of God, not just the mother of a man. If she had not conceived the Logos in his human nature, then she could not truthfully be called the Mother of God; she would be only the mother of a man. But it is the infallible teaching of the Church, confirmed by the early councils, that Mary is truly the Mother of God. This is another proof that the Hypostatic Union of Christ's human nature with the second Person of the Trinity took place at the moment of his conception.

Catholic thinkers have also asked whether or not the Hypostatic Union ceased for a time, namely, from the time of his death to his glorious Resurrection. The Apostles' Creed says that the Son of God suffered, was crucified, died, was buried (his body) and descended into hell (his soul). Death means the separation of the soul from the body. Since Christ truly died, it follows that his soul was separated from his body from the moment of his death until his Resurrection. The question arises whether or not the Logos remained united to the body and the soul during those three days. It is a common teaching of Catholic theologians that the divine Logos remained hypostatically united to both the body and the soul after Jesus' death. This means that Jesus' body in the tomb on Holy Saturday was worthy of full adoration.

Some Gnostic heretics have maintained that the Logos abandoned Jesus before his passion. By this they mean that the Hypostatic Union ceased before he began to suffer. But the Hypostatic Union did not cease before or during the passion. This is shown by the statement of St. Paul, "If they had known the concealed wisdom of God they would never have crucified the Lord of Glory" (1 Cor 2:8).

The Gnostics try to prove their point by quoting Matthew 27:46, "My God, my God, why have you deserted me?" There is no doubt that the passage has troubled many devout Christians. St. Thomas Aquinas and other theologians explain it in the sense that the Father withdrew certain aspects of his protection of Jesus, but not that the Logos abandoned Jesus. Here Jesus experiences the depths of human suffering and anguish, but he is and remains the Son of God.

Another question that suggests itself in this connection is whether or not the divine Logos, after the end of the world and the judgment of the living and the dead, will cast off his human nature and cease to be hypostatically united to flesh and blood. In the past some have also held this opinion, but it was rejected as heretical by the First Council of Constantinople in 381. In order to make sure that this error did not recur the Council ordered the following addition to the Creed that we pray at Mass, "and His Kingdom will have no end". Another indication that the Hypostatic Union will continue for all eternity is contained in the words of the angel Gabriel to Mary: "The Lord God will give him (= Jesus) the throne of his ancestor David; he will rule over the house of Jacob for ever and his reign will have no end" (Lk 1:33).

11

# THE HYPOSTATIC UNION

In the attempt to learn more about our Catholic faith, it is most important to understand clearly what the Church means by the expression, *Hypostatic Union*. The correct understanding of the Catholic faith, and indeed of Jesus Christ, depends directly on the meaning of this phrase.

The word "hypostatic" comes from the Greek "hypostasis" and it means "personal". The expression "Hypostatic Union" was developed by the early Fathers of the Church to describe the wonderful union of the divine and human natures in the one Person, Jesus Christ.

We all know what it means to be a person because that

is what we are. But it is not at all easy to describe it or to explain it. The philosophers say that it is the ultimate subject of predication. Thus, whatever is said about "me" refers to the "I" in me. Each and every human being is also a human person. In our daily experience person and human nature always go together. Animals, plants and minerals do not qualify as "persons" because they are lacking intelligence and free will—the two attributes that are characteristic of persons.

From revelation we know that angels and devils exist and that they too are personal beings. In the most perfect sense God is personal. Here again we know, but only from revelation, that what we mean by "person" is found multiplied in God, that is, God is a Trinity. According to our Christian faith, there are three Persons in one God—Father, Son and Holy Spirit.

When the Church uses the expression "Hypostatic Union" to describe the great mystery of the Incarnation of God, she is telling us that Jesus' human nature is united with his divine nature in the one Person of the Word or second Person of the Blessed Trinity. This means that Jesus is a divine Person. But he is not a human person. I have mentioned that before in previous sections, but I wish to emphasize it here.

In virtue of the Hypostatic Union Jesus Christ is both God and man. Here is how the famous Athanasian Creed of the fifth or sixth century puts it:

> As God He was begotten of the substance of the Father before time; as man He was born in time of the substance of His mother. He is perfect God; and He is perfect man, with a rational soul and human flesh. He is equal to the Father in His divinity but He is inferior to the Father in His humanity. Although He is God and man, He is not two but one Christ.

> And He is one, not because His divinity was changed into flesh, but because His humanity was assumed to God. He is one, not at all because of a mingling of substances, but because He is one person.

This of course is the central mystery that surrounds the Person of Jesus Christ—how he can be both God and man at the same time. Revelation tells us that the Word of God became man in Jesus Christ (Jn 1:14), but it does not tell us *how* that was accomplished.

The more we reflect on the Hypostatic Union, the more we realize that the assumption of a created human nature into the unity of a divine Person is absolutely supernatural. It is a *grace* in the full sense of that word, that is, an unmerited and unmeritable supernatural gift of God. It is sometimes referred to as "the grace of union".

The Hypostatic Union is an absolute mystery of faith; so also is the Holy Trinity. An absolute mystery is one whose reality could not be known before its divine revelation; even after its revelation one cannot prove the intrinsic possibility of an absolute mystery of faith. Accordingly, it is beyond the power of human reason, but, since it has been revealed by God who is absolute truth, it is not contrary to reason. St. Paul calls the Incarnation "a mystery hidden from eternity in God" (Eph 3:9).

The Hypostatic Union is a fundamental mystery of the Christian faith. If it is properly grasped, then one has the right understanding of Christianity. If it is distorted in some way, then one falls immediately into error. Many of the great heresies in the history of the Church involved errors with regard to the Hypostatic Union: some denied the true humanity of Jesus; some denied his divinity; others had a false understanding of the manner of the union between the divine and human natures.

It is most important for us Catholics to know clearly who Jesus Christ is. He is both fully divine and fully human; the two natures come together or are united in the Person of the Word. He is a human being like us in all things except sin, but he is not a human person. He is a divine Person and therefore worthy of our adoration, since he is our Creator and also our Redeemer. By reason of his human nature he has a history; he is a member of the human race and one of us. He is also our "window" on divinity and eternity, for he says to Philip in St. John's Gospel, "To have seen me is to have seen the Father" (14:9).

12

# THE WHOLE TRINITY BROUGHT ABOUT THE INCARNATION

We have already treated the Church's teaching on the most Holy Trinity. At present I am trying to explain the most important aspects of Christology or the theological doctrine about Christ our Lord. There is of course an essential connection between Christology and the Trinity since, according to our faith, Jesus Christ is the second Person of the Blessed Trinity.

Careful readers of the New Testament will have noted that Holy Scripture attributes the Incarnation (or Hypostatic Union) to the Father (Heb 10:5), to the Son (Phil 2:7), and to the Holy Spirit (Mt 1:18, 20; Lk 1:35). A question I would like to treat today is this: Who caused or brought about the Incarnation of the Word of God? The Bible attributes it to each of the three divine Persons.

The official teaching of the Church is that the Incarnation or Hypostatic Union was effected by the three divine Persons acting in common. An important Creed from the seventh century says on this point: "It should be believed that the whole Trinity effected the Incarnation of this Son of God, because the works of the Trinity cannot be divided" (*Denzinger* 284). The Fourth Lateran Council in 1215 said the same thing: "The only begotten Son of God, Jesus Christ, was made incarnate by a common action of the Holy Trinity" (*Denzinger* 429).

The basic reason for this Catholic teaching is that the divine nature, which is common to the three divine Persons, is and must be the active principle of all operations, such as creation, which take place outside the inner trinitarian life. The Incarnation of the Son of God in space and time is just such an activity. Therefore, it is common to Father, Son and Holy Spirit. Accordingly, in different contexts the New Testament attributes the Incarnation to each of the three divine Persons.

A little reflection on the Incarnation will reveal that it must be the work of the whole Trinity. For, the Trinity of Persons is also a unity of nature; there is only one God in three divine Persons. But the divine Persons do not act as separate individuals; they are not like human persons, each with his or her own nature. Everything they do in the created world is common to all three Persons. Thus,

St. Augustine says: "Mary's conceiving and bringing forth is the work of the Trinity, through whose creative activity all creation is made."

A second point I would like to make is that only the second divine Person became man; he is also called the Son of God or the Word or the Logos. Stated negatively, this means that the Father and the Holy Spirit were not incarnated.

In this difficult matter, one might be tempted to think that the whole Trinity was incarnated in Jesus of Nazareth. Since Father, Son and Holy Spirit act in common in the created world, it might seem that, if one Person becomes man, then all of them become man. Some of the early heretics actually held that erroneous opinion, but they were condemned by various Church councils. For, the New Testament refers to the Son of God *only* when it says that he became flesh and dwelt among us (Jn 1:14). The Creed says clearly that only the Son of God "came down from heaven . . . was born of the Virgin Mary, and became man".

Since the high Middle Ages there has been considerable speculation among Catholic theologians about whether or not the Father and the Holy Spirit could be incarnated, that is, assume a human nature and so become man. Some theologians have been of the opinion that any divine Person could become man.

In recent years, however, this opinion has become less common. Most contemporary dogmatic theologians would hold that only the second Person of the Blessed Trinity, the Son of God, could become man. The reason for this opinion is that the incarnate God is the revelation, the visibility of the infinite and invisible God. The Incarnation is a manifestation of God to personal beings endowed with intelligence and free will. In a very true sense the God-man Jesus Christ leads us to the Father; he is the *image* of the Father (see Jn 14:9). Now we know from our study of the Trinity that the Father generates the Son and that the Son is therefore the image or reflection of the Father. He is the expression of the Father.

The incarnate God-man is the external expression of God. Since the second Person of the Trinity is by nature the *image* of the Father, the *Word* of God, it would seem that only he could become man.

13

## "WE ADORE THEE, O CHRIST..."

In the previous essay we saw that the Holy Trinity effected the Incarnation. The result of the trinitarian activity was that the Word of God, the second Person of the Blessed Trinity, became man in Jesus Christ of Nazareth. We saw also that only the Word became man, not the Father or the Holy Spirit.

Jesus Christ, therefore, is God made man; he is the visibility of God in the material world. What does this say about our relationship towards him? Since he is God and we are poor creatures, and since the creature is required by nature to show respect and adoration for its creator and God, it follows that Jesus Christ has the right to our respect and adoration.

In the history of the Church the question has often been raised about whether or not Jesus should be revered and honored as a very holy man, or whether he should be adored as God Almighty, with the same adoration that we offer to God the Father.

Some have held that as God Jesus was the natural Son of God and as man he was the adopted son of God. They say that in the Baptism in the Jordan Jesus was adopted by God through grace. This theory of a double sonship in Jesus Christ implies that there are two persons in him, one divine and one human. This is the error of Nestorianism which has been condemned by the Church many times. The Church says that there is only one Person in Jesus Christ and that is the Logos or Word of God. This means that not only as God, but also as man, Jesus Christ is the natural Son of God. So we owe him the worship due to God alone.

"Worship" is a kind of honor or esteem given to a person because of his excellence. In religious matters, worship adds to honor or esteem the sense of one's own inferiority with regard to the person honored. Since God is the supreme being, worship in the highest degree is due to him. The correct name for this type of worship is "adoration". The Latins and Greeks called it *latria*, which meant the service given to the gods. That word makes up the second part of the English word "idolatry".

The teaching of the Catholic Church in this matter is that the God-man Jesus Christ is to be venerated with one single mode of worship—the absolute worship of adoration which is due to God alone. Jesus Christ is one divine Person subsisting in a divine nature and a human nature. He is therefore *One*. Adoration of Jesus is adoration of the second Person of the Blessed Trinity by reason of the Hypostatic Union, which has already been explained. Through the Hypostatic Union Christ's humanity is a part of, belongs to the incarnate Logos and so is adored in and with the Logos. The human nature of Christ is clearly a creature but it is still the object of our adoration, not because it is a creature, but because of its Hypostatic Union with the Logos.

There are a number of instances related in the Gospels in which individuals worship Jesus by kneeling before him (Mt 28:9, 17). Jesus also claims for himself the same veneration which is due to the Father: " . . . that all may honor the Son as they honor the Father' (Jn 5:23). St. Paul witnessed to the divine adoration owed to Christ in his humanity: " . . . so that all beings in the heavens, on earth and in the underworld, should bend the knee at the name of Jesus" (Phil 2:10).

Some early heretics accused the Church of adoring just the flesh of Christ or simply the man Jesus. The Fathers of the Church rejected the charges on the ground that adoration is shown to Christ's humanity, not on its own account and as something separated from the Word, but on acccount of its Hypostatic Union with the second Person of the Blessed Trinity.

In the proper sense, veneration is shown to a person only. There is only one divine Person in Christ, so we offer him one adoration only. Since the human nature of Jesus Christ is inseparably united with the divine Person of the Word, adoration directed to that divine Person must include the human nature. St. Thomas Aquinas sums up this matter in the following words: "The honor of adoration belongs in the proper sense to the subsisting person. . . . The adoration of Christ's flesh means nothing else than the adoration of the Word become Flesh" (*Summa Theologica*, III, q. 25, art. 2).

What this means in the realm of the liturgy is that by adoring Christ we are adoring the incarnate Word. Christ's human nature is included in our adoration because it is hypostatically and eternally united to the second Person of the Blessed Trinity. The fundamental reason for our adoration is the infinite perfection, being and beauty of the divine Person. Thus, when we adore Christ we are adoring God Almighty because Jesus Christ is God.

14

# HEART OF JESUS
# BURNING FURNACE OF LOVE

In a previous essay we considered the religious act of adoration. We saw that worship in the strict sense, or adoration, is due to God alone. We also saw that, since Jesus is both God and man, he deserves our adoration. For, in Jesus, the human nature is hypostatically and eternally united to the second Person of the Blessed Trinity. This means that the humanity of Jesus is the humanity of the Word, the Son of God. Thus when we worship Jesus Christ we are worshipping the second Person of the Blessed Trinity.

Now if adoration is due to the whole Christ, one can raise a question about his individual parts. May we, should we adore certain parts of Jesus' sacred humanity? Why raise this question? Well, there is an ancient Catholic tradition of showing special veneration or adoration for individual parts of Jesus' human nature—for the Five Holy Wounds, for the Most Precious Blood, for the Holy Face, for his Most Sacred Heart. The Church has approved of these devotions for centuries. The reason for the special veneration of these parts of Jesus' human nature is found in the fact that in them the redeeming love of Christ is revealed very clearly.

We can say with certainty that, just as adoration is due to the whole human nature of Christ, so also is it due to the individual parts of his nature. For, they are all hypostatically united to the Person of the Word. For our present consideration I wish to apply this principle to the Sacred Heart of Jesus. Thus, just as we ought to adore the whole humanity of Christ, so also may we and should we adore the Heart of Jesus Christ. That Heart beats in love for us with human and divine love.

Devotion to the Sacred Heart of Jesus originated with the German mystics of the Middle Ages. It has its scriptural foundation in John 19:34, "One of the soldiers pierced his side with a lance; and immediately there came out blood and water." Pope Pius VI declared in 1794 that the Heart of Jesus is not separated from the Godhead, but rather is adored as "the heart of the Person of the Word, with which it is inseparably united".

When we worship the Heart of Christ, what precisely do we worship? Is our worship directed to the physical Heart of Jesus? Or do we worship the divine love for us and use the Heart of Jesus merely as a symbol for that love? It may surprise some, but the object of the devotion is the corporeal Heart of Jesus as an essential part of the human nature of Christ which is hypostatically united to the Person of the Word. We worship the Heart of

Jesus because it is the Heart of God, the second Person of the Blessed Trinity.

Jesus' Heart has been singled out for special veneration because the heart is the most perfect symbol of his redeeming love for mankind. Both in the Bible (see Dt 6:5; Prov 2:2; Mt 22:37; Jn 16:6, 22; Rom 5:5) and in popular language the heart is the center of our affections, especially the affection of love. Since love is the motive of our redemption (see Jn 3:16), special love and adoration are shown to the physical Heart of Jesus our Redeemer because it is the symbol of his love for us.

The purpose of the devotion to the Sacred Heart of Jesus is that we will be moved to return love for love, to imitate the virtues of the human Heart of the incarnate God, and to promote a desire to atone for the insults offered by men to the Heart of Jesus.

It is regrettable that the devotion to the Sacred Heart of Jesus has declined so much among Catholics since the Vatican Council. For, this devotion touches the very roots of Christianity. Ultimately, what life and religion are all about is love. Through human love we get a taste of absolute, divine love. In Christ Jesus the love of God for man is fully revealed. There is no better symbol of God's infinite love for sinful mankind than the physical Heart of the God-man Jesus Christ.

"Heart" is a universally understood symbol of love. Thus, when we speak of the Heart of Jesus we are referring to the boundless love of God's only-begotten Son for us. By honoring the Heart of Jesus we are directly honoring the love of the second Person of the Blessed Trinity for mankind; we are also, through Jesus, honoring the love of the Father and the Holy Spirit for us.

Prayer and love are major concerns of Catholics today. A rightly understood and practiced devotion to the love of Jesus Christ can satisfy that concern to the highest degree. Devotion to the Sacred Heart of Jesus has been highly recommended by the last fifteen popes. Pius XI called it "the synthesis of all religion, the norm of the more perfect life". Pius XII said that it is "a most perfect way of professing the Christian religion". In a time of growing cynicism, despair, violence and atheism there is no better way to live the fullness of the Catholic faith, it seems to me, than by consecrating oneself to the Heart of Jesus, which the Litany refers to as "the burning furnace of love".

## 15

## TALKING ABOUT JESUS

So far we have pondered the Church's teaching on the Hypostatic Union, that is, the union of the divine nature and the human nature of Jesus Christ in the Person of the Word. We have also reflected on some of the consequences for Jesus of the Hypostatic Union, namely, that he is the natural Son of God and that he is worthy of our adoration.

A further consequence of the Hypostatic Union concerns the way in which we talk about Jesus. Careful analysis of the New Testament reveals that both human and divine attributes or qualities or properties are predicated of him. Since Jesus Christ is both God and man, it follows that we can attribute to him both divine and human qualities. In this we are merely following the example of the Bible.

If you run over in your mind the first part of the Apostles' Creed you will note that it attributes to the Son of God the human properties of conception and birth, of suffering and crucifixion, of dying and being buried. The Bible and the Church also attribute divine qualities to Jesus Christ, such as divinity, creation, eternity. Some of the ancient heretics, called Nestorians, said that there were two persons in Christ—one human and one divine. They said, falsely, that the human qualities belonged to the human person in Jesus and that the divine qualities belonged to the divine Person in Jesus. The Council of Ephesus in 431, however, taught that the biblical statements about Christ may not be divided between two persons, the Word of God and the human Christ, but must be referred to the one Word made flesh.

It must be remembered that Christ's divine Person exists in two natures, one divine and one human, and that it may be referred to either of these two natures. This means, therefore, that human things can be asserted of the Son of God and divine things of the Son of Man.

Perhaps a few examples from the New Testament will help to make this difficult teaching of the Bible and the Church more clear. We read in John 8:58, "Before Abraham ever was, I am" (the man-Christ). In Acts 3:15 St. Peter says to the people in Jerusalem, "You have killed the author of life." In Acts 20:28 St. Paul tells the elders of Ephesus "to feed the Church of God which he bought with his own blood". And Paul writes in 1 Corinthians

2:8, "It is a wisdom that none of the masters of this age have ever known, or *they would not have crucified the Lord of Glory*" (i.e., God). In these passages we find both divine and human predicates attributed to Jesus Christ. The reason for this is that whatever is true of either the divine nature or the human nature of Jesus Christ can truthfully be said of him.

To say that the Lord of Glory has been crucified seems to be a contradiction. For, how can God, the Lord of Glory, possibly undergo crucifixion? The answer is that he cannot in his divine nature, but he can in his human nature. Both natures are united in the one Person of the Word. Since the man Jesus is a divine Person, the Fathers of the Church, basing themselves on Holy Scripture, were bold enough to speak of the blood of God, the sufferings of God and the birth of God from Mary.

Qualities pertaining to both the divine and the human nature can be attributed to the Person of Christ, but it is to be noted that qualities belonging specifically to one nature cannot be said of the other nature. Thus, it is true to say that the Son of Man died on the Cross and that Jesus created the world. In both cases the activity is referred to the one Person of Christ. But it would be false to say "Christ suffered as God." For, Christ suffered in his human nature, not in his divine nature which is not capable of suffering. Likewise, it would be false to say, "Christ created the world as a human being." He did create the world, but not "as a human being"; he created it as God.

For the same reasons it would be false to say, "Christ's soul is omniscient", or "Christ's body is everywhere."

We must beware of negative statements about Jesus since nothing may be denied to Jesus Christ which belongs to him according to either nature. Thus, it is false to say, "The Son of God has not suffered", or, "Jesus is not divine." In order to be perfectly clear it is often helpful to add qualifications like "as God" or "as man", depending on which nature is being referred to. Thus it is correct to say, "Christ, as man, is a creature."

The two natures of Jesus Christ, despite the real distinction between them, do not exist side by side but in a most close and intimate union. From the mysterious Hypostatic Union there derives a mutual intimate union and penetration of one nature by the other. The power which unites the two natures and holds them together proceeds exclusively from the divine nature. The divinity, which itself is impenetrable, penetrates and inhabits humanity, which is thereby deified without suffering any change.

16

## JESUS' SOUL POSSESSED THE IMMEDIATE VISION OF GOD

The Hypostatic Union had a profound effect on Jesus' human nature. As we have seen, Jesus Christ is a true man, but, because he is also God, he is no ordinary man. He is like us in all things except sin, but he is also unlike us in that his human nature is hypostatically united to the Word of God. It is important to remember that Jesus is not a human person like us; he is a divine Person—the second Person of the Blessed Trinity. Because of the Hypostatic Union, Jesus' human nature was endowed with an abundance of supernatural gifts. This raises questions about his human knowledge, human will and human power. Here I would like to make a few points about Jesus' human knowledge.

There is a long tradition in the Church, going back to the early Fathers, that the human soul of Jesus possessed the immediate or Beatific Vision of God from the first moment of its existence in the womb of the Virgin Mary. The immediate vision of God is absolutely supernatural; it is granted to the angels in heaven and to the saints in heaven. What the Fathers and the theologians have said and say is that Christ's soul possessed the immediate vision of God from the first moment of its union with the divine Person of the Word, that is, from its conception in Mary. This means that Jesus was, at the same time, both a pilgrim on earth like us and a possessor of the immediate vision of God like the blessed in heaven. One of the consequences of his immediate vision of God is that he did not have the theological virtues of faith and hope, since faith and hope cease once there is vision and possession of God.

Over the centuries there have been many theological disputes about the human knowledge of Christ. Thus in 1918 Pope Benedict XV declared that the following three propositions are incompatible with the Catholic faith:

> 1. It is not certain that there was in the soul of Christ, during his life among men, the knowledge possessed by the blessed or those in glory.
> 2. Equally uncertain is the statement which claims that the soul of Christ was ignorant of nothing, but that from the beginning

> it knew in the Word all things, past, present, and future; in a word, that it knew all things which God knows by the knowledge of vision.
> 3. The position of some recent spokesmen about the limited knowledge of the soul of Christ should be no less acceptable in Catholic schools than the statement of the ancients about its universal knowledge.

Please note that the Pope said the above statements cannot be taught as true. That means that the opposite is true, namely, that Jesus has the immediate vision of God, that he knows all things—past, present and future, and that his human knowledge is unlimited in some respects.

There are a number of indications in the New Testament that Jesus has immediate knowledge of the Father. Thus, we read in John 1:17-18, ". . . grace and truth have come through Jesus Christ. No one has ever seen God; it is the only Son, who is nearest to the Father's heart, who has made him known." Jesus says in John 8:55, "I know him (the Father), and if I were to say: I do not know him, I should be a liar, as you are liars yourselves. But I do know him, and I faithfully keep his word."

That Jesus had the Beatific Vision from the moment of his conception is a conclusion that the Fathers of the Church and theologians like St. Thomas Aquinas arrived at by examining who and what Jesus is. The Beatific Vision is the consummation of sanctifying grace; also, the attachment of the soul to God through grace and glory is an accidental union or perfection of the created soul. The attachment of Christ's soul to God, however, is a substantial union because it is hypostatically united to the Word of God. Such a substantial union is more intimate than the union of the saints in heaven with God. Thus, if Christ's soul on earth was already more intimately united to God than the blessed are in heaven, it follows that it must have at least the same immediate knowledge of God that the saints and angels have.

St. Thomas also argues that, since Christ by his life and death is the source of salvation and heaven for all mankind, he must have what he gives to others. Since he communicates the Beatific Vision to others, he must have it himself.

According to Hebrews 12:2 Jesus "leads us in our faith and brings it to perfection". If he leads us and perfects us in faith, then he knows perfectly what he is doing and does not himself walk in the darkness of faith, as I mentioned above. The perfection of the knowledge and self-consciousness of the man Jesus can be explained only by the fact that he possessed immediate knowledge of the divinity with which he was substantially united.

In concrete terms this means that Jesus' soul had the immediate vision of God from the first moment of its existence. He already had in this life what we hope to attain in the next life.

## 17

## JESUS' SUFFERING AND GLORY

We have seen that Jesus, because of the Hypostatic Union, possessed the immediate or Beatific Vision of God from the first moment of his conception. This means that Jesus had during his earthly life what we hope to attain in heaven. It is quite certain that Jesus enjoyed the Beatific Vision. For, in 1943 Pope Pius XII said in his famous encyclical letter on the Mystical Body: "For hardly was he (Jesus) conceived in the womb of the Mother of God, when he began to enjoy the beatific vision; and in that vision all the members of his mystical body were continually and unceasingly present and he embraced them with his redeeming love."

In the Beatific Vision Jesus saw everything that pertained to his mission as Redeemer of the world. He saw you and me; he saw all of our deeds and knew all our thoughts. How could this not be since the Father has established him as our Eternal Judge?

The teaching about Jesus' Beatific Vision raises a number of difficult and fascinating questions about his human knowledge and his ability really to suffer, especially in his passion. For, the immediate vision of God causes supreme happiness in rational creatures, such as angels and men. If that is so, and if Jesus possessed the Beatific

Vision all during his life, how can that be reconciled with his profound sorrow during his agony in the Garden of Gethsemane? And how can it be reconciled with his cry of agony on the cross? Can both beatitude and extreme suffering be present in Jesus at the same time?

These are very difficult questions which touch immediately on the mystery of Christ, the mystery of the Incarnation of God. The classical explanation of the difficulty was given by St. Thomas Aquinas and has been adopted, in one form or another, by most theologians since his time. He made a distinction between the spiritual powers of the soul and the sensitive powers of the soul. By a special divine ordinance, he said, the joy deriving from the Beatific Vision was limited in Christ to his spiritual soul. According to Thomas, the overflow of bliss into the body does not belong to the nature of glory; it is an accidental consequence of it which was suspended by God in the special case of Jesus Christ during his earthly life. There was a brief exception to this, however, during his Transfiguration on Mount Tabor when the divine glory shone through his body.

Thus, since by the miraculous intervention of God the bliss proceeding from the immediate vision of God did not overflow from the higher powers of the soul to the lower, nor from the soul to the body, Jesus remained sensitive to sorrow, sadness and suffering. How this was accomplished remains ultimately mysterious, since we are dealing with the mystery of the Incarnation, but at least it offers some explanation.

In this matter we must hold on to two truths: 1) Jesus had the Beatific Vision during his whole life and passion; 2) Jesus truly suffered both in body and soul. The witness of the Gospels is clear that Jesus truly suffered not only physically but also mentally. "And he said to them, 'My soul is sad, even unto death. Wait here and watch' " (Mk 14:34). "And at the ninth hour Jesus cried out with a loud voice, saying, 'Eloi, Eloi, lama sabacthani?' which, translated, is, 'My God, my God, why have you forsaken me?'" (Mk 15:34).

The mystery seems to be that, even though Jesus possessed perfect psychological unity, he could enjoy the Beatific Vision in one part of his soul and suffer intense agony and abandonment by God in another part of his soul.

It has been pointed out here before that Jesus Christ is a divine Person, not a human person, with two natures—the divine nature and a human nature. This means in the concrete that Jesus has two intellects (divine and human) and two wills (divine and human). It also means that he has a divine consciousness and a human consciousness—both united in the one Person of the Word. It is very difficult, if not impossible, for us to imagine how two consciousnesses can achieve psychological unity. Nevertheless, our faith does affirm that Jesus possessed that psychological unity.

The Gospels present Jesus as a Person who is fully integrated, wise, self-possessed, with a perfect knowledge of the Father and his relationship to the Father. Since he revealed the Father and the Holy Spirit to us, he had an intimate knowledge of them that comes only from union and vision.

Thus, our Catholic faith urges us to hold fast to these two truths: Jesus enjoyed the immediate vision of God during his earthly life; he also truly suffered for us both in his body and in his soul.

## 18

# DID IGNORANCE OR ERROR EXIST IN CHRIST?

We have been considering some of the effects of the Hypostatic Union in Jesus Christ, that is, the marvelous union of his divine nature and his human nature in the one Person of the Word. One consequence was that Jesus possessed the immediate and Beatific Vision of God throughout his earthly life, from the first moment of his conception to his death in agony on the Cross.

The primary object of the immediate vision of God is the divine essence—that is what Christ saw with his human intellect. Because of the finiteness of human nature, however, Christ as man did not have a comprehensive knowledge of God. That means that Jesus' human mind did not know everything knowable about God. For, the finite cannot contain the infinite, and the soul of Christ is a finite entity.

The secondary object of the immediate vision of God is found in those things that are external to God and are seen in him as the origin of all things. The extent of this kind of knowledge depends on the perfection with which God is known. For the angels and the saints in heaven it includes all the knowledge that pertains to them.

By reason of the Hypostatic Union Christ's soul is more closely united to God than are the angels and saints. Therefore, he knew everything that pertained to him and to his mission as the Redeemer of the world. Thus, during his earthly life Christ's soul knew all extra-divine things in the divine essence, to the extent that such knowledge was necessary for his mission as Redeemer. St. Thomas Aquinas concluded that, since Christ is the Lord of all creation and the Eternal Judge of all mankind, his soul knew in the divine essence all real things of the past, present and future, including the thoughts of all men of all times.

The limitation on Christ's human knowledge was that he did not know all the possible things that God could do. The way theologians explain it, that kind of knowledge is equivalent to comprehensive knowledge; only God knows himself in that way. No creature can have comprehensive knowledge of God, not even Christ's human soul.

Christ's soul therefore possessed, as St. Thomas says, a relative omniscience, not an absolute one. He knew all real things—past, present and future. In order to protect this truth, the Holy See in 1918 in the time of Pope Benedict XV rejected the following proposition: "Nor can the opinion be said to be certain which holds that Christ's soul was not ignorant of anything but from the beginning knew in the Word all things past, present, and future, that is, everything that God knows with the knowledge of vision."

It follows then that Christ's human knowledge was free of all ignorance and error. Let us look at the New Testament. Jesus calls himself "the light of the world" (Jn 8:12), which came into the world to bring true knowledge to mankind (Jn 12:46). He calls himself "the truth" (Jn 14:6), and says that he came into the world to give testimony to the truth (Jn 18:37). In him are hidden "all treasures of wisdom and knowledge" (Col 2:3). He knows things which take place far away (Jn 1:48), and he sees through the heart of man (Jn 1:47; 2:24ff.; 6:71). The idea that Jesus' human knowledge was defective in any way, or that he was in error, cannot be reconciled with these statements of the Bible.

Among the ancient heretics there were some who said that Jesus was ignorant of many things; others said that he was in error on some points, especially about the Parousia and the end of the world. The text that occasioned much dispute on the point is Mark 13:32, which refers to the Second Coming of Christ: "But as for that day or hour, nobody knows it, neither the angels of heaven, nor the Son; no one but the Father." The problem arises because Jesus said that "the Son" does not know when the Parousia will occur.

The Fathers of the Church attempted a number of different explanations of the text. The explanation of St. Augustine is the one that was generally adopted. He said that Christ, in his human intellect, possessed divine knowledge that was communicable and non-communicable. In other words, what pertained to his mission as Redeemer he could communicate to us; what did not pertain to that mission was non-communicable knowledge. Thus, it was not in accordance with the Father's will that Jesus reveal when the end of the world will take place (see Acts 1:7). St. Augustine says, "It was not part of His teaching duty to make it (the Day of Judgment) known to us."

In all of this it is important to remember that the basic

reason for the impossibility of ignorance or error in Christ's human soul is found in the most mysterious Hypostatic Union. For, it is irreconcilable with the dignity of the divine Person to ascribe to him such imperfections.

19

# JESUS POSSESSED BOTH INFUSED AND ACQUIRED KNOWLEDGE

For many centuries theologians have been arguing about the nature and extent of Jesus' human knowledge. We have already seen that he possessed the immediate vision of God. A further question has been raised about infused knowledge. It is an accepted point in Catholic teaching that the angels do not learn from experience as we do; they do not have bodies and so they do not have sense experience. Their knowledge was given to them, or infused into them, at the moment of their creation.

We come into this world with certain faculties or powers of learning, but we do not have actual knowledge. This comes from experience of the world. At birth our minds are a blank, a *tabula rasa*. Must we say that Jesus Christ came into this world lacking all knowledge? or did he possess certain gifts of knowledge because of the Hypostatic Union and because he was the Redeemer of the world?

It has been the common teaching of the theologians since St. Thomas Aquinas that, from the beginning of his life, Jesus' soul possessed infused knowledge. By "infused knowledge" is meant spiritual concepts which are immediately and habitually communicated to the mind by God. Thus, infused knowledge does not depend on sense experience in its acquisition. There seem to be many examples of this kind of knowledge in the lives of the great mystics who have been illuminated about divine things directly by God.

It is not possible to offer a strict proof from Scripture for this kind of knowledge in Jesus Christ, but there are some indications of it. Thus, St. Paul says of him that "in him are hidden all the treasures of wisdom and knowledge" (Col 2:3). He is also the Wisdom of God (1 Cor 1:24) and the Mystery of God (1 Cor 2:7).

St. Thomas says that the dignity of the human nature assumed by the Word of God requires that it should lack no perfection which human nature is capable of. That would seem to require the perfection of knowledge. Also, since he is the Head of all creation, it seems appropriate that he should not be lacking in any knowledge. Moreover, as the Revealer of the intimate secrets of God and God's plan for mankind it seems fitting that Jesus Christ should know all things, past, present and future.

Another argument for Jesus' infused knowledge is given by St. Thomas. He points out, on the basis of his theory of knowledge borrowed from Aristotle, that the human mind, as spirit, has the capacity to know all created things. Lack of knowledge is considered an imperfection, and actual knowledge a perfection of the mind. Thomas argues that the union of Jesus' soul with the Word of God, and his mission as Redeemer and Revealer, require that he have the perfection of all human knowledge. Therefore, he argues, Jesus' soul possessed the fullness of infused knowledge from the first moment of its creation.

What about acquired or experiential knowledge? Did Jesus have that kind of knowledge too? By "acquired knowledge" is meant the human knowledge which proceeds from the unique combination of sense perception with the abstracting activity of the intellect which produces concepts or universal ideas. Since it is a defined dogma of the Church that Jesus was fully human—possessing both body and soul—it follows necessarily that he had human acquired or experiential knowledge. As St. Thomas remarked long ago, the denial of experiential knowledge in Christ leads eventually to the heresy of Docetism, that is, the theory that Jesus was not really a human being but merely "appeared" to be such.

The Gospels give many indications that Jesus made progress in human knowledge. In fact, St. Luke says in 2:52 that "Jesus increased in wisdom, in stature, and in favor with God and men." In what sense did he make progress in human knowledge? It was not possible for him to "progress" in the immediate vision of God or in his infused knowledge since both of these types of knowledge, from the very beginning, encompassed all real things of the past, the present and the future, as we have seen. With regard to these two types of knowledge, we can speak of "progress" only in the sense of a gradual manifestation which corresponded to the various stages of his physical growth. Thus, Jesus did not speak like an adult when he was a child, except perhaps on rare occasions. For example, his wisdom shone through at the age of twelve in the Temple when he said, "Did you not know that I must be about my Father's business?" (Lk 2:49).

That Jesus had acquired knowledge and that he made progress in human knowledge, we know from Scripture. *How* this was possible is another matter. There have been many theories to explain it; none of them is fully satisfactory. St. Thomas said that Jesus made progress in his human knowledge because he learned by experience what he already knew through his infused knowledge. Thus, he said that it was new, not in its content, but only in the way in which Christ acquired it. You may or may not find that explanation satisfactory. I have studied many of the modern theories, some quite different from that of St. Thomas, but I have not found one that is better.

In any event, to be in tune with the thinking of the Church, it is best, in my view, to hold that Jesus possessed both infused knowledge and acquired or experiential knowledge. We can leave the more subtle explanations to the theologians.

20

# JESUS WAS FREE FROM ALL SIN AND COULD NOT SIN

We have seen that Jesus possessed, during his earthly life, the fullness of wisdom and knowledge. The next step in our consideration of Christ is to examine his will. It is by our wills that we adhere to God or separate ourselves from him. Sin, or rebellion against God, resides in the will.

With this in mind we can ask at this point: Did Jesus ever sin? Was he capable of sinning? To those questions most Catholics would reply instinctively "No". That answer is perfectly correct. In this essay I would like to show why that answer is right.

The New Testament attests in many places to the absolute sinlessness of Jesus Christ. "He did no sin; neither was deceit found in his mouth" (1 Pet 2:22). "For we have not a high priest who cannot have compassion on our infirmities, but one tried as we are in all things except sin" (Heb 4:15). And Jesus himself challenged his enemies: "Which of you can convict me of sin?" (Jn 8:46).

Various General Councils of the Church have declared that Jesus was free of all sin. The Council of Chalcedon in 451 said that he is "like us in every respect except sin"; here the Fathers quote Hebrews 4:15 cited above. In the further explanation of Jesus' sinlessness the Fathers and theologians deduce Christ's freedom from original sin from the Hypostatic Union—that totally marvelous union of the human nature and the divine nature in the one Person of the Word. This most intimate connection with God excludes the condition of separation from God which is the result of original sin.

According to Luke 1:35 Jesus entered into this world in a state of holiness: "The child will be *holy* and will be called Son of God." The Council of Trent defined that original sin is transmitted from one generation to the next by natural generation. Since Jesus Christ entered into this world in a supernatural way because of his conception by the Holy Spirit (Mt 1:18ff.; Lk 1:26ff.), it follows that he was not subject to the general law for the transmission of original sin.

The sad consequences of original sin are our inclinations towards sin, our unruly passions, our difficulty in controlling ourselves, even when we interiorly want to obey God. This inclination is called "concupiscence" in theological tradition; I have already explained this on a previous occasion. Trent also defined that concupiscence flows from original sin: it comes from sin and it leads us into sin. Thus, where there is no original sin there is no concupiscence. That is one of the aspects of Mary's Immaculate Conception. She was conceived without original sin, so she was not burdened with concupiscence and never committed any sin, not even a venial sin. Since Christ was not subject to original sin, he was free from concupiscence. Thus his sensual nature and his passions were completely subject to the direction of reason. Thus, the Fifth Council of Constantinople officially rejected the false teaching of some theologians that Christ "was burdened with the passions of the soul and with the desires of the flesh".

So it is a defined dogma of the Faith that Jesus never committed a sin. But was Jesus capable of sinning? Although it is not defined, it is a matter of Catholic faith that Jesus in his humanity was not merely sinless, but also that he was impeccable, that is, incapable of sinning. There are indications of this in the New Testament, some of which were cited above. The Bible, however, says that there was no sin in Jesus; it does not say explicitly that he was *incapable* of sinning.

The Fifth Council of Constantinople (553) condemned a certain teaching which maintained that Christ became completely impeccable only after the Resurrection. We may conclude from this that he was already impeccable before his death and Resurrection.

The basic reason for Jesus' impeccability is found again in the marvelous Hypostatic Union. What this means in practice is that the human acts of Jesus are the acts of the second Person of the Blessed Trinity. Clearly, it is contradictory to the absolute sanctity of God—the source of all sanctity—that a divine Person should be the responsible subject of a sinful act. Also, because of the Hypostatic Union, Christ's human will was totally penetrated and controlled by the divine will.

When it comes to explaining *how* Jesus' impeccability was brought about, the theologians are divided. The followers of St. Thomas teach that it was accomplished by the Beatific Vision possessed by Jesus from the first moment of his conception. In this view, the Beatific Vision by itself always renders sin absolutely impossible.

For, one who sees God as he is in himself cannot turn away from him in sin. For this reason, the blessed saints in heaven can never sin and be cast out of the presence of God.

21

## JESUS POSSESSES THE FULLNESS OF GRACE

The goal of human life is personal union with God for all eternity in knowledge and love. Union with God is called sanctity or holiness, for God is the essence of holiness. Thus, the closer one is to God, the holier one is.

Our Lord Jesus Christ is both God and man. The union of his human nature and his divine nature is effected in the Person of the Word, the second Person of the Blessed Trinity. Because of the Hypostatic Union, Christ's human nature is said to be substantially holy. The reason for this is that the Word of God, who is uncreated holiness itself, imparts a special holiness to his own created human nature. Since the relationship between Jesus' human nature and the Word of God is in the substantial order by virtue of the Hypostatic Union, then it is legitimate to say that his humanity is endowed with substantial sanctity or holiness. For, it is impossible to have a more intimate union between a creature and

God than the Hypostatic Union in Jesus Christ. A suggestion of Jesus' substantial holiness is given in Luke 1:35, "And so the child will be holy and will be called Son of God."

In addition to the special "grace of union", as the above is called, Christ's soul is also holy by reason of the fullness of sanctifying grace with which it is endowed. By "sanctifying grace" here is meant the created habitual grace that inheres in the soul of the justified. Jesus possesses the fullness of that grace. Thus Pope Pius XII said in his encyclical letter on the Mystical Body in 1943: "In Him (Christ) dwells the Holy Spirit with such a fullness of grace that greater cannot be conceived." Basing their opinion on the Gospel of St. John, all theologians ascribe sanctifying grace in its fullness to the human soul of Christ: "And the Word was made flesh and dwelt among us . . . full of *grace* and truth. . . . And of his fullness we have all received, *grace for grace*" (Jn 1:14, 16). In Acts 10:38 we read that "God anointed him with the Holy Spirit"; in St. Luke we find that Jesus was "filled with the Holy Spirit" (4:1); he also quoted Isaiah and said, "The spirit of the Lord has been given to me, for he has anointed me" (4:18).

St. Thomas Aquinas (*Summa Theologica* III, q. 7, art. 1) bases the sanctification of Jesus' humanity through sanctifying grace on three facts: 1) on the Hypostatic Union which demands the fullness of grace in Christ's soul according to the principle, "The nearer an effect is to its cause, the more it partakes of its influence"; 2) on the nobility of Christ' soul which enjoys the immediate vision of God; 3) on the relationship of Christ to all men since he is the Head and source of their grace.

Because Christ possesses the fullness of all grace, he is

able to bestow it on all the members of his Mystical Body, past, present and future. In his wisdom and divine plan God the Father has seen fit to dispense all grace to men through his only-begotten Son, Jesus Christ. Thus, all grace is the grace of Christ; all grace comes to us from and through him. In this regard, Pius XII said in the Letter quoted above: "From Him there flows out into the body of the Church all light through which the faithful receive supernatural enlightenment, and every grace, through which they become holy, as He Himself is holy. . . . Christ is the founder and the originator of holiness. . . . Grace and glory well up from His inexhaustible fullness."

With regard to the same point, St. John says: "And of his fullness we have all received, grace for grace" (1:16). St. Paul says that Christ as man is the Head of the Church, which is his Mystical Body: "He has put all things under his feet, and made him, as the ruler of everything, the head of the Church, which is his body" (Eph 1:22–23). Just as among human beings the life and control of the body is thought to be located in the head, so also the supernatural life of grace—in the spiritual order—flows from Christ the Head to the members of his Mystical Body. As God, Christ is the author and source of grace; through his human nature, as the instrument of the divinity, he confers grace upon individual persons through the Church and the sacraments.

The activity of Christ in bestowing grace extends to all men of all times; to the actual members who are united to him through sanctifying grace; to those who have faith; and to the potential members who do not yet have either sanctifying grace or faith. The only one excluded from his grace are the damned in hell. The reason for their exclusion is that, since they have freely rejected God and his grace, they no longer have the capacity to receive grace.

It is very helpful to recall from time to time that our grace and salvation come from Jesus Christ and only from him. Without him there is no grace and no salvation.

22

# THE POWER OF CHRIST

We have considered the knowledge of Jesus Christ, his sinlessness and his fullness of grace. The next point I would ask you to reflect on is the *power* of his humanity. In the Gospels we read about the many marvelous and miraculous things that Jesus did.

Let me mention just a few of them. Jesus performed many miraculous cures of the sick and the infirm—by the touch of his hand or by a mere word. St. Luke says in 6:19 about the crowds that followed him, "and everyone in the crowd was trying to touch him because power came out of him that cured them all." Even during his earthly life Jesus had power over nature—over the mysterious power of gravity, over the fish, over the wind and the waves. St. Matthew related in 14:25, "In the fourth watch of the night he went towards them, walking on the lake, and when the disciples saw him walking on the lake they were terrified."

In addition to his power over nature he also had power over the spiritual realities that concern man's relationship with almighty God. Thus, Jesus attributed to himself as the Son of Man the power to forgive sins: "The Son of Man has power on earth to forgive sins" (Mt 9:6). "He who eats my flesh and drinks my blood lives in me and I live in him. . . . anyone who eats this bread will live for ever" (Jn 6:56–58). In his High Priestly prayer before his passion Jesus confesses that the Father has given him power over "all flesh" or all mankind: "and, through the power over all mankind that you have given him, let him give eternal life to all those you have entrusted to him" (Jn 17:2).

We know from our many years of reading the Scriptures, from hearing them read each Sunday at Mass, and from our study of the catechism that Jesus possessed extraordinary powers and that he performed many miracles. How did he do that? Did his human soul and body possess the omnipotent power of God so that he could do such remarkable things?

In order to get a clear picture of this mysterious reality, it is important to remember that God confers certain powers on the natures of the things he has created. Occasionally, for a spiritual purpose, he goes beyond the normal powers of nature; that is what we mean by a "miracle". Christ's human nature was endowed with certain powers of nature and grace, but those powers were finite, not infinite. In his human nature, which was created and finite, Jesus was not omnipotent. Omnipotence is a perfection which pertains to the divinity alone.

But with regard to producing supernatural effects, such as miracles, prophecies and the forgiveness of sins,

Jesus' human nature functions as an instrument of the Word. So he has instrumental power to produce supernatural effects in the physical order and the moral order which serve the purpose of redemption, that is, the salvation of mankind.

The key here to understanding Jesus' supernatural power is the Hypostatic Union, which has been referred to many times in this series of essays on Christology. This means that the humanity of Jesus is substantially united to the second Person of the Blessed Trinity or the Word of God. The Person of Jesus is that Word. The principal cause of the supernatural effects produced by Jesus is therefore the Word of God who operates in and through the humanity. There is a certain similarity here to the painter who uses a brush to paint a beautiful picture. The painter is the cause of the picture, but he uses the brush as an instrument. The main cause of the picture is the creative power of the artist, although the brush also contributes something. Likewise, the divine power operates in and through Jesus Christ, but the principal cause is the divinity of the Word while the humanity functions as the instrumental cause.

The Fathers of the Church looked upon the humanity of Christ as an instrument of the Godhead. Therefore, they said that the flesh of Christ has the power to give life. St. Cyril of Alexandria said of the Eucharist which is the Body and Blood of Christ: "As the flesh of the Redeemer, through His union with substantial life, that is, with the Word stemming from God, is become life-giving, we, when we enjoy it, have life in us."

The point of this consideration is to realize that Jesus possesses divine power to produce supernatural effects in the order of nature and in the order of grace. Jesus, however, who is both God and man, possesses infinite power because he is God, not because he is man. Thus, Christ's humanity, as instrument of the divine Word, produces and can produce supernatural effects through the power received from God.

Christ is the Head of the Church which is his Body. The glorified Christ continues to pour out his Spirit on the faithful. He showers his grace on us through his sacraments, especially through the reception of his Body and Blood in the Eucharist.

## 23

## JESUS' SUFFERING AND HUMAN FEELINGS

Having considered Jesus' unsurpassable knowledge, sanctity and power, the next point to reflect on is the question of the defects he labored under in both body and soul. By "defects" in this context I do not mean moral faults, but merely certain aspects of the human condition as the result of which we are able to suffer either in the body or in the soul.

The questions I hope to answer in this essay are: Did Jesus really suffer pain in his body as we do? Also, did Jesus endure mental suffering such as we are exposed to, for example, sadness and fear? We ask these questions because, now aware of his infinite dignity by reason of the Hypostatic Union, we might be led to think that he did not suffer under the same weaknesses and defects that we do.

There were some heretics in the early Church, called "Docetists", who said that Jesus did not have a human body and soul like ours and that therefore he could not suffer as we do. The Church reacted strongly against this error and repeatedly condemned it. For, if that were true, then Jesus would not truly be one of us—be our Brother; it would mean that he did not really suffer and die for our salvation; it would in effect mean the end of the Church and the sacraments.

Against that heretical view the Church in her Creed professes that Jesus really suffered and died under Pontius Pilate. The Fourth Lateran Council in the year 1215 declared that Jesus "in His humanity was made capable of suffering and death". Thus, it is the defined teaching of the Catholic Church that Jesus could and did suffer bodily pains just as we do. The fact that he was God—the second Person of the Blessed Trinity incarnate—did not prevent him from suffering and dying as we do.

Since Jesus was free of all sin, however, including original sin, his bodily defects were not the consequence of sin as they are for us. The defects we are talking about are hunger, thirst, weariness, feeling of pain and mortality. Jesus voluntarily assumed these common human weaknesses for three reasons: 1) to satisfy for the sins of mankind by undergoing the punishment due to sin, such as fatigue, pain and death; 2) to confirm the faith of mankind in the truth of the Incarnation; 3) to give Christians an example of those virtues of patience and endurance that they ought to imitate in their own lives.

It would not be correct to say that these defects were unnatural in Christ because he is God. They were natural because they belong to human nature as such. The point is that he *freely* assumed them. Because he was God incarnate he could have assumed a human nature without them.

We might note, though, that Jesus' work of redemption required only that he assume the general human defects of human nature as such, i.e., hunger, thirst, fatigue, pain and death. He did not assume particular defects that often are the result of moral faults, like illness of body or soul, or that are opposed to the perfection of the soul, like ignorance.

At this point I would ask you to recall that Jesus, already in his earthly life, possessed the immediate vision of God and infused knowledge of all things past, present and future. Consequently, he was absolutely free of all ignorance and error. This situation suggests a question about Jesus' emotions and feelings. Our passions and emotions often induce us to do or say things (for example, in a fit of anger) that are contrary to reason and that we later regret. So did Jesus have emotions? Did he experience the push and pull of feelings as we do?

For those familiar with the New Testament the answer is clear: Yes, Jesus was subject to emotions. We find various emotions explicitly attributed to him in the Gospels. "He began to grow *sorrowful* and be *sad*" (Mt 26:37). "He began to *fear* and be heavy" (Mk 14:33). "He looked round about on them with *anger*" (Mk 3:5). "I am *glad* for your sake" (Jn 11:15).

It is not surprising that it should be so since Jesus was fully human, just as we are, except for sin. The soul and the body form one human person. What happens to the body affects the soul and vice versa. That is the whole point in contemporary psychosomatic medicine. We have already shown that Jesus suffered bodily ills; it follows, then, that he also felt human emotions.

Because of Jesus' freedom from concupiscence, however, his passions or emotions could not be directed to a sinful object, could not even arise in him without his consent—they were completely under the control of his will and could not obscure or dominate his mind. In this regard there is a significant difference between his emotions and ours. For, our emotions arise spontaneously, often against our will, and sometimes totally dominate our power of reason. Thus, they can lead us into sin. Not so with Jesus. Jesus was capable of suffering and experienced emotions, but everything was under the control of his will which was totally obedient to his Father.

24

# WHY DID GOD BECOME MAN?

We have been considering the Person of our Redeemer, the Lord Jesus Christ. Now we will reflect on what it is he came to do in this world, that is, the work of our redemption or salvation.

We sometimes refer to Jesus as "our dear Savior"—and indeed he is. Even a short reflection on the Incarnation—the implications of the Hypostatic Union—necessarily lead one to ask in a state of wonder: "Why did God do it?" "Why did God humble himself to such an extent that he actually assumed our weak human flesh?"

The Bible and the Church, which alone can authentically interpret the Bible, say clearly that the Son of God—the second Person of the Blessed Trinity—became man in order to redeem mankind. In other words, the *purpose* of the Incarnation was our redemption from sin.

We are all familiar with that idea from the Creed that we profess at Mass each Sunday: "We believe in one Lord, Jesus Christ. . . . For us men and for our salvation he came down from heaven."

The New Testament says often that Christ came into the world to save all men, to redeem them from their sins. The very name of "Jesus", which means "Savior", affirms his redemptive task. Thus, we read in Matthew 1:21, "you must name him Jesus, because he is the one who is to save his people from their sins." Speaking of himself and his work, Jesus said: "for the Son of Man has come to seek out and save what was lost" (Lk 19:10). In Matthew 20:28 he said something quite similar: "the Son of Man came not to be served but to serve, and to give his life as a ransom for many."

We find the same idea often in St. John's Gospel: "For God sent his Son into the world not to condemn the world, but so that through him the world might be saved" (3:17).

St. Paul is probably the most outspoken writer in the New Testament about the redemptive purpose of the Incarnation. "God sent his Son, born of a woman, born a subject of the law, to redeem the subjects of the law and to enable us to be adopted as sons" (Gal 4:4). Again, Paul says very clearly in 1 Timothy 1:15, "Here is a saying that you can rely on and nobody should doubt: that Christ Jesus came into the world to save sinners."

Everything that God does outside himself is for his

own glory in one way or another. Thus the New Testament mentions another purpose of the Incarnation. It is the Glory of God which is the ultimate purpose of all God's works. Thus, the angels sing at Bethlehem, "Glory to God in the highest heaven" (Lk 2:14). And before he goes to his death Jesus prays, "I have glorified you on earth and finished the work that you gave me to do" (Jn 17:4).

For centuries there has been a controversy among Catholic theologians about God's primary purpose in becoming man. Most, following St. Thomas Aquinas, say that the primary motive was the redemption of mankind from sin. They conclude from this position that, if Adam and Eve had not sinned and so transmitted original sin to all their descendants, the Incarnation would not have taken place. Other theologians, following the Franciscan, Duns Scotus, maintain that the primary motive of the Incarnation was the primacy of Jesus Christ over all creation—angels, world and men. They say that the Son of God, in order to crown the work of creation, would have become man even without the Fall.

The testimony of the New Testament favors the view of St. Thomas (*Summa Theologica*, III, q. 1, art. 3), as is clear from the citations given above. There are many texts in the New Testament which say explicitly that the purpose of the Incarnation was the redemption of mankind. On the other hand, there is not one text in the New Testament which says that the Incarnation would have taken place even without the Fall of our first parents.

The Fathers of the Church are practically unanimous in the same opinion. St. Augustine said: "If mankind had not fallen, the Son of Man would not have come. . . .

Why did He come into the world? To save sinners (1 Tim 1:15). There was no other reason for His coming into the world."

The Incarnation is God's most sublime work. The followers of Scotus find it inappropriate that sin, which God hates, should be the occasion for the greatest revelation of God. The Thomists see in that an even greater proof of God's infinite love and mercy.

The Scotists try to find the biblical proof for their view in the teaching of St. Paul that all creation is ordered to Christ as its head and crown. The main text they use is Colossians 1:15–20, where Christ is said to be "the first-born of all creation" (v. 15). "All things were created through him and for him" (v. 16). "As he is the Beginning, he was the first to be born from the dead, so that he should be first in every way" (v. 18). The Thomists reply that these texts prescind from the Incarnation and refer to the second Person of the Blessed Trinity who is the eternal and infinite God.

The view of St. Thomas is not as lofty and all-encompassing as that of Scotus, but it is more in accord with the data of revelation, that is, what God told us about himself.

We are not in a position to say what God would have done if Adam and Eve had not sinned. He did not reveal that to us. Scripture says that "Christ Jesus came into the world to save sinners."

# 25

# JESUS CHRIST—REDEEMER AND LIBERATOR OF MANKIND

In the last essay we asked the question: Why did God become man? We arrived at the answer: In order to save us from our sins, in order to redeem us. One of the common titles we give to Jesus is that of "Redeemer". In this chapter I would like to explain what the Church means by the word "redemption".

In ordinary usage we say that one can redeem something, such as a coat or a suitcase, by making a payment or by presenting a ticket that one has paid for in advance. The idea is related to what is meant by the word "ransom". We use this word in reference to a payment made to a kidnapper for the release of the person or thing taken and held.

Both of these ideas have been used by theologians to explain what is meant by the redemption of mankind by Jesus Christ, the God-man. Other ideas used to explain it include liberation and deliverance. Jesus is the Great Liberator who frees us from our sins and restores us to friendship with Almighty God who was offended by the sin of Adam and by our own personal sins.

The term "redemption" in Christian theology, therefore, refers to the mystery of God's deliverance of mankind from the evil of sin and his restoration of man to the state of grace by an act of divine power and merciful love. God's redemptive act in Jesus Christ includes the whole of man's history from the time of his first sin and fall from grace, as St. Paul intimates in 1 Timothy 2:4, "God . . . wants everyone to be saved and reach full knowledge of the truth."

There are two ways of looking at the work of redemption. First, we can consider it as the work done on our behalf by the God-man, Jesus Christ. In this sense it includes the Incarnation of the second Person of the Blessed Trinity, the life, passion, death and Resurrection of Jesus. His work of redemption effected the salvation of mankind from the burden of sin, which includes separation from God, suffering, death and subjection to the power of the devil. St. Paul expresses this idea clearly in Romans 3:23-24, "Both Jew and pagan sinned and forfeited God's glory, and both are justified through the free gift of his grace by being redeemed in Christ Jesus who was appointed by God to sacrifice his life so as to win reconciliation through faith."

Second, we can consider the redemption as the application of the grace of Jesus Christ to individual men and women. Thus, those who believe in Jesus Christ, repent of their sins and are baptized into the community of the faithful receive the grace of Christ which makes them children of God and heirs of heaven.

Redemption is directed against sin and its power over the soul. Its purpose is to liberate us from sin and the power of the devil. By its very nature sin is a turning away from God and a turning towards creatures. The work of redemption, therefore, must consist in turning men away from a disordered attachment to creatures and turning them towards God. On this point St. Paul says that the heavenly Father "has taken us out of the power of darkness and created a place for us in the kingdom of the Son that he loves, and in him we gain our freedom, the forgiveness of our sins" (Col 1:13–14).

Our redemption, objectively considered, was accomplished by the teaching, life, death and Resurrection of Jesus Christ. In a very special way, however, it was effected by the vicarious atonement of the merits of Christ in his sacrificial death on the Cross. Through the Atonement the offense offered to God by sin was counterbalanced and the injury to the honor of God was repaired. By his death Christ merited a superabundance of grace which is dispensed to all men of all time to bring about their redemption.

Because the offense of sin is against the infinite dignity of God, and because man—as a creature—is totally dependent on God, he is not able to save himself. Thus, he needs assistance from God; he needs a mediator who can reconcile him with God.

Jesus Christ was able to redeem mankind because he is both God and man. He is a divine Person—the second Person of the Blessed Trinity—substantially united to a human nature. In virtue of his divine-human constitution Jesus is the Mediator between God and mankind, as Paul says in 1 Timothy 2:5, "For there is only one God, and there is only one mediator between God and mankind, himself a man, Jesus Christ, who sacrificed himself as a ransom for them all."

In the order of being and activity the God-man Jesus Christ is the only Mediator between God and man. Other mediators, such as the angels and the saints, are all subordinated to the mediation of Christ. Jesus Christ mediated and mediates for us through the actions of his human nature. Because of the real distinction between his two natures—divine and human—it was possible for him to perform mediatory acts as man and receive them as God. This answers the objection that Christ could not act as mediator between himself (as God) and mankind.

26

## FALLEN MAN CANNOT SAVE HIMSELF

Jesus Christ is our great Redeemer. This means that he liberated us from sin—both original sin and our own personal sins. In order to stir up sentiments of gratitude to God for such a Redeemer, it might be helpful to reflect for a few moments on the necessity and freedom of our redemption.

Given Adam's sin, which is open rebellion against God, and our own personal sins, what can man do when he comes to the realization of his own evil and wishes to be reconciled with his Creator and God? The Church answers: By his own efforts man can do nothing to save himself, to redeem himself, to regain the lost friendship with God. Here is what the Council of Trent had to say on this point:

> It is necessary to admit that all men had lost innocence in the sin of Adam. They became unclean. . . . They 'were by nature children of wrath' (Eph 2:3). . . . So completely were they slaves of sin and under the power of the devil and death, that

neither the power of nature for the Gentiles nor the very letter of the Law of Moses for the Jews could bring liberation from that condition (*Denzinger* 793).

In other words, the Catholic Church teaches infallibly that fallen man, namely all of us, cannot redeem himself. If he is to attain his final end in the face to face vision of God, he is in desperate need of God's help. Just as all are under the curse of sin, so also all need the grace of Jesus Christ. Here is how St. Paul expresses the same truth: "Both Jew and pagan sinned and forfeited God's glory, and both are justified through the free gift of his grace by being redeemed in Jesus Christ" (Rom 3:23–24).

Jesus Christ is the second Adam. Just as the first Adam lost for himself and for us the grace of God, so the second Adam, by his sacrificial suffering and death, regained for us what the first Adam had lost. It is important to note that sanctifying grace is wholly supernatural. That means that it is a free personal gift of God over and above the first gift of natural existence. In theological terms, this means that God could have created man in a purely natural state, with a natural end, without ordaining him to the Beatific Vision. But to the first gift of nature, he added the second gift of sanctifying grace which is wholly supernatural and not required by the first gift.

God came into our world and became incarnate in order to restore the supernatural gift of sanctifying grace. This is what we mean by redemption and this is something that man could not accomplish by his own powers.

In trying to understand our redemption it helps also to consider the nature of sin. Sin is rebellion against God, violation of his will and his Law. Man is a finite, limited creature; God is infinite goodness and perfection. Personal offenses are measured not only by what is done, but also by the dignity of the person offended. Thus, an insulting word offered by one child to another is not as serious as the same insulting word uttered by a son against his father. Likewise, the offense of one man against another is not the same as an offense of a man against God. For, the dignity of God infinitely surpasses the dignity of the human person.

Thus, the basic reason for the absolute necessity of redemption for fallen man is found both in the supernaturalness of sanctifying grace and in the infinity, in one sense, of man's guilt that is found in sin. As an action of a creature, sin is certainly finite; but if we consider sin as an insult to the infinite God—which it is—then it is infinite. It should be obvious that an infinite offense requires infinite satisfaction or atonement. Man is not capable of that because he is utterly finite. Therefore, only God can make adequate satisfaction to himself—only a divine Person can do that.

We Catholics believe—and we profess in our Creed—that the Son of God became man to redeem us and to save us from the power of Satan, sin and death.

Was God under any compulsion to redeem us? No. Our redemption was a perfectly free act of divine love and mercy.

Another question that occurs is this: On the supposition that God resolved to redeem man, was the Incarnation of the second Person of the Blessed Trinity absolutely necessary in order to accomplish this? St. Thomas Aquinas asked this question and replied that God, because of his omnipotence, could have redeemed mankind in many other ways. It would be an unwarranted limitation on his power and mercy to say that the

Incarnation was his only means of redeeming us. Without injury to his justice, God can grant forgiveness to the repentant sinner even without adequate satisfaction.

The Incarnation of the second divine Person, however, was most fitting. It was the most appropriate means of redeeming us because it reveals the perfections of God in a most glorious manner and also offers the strongest motives and best example to men and women to strive for religious and moral perfection by imitating Jesus Christ, the incarnate Word.

# 27

# THE DIVINE TEACHER

Jesus Christ is our divine Redeemer. By his death and Resurrection he triumphed over the powers of Satan, sin and death. He actually accomplished our redemption through his three offices or functions, which are traditionally called his prophetic office, pastoral or kingly office, and priestly office. Thus, in many Church documents reference is made to our Lord as prophet, pastor or king, and priest. For example, the Second Vatican Council in its Constitution on the Church speaks explicitly about these three offices of Jesus Christ. They are indicated also in John 14:6, "I am the way (pastor), the truth (teacher) and the life (priest)."

In this essay we will consider a few aspects of Jesus'

prophetic or teaching office. Certainly we get our best picture of the Lord in the four Gospels, and there he is most frequently presented as a teacher of the truth. We see him teaching his disciples, instructing the people. One of the most memorable passages in the New Testament is the Sermon on the Mount in Matthew, chapters five to seven. There Jesus is presented as a second Moses, teaching the people about God and the way to God.

A consequence of original sin, ratified by personal sin, is that man is caught up in religious ignorance. This ignorance came into the world through the deception of the devil who is "a liar and the father of lies" (Jn 8:44). The Redeemer came into the world "to destroy the works of the devil" (1 Jn 3:8) and to free mankind from his slavery, a part of which is both ignorance about God and false ideas about God's nature and existence. An essential part of this task was to remove man's spiritual darkness, which is the result of sin, and to bring the bright light of true knowledge about God. Hence, one of Jesus' major tasks as our Redeemer was to instruct us about the nature of God and about his divine plan for the salvation of mankind.

Truth of itself possesses tremendous liberating power. Jesus proclaimed the redeeming power of truth when he said, "You will know the truth and the truth will make you free" (Jn 8:32). Jesus both speaks the truth and is the truth.

Some readers may not immediately perceive the connection between "teacher" and "prophet". In biblical terms, the prophet is simply one who speaks in the name of God, whether to express his demands or his promises. He proclaims to the people what God's will is for them and what he expects them to do. Predicting the future—a notion often associated with prophecy—is only one aspect of the prophetic office. But since God's plan will be fully realized only in the future, when the prophets advert to that there is always an element of prediction in their prophecies.

The Jews of Jesus' time were expecting another great prophet. For, Moses had said in Deuteronomy 18:15, "The Lord your God will raise up for you a prophet like myself, from among yourselves, from your own brothers; to him you must listen." The New Testament writers refer this text to Jesus (see Acts 3:22; 7:37; Jn 1:45). So Jesus is often spoken of as a prophet.

Christ calls himself "the light of the world" (Jn 8:12), "the truth", and considers the proclamation of the truth as one of his principal tasks: "I was born for this, I came into the world for this: to bear witness to the truth; and all who are on the side of truth listen to my voice" (Jn 18:37).

Jesus is often called "Rabbi", which means "teacher", and he claims to be the only teacher of men: "Nor must you allow yourselves to be called teachers, for you have only one teacher, the Christ" (Mt 23:10). So Jesus is the teacher of mankind. His teaching, of course, does not concern human affairs and human science. Jesus is exclusively concerned about God and man, and man's way to God.

There is no doubt that Jesus' teaching made a powerful impact on his listeners. The Gospels often use the word "amazement" to describe the reactions of his audience. When the police sent to arrest Jesus returned empty-handed, they said to their angry superiors, "There has never been anybody who has spoken like him" (Jn 7:46). At the conclusion of the Sermon on the Mount St.

Matthew says, "Jesus had now finished what he wanted to say, and his teaching made a deep impression on the people because he taught them with authority, and not like their own scribes" (7:28–29).

The foundation of Jesus' unique teaching authority lies, again, in the mysterious Hypostatic Union. In virtue of that union he possesses the immediate vision of God and infused knowledge of all things past, present and future. Because of that knowledge he is "the Truth" and speaks the truth with absolute confidence and authority. Aware of his supreme teaching authority, Jesus gave his right to teach all men to his Apostles and their successors: "All authority in heaven and on earth has been given to me. Go, therefore, make disciples of all the nations . . . and teach them to observe all the commands I gave you. And know that I am with you always; yes, to the end of time" (Mt 28:18–20).

28

# KING OF KINGS, AND LORD OF LORDS

Our heavenly Father sent Jesus Christ into this world to teach all men the way of salvation, to rule and to sanctify. These offices or tasks of the Lord were indicated by himself when he said, "I am the way, the truth, and the life" (Jn 14:6). Accordingly, Church documents often refer to Jesus as prophet, king and priest. In the previous article we considered Jesus' prophetic or teaching office; now we will reflect for a few moments on his pastoral office or "kingship". In further essays we will treat his priesthood.

Jesus Christ is king, there is no doubt about that. In reply to Pontius Pilate who asked Jesus if he was a king, he said, "Yes, I am a king" (Jn 18:37). It is perhaps difficult for Americans to grasp easily what a king is, since we have experienced over two hundred years of democratic government. Our ancestors declared independence from the English King because of certain grievances that were not redressed.

We might ask ourselves: "What is a king?" The Webster's Dictionary defines it thus: "a male monarch of a major territorial unit; esp.: one who inherits his position and rules for life." An absolute monarch, like Louis XIV of France, incorporates in his own person all three functions of normal government—legislative, judicial and executive. Various limits can and have been put on kings and their heirs. There are current examples of this in constitutional monarchies such as England or Belgium. In the course of history kings in those countries have been stripped of most of their powers so that their function has become ceremonial for the most part.

We know from the New Testament that Jesus Christ is a king—he said so himself. Jesus is also the shepherd or pastor of his flock, that is, all those who believe in him and follow him. In Church language the words "king" and "pastor", when used of Jesus, have more or less the same meaning. They refer to his power or authority to rule over the people of God. Just as a shepherd or pastor rules over his flock of sheep, and just as an earthly king rules over the people in his territory, so also Jesus Christ,

King of Kings and Lord of Lords, rules over his Church. Accordingly, Christ's pastoral or kingly office manifests itself in legislation, in judicial functions and in the execution of his judgments.

The Old Testament prophecies proclaimed a great messianic king who would be sent to redeem God's people (see Ps 2; Is 9:6ff.; Dan 7:13ff.). The New Testament says that those prophecies have been fulfilled in Jesus of Nazareth. Thus the angel Gabriel said to Mary at the Annunciation: "The Lord God will give him the throne of his ancestor David; he will rule over the House of Jacob for ever and his reign will have no end" (Lk 1:32). Before Pilate, as we have seen, Jesus openly proclaims himself to be a king. At the same time, however, he makes it clear that his kingdom is spiritual and not earthly: "My kingdom is not of this world" (Jn 18:36). Before his Ascension, when he gave his Great Commission to his Apostles, Jesus stated that his royal power embraces both heaven and earth: "All authority in heaven and on earth has been given to me" (Mt 28:18).

Jesus confirmed his legislative or lawgiving power when he promulgated the basic law of his kingdom in the Sermon on the Mount. He preached the arrival of the kingdom of God on earth and gave it visibility in his Church which was founded on Peter and the Apostles (Mt 16:18–19; 18:18). He established the new commandment of love (Jn 13:34) and demanded strict observance of his commandments (Jn 14:15; Mt 28:20).

Jesus also possesses supreme judicial power: "The Father judges no one; he has entrusted all judgment to the Son" (Jn 5:22). We also pray in the ancient Apostles' Creed, "From thence he shall come to judge the living and the dead." So Jesus is the supreme and eternal Judge of all men of all time. The judgment that the Son will hand down on the last day will be executed or carried out immediately: "And they (the evil ones) will go away to eternal punishment, and the virtuous to eternal life" (Mt 25:46).

Martin Luther said that Christ did not give any commands, but only promises. In opposition to that teaching the Council of Trent declared in the sixteenth century: "If anyone says that God has given Jesus Christ to men as a redeemer in whom they are to trust, but not as a lawgiver whom they are to obey: let him be anathema", that is, expelled from the Church. So Jesus is a lawgiver—one of the functions of a ruling king.

Since the time of the early Fathers Jesus has been addressed and adored as a king. Some saw him as a king ruling from the wood of the Cross. In 1925 Pope Pius XI published a beautiful encyclical letter on the universal kingship of Christ, entitled "Quas Primas". By order of the same Holy Father the feast of Christ the King was instituted for the universal Church. Until the liturgical reform of Pope Paul VI it was celebrated on the last Sunday of October. It is now celebrated on the last Sunday of the liturgical year, which is usually the third or fourth Sunday of November.

## 29

## JESUS IS A PRIEST FOREVER

The third office attributed to Jesus by Holy Scripture is that of priest. The Old Testament text most often applied to Jesus in the New Testament is Psalm 110:4 which affirms his eternal priesthood: "The Lord has sworn an oath that he never will retract, 'You are a priest of the order of Melchizedek, and for ever.'"

In order to understand why Scripture and the Church affirm that the God-man Jesus Christ is a priest, it is necessary to have a clear idea of what a priest is. A basic notion of priesthood is "mediation" or "to be a mediator". A mediator is one who stands in the middle between two extremes; he is a go-between. Thus, when a child has a serious conflict with his father, he will often plead with his mother to act as a "mediator" between himself and his father. The function of a mediator is to bring about a reconciliation between two opposed parties. Acceptable to both sides, he is able to facilitate communication back and forth and to work out an agreement or "reconciliation".

That is exactly what Jesus is—a mediator between God and men. Offended by the sin of Adam and by our own personal sins, God punished man with death and became inaccessible. In order to get back into God's good graces, man needed to be reconciled with him. Being finite and sinful, man needed a "bridge builder" or mediator who could establish contact with God and work out a settlement. That is where the God-man Jesus Christ comes into the picture. St. Paul expresses this thought beautifully in 1 Timothy 2:5, "For there is only one God, and there is only one mediator between God and mankind, himself a man, Christ Jesus, who sacrificed himself as a ransom for them all."

Another essential notion involved with priesthood is that of "sacrifice". A priest is more than one who "ministers" to others by proclaiming to them God's Word, by teaching them and by leading them in prayer. That is the Protestant idea of a minister. The Catholic idea of the priesthood includes all that, but also adds the reality and function of "sacrifice". "Sacrifice" in this sense means to offer something good and precious to God, to remove it from our possession and place it in God's hands; the purpose of this act is to give visible expression to our obedience and subjection to his will.

Mediation between God and mankind is a two-way street. The priest offers gifts and sacrifices to God on behalf of mankind; he also brings gifts and blessings from God back to the human family. Thus, we read in Hebrews 5:1, "Every high priest has been taken out of mankind and is appointed to act for men in their relations with God, to offer gifts and sacrifices for sins." In the Catholic faith and understanding, the priest brings God's gifts and graces to mankind by administering the holy sacraments, especially by offering the Holy Sacrifice of the Mass and by bringing Christ to the faithful in the Holy Eucharist as the food for their souls.

It is a truth of the Catholic faith that Jesus is a priest; in fact, the Bible and the Church documents refer to him as our "high priest", that is, principal, leading or supreme priest. The Letter to the Hebrews offers us a whole treatise on Jesus' priesthood. In 3:1 we read, "All you who are holy brothers and have had the same heavenly call should turn your minds to Jesus, the apostle and the high priest of our religion." Basing themselves on this text and others like it, the Fathers at the Council of Ephesus in 431 A.D. said, "If anyone, therefore, says that it was not the Word of God himself who was born to be our high priest and apostle when he was made flesh (see Jn 1:14) . . . let him be anathema."

In 1562 the Council of Trent declared that the Levitical priesthood of the Old Testament was insufficient. Then the Council said: "It was, therefore, necessary (according to the merciful ordination of God the Father) that another priest arise according to the order of Melchizedek (see Gen 14:18; Ps 110:4; Heb 7:11), our Lord Jesus Christ, who could perfect all who were to be sanctified (see Heb 10:14) and bring them to fulfillment."

What is it that constitutes Jesus as our mediator or high priest? It is the Hypostatic Union—the unique and eternal union of the divine nature and the human nature in the Person of the Word—which commenced at the moment of the Incarnation when Mary consented to be the Mother of God. By reason of the Hypostatic Union Jesus Christ stands, as it were, in the middle between God and man. He can offer a sacrifice that is wholly pleasing to the Father and he can bring the grace of God to all mankind because he is our Brother. Finally, because the Hypostatic Union will last for all eternity, so also is Jesus our eternal high priest.

## 30

# JESUS' SACRIFICE ON THE CROSS

We have seen that Jesus is a priest and that his priesthood will last forever, because the mysterious union of the human nature and the divine nature in Jesus Christ will last for all eternity. It is very important to note that the most essential function of the priestly office is to offer sacrifice to God for the sins and failures of mankind. Thus, we read in Hebrews 8:3, "It is the duty of every high priest to offer gifts and sacrifices."

What I would like to communicate to you here is the Church's belief and teaching that Jesus' bloody death on the Cross was a true *sacrifice*. We all have some idea of what a "sacrifice" is in the secular sense, that is, the giving up of some present good for the sake of something better. Thus, many parents deny themselves certain luxuries, such as a new car or a trip to Europe or a pleasure boat, in order to have the necessary money to send their children to college. Real accomplishment and perfection in any line of human endeavor, whether it be tennis, biology or playing the piano, requires giving up or sacrificing other things, often much more pleasant, that one would like to do.

In the liturgical sense, such as we find in the Old Testament, a sacrifice is an external religious act in which a gift perceptible to the senses is offered to God by a specially designated person in recognition of his absolute sovereignty and in atonement for sins. Thus we distinguish four elements in every true sacrifice: the person to whom it is offered, the one who offers, the visible gift and the purpose for which the offering is made.

All of these elements are present in Jesus' death on the Cross. For, Jesus himself is both the priest and the victim; he offered himself to the Father in atonement for the sins of all mankind.

The Council of Ephesus in 431 A.D. taught that Jesus offered himself up as a pleasing sacrifice to our God and Father. In that teaching they relied on the words of St. Paul to the Ephesians as found in 5:2: "Follow Christ by loving as he loved you, giving himself up in our place as a fragrant offering and a sacrifice to God" (see Ex 29:18).

Some of the Fathers of the Church looked upon the Cross of Jesus as a type of altar of sacrifice. This idea was picked up and incorporated into the official teaching of the Church by the Council of Trent in 1562. In pointing out the relationship between Jesus' bloody sacrifice on the Cross and the Holy Mass, the Fathers said: "In the divine sacrifice that is offered in the Mass, the same Christ who offered himself once in a bloody manner *on the altar of the cross* is present and is offered in an unbloody manner" (*Denzinger* 940).

In the New Testament there are many references, both direct and indirect, to the sacrificial character of Jesus' death on Calvary. Thus, St. John the Baptist, following the prophet Isaiah, sees in Jesus the Lamb of sacrifice, who took on himself the sins of all mankind, in order to atone for them. Seeing Jesus approach the Jordan, St. John exclaimed to his followers: "Look, there is the Lamb of God that takes away the sin of the world" (Jn 1:29). St. Paul says of him in 1 Corinthians 5:7, "Christ, our passover, has been sacrificed."

In the Gospels Jesus, on a number of occasions, speaks of "giving" his life for us, and of "shedding" or "pouring out" his blood for us. The Greek words used for these expressions are the same ones used in the Septuagint or Greek version of the Old Testament which was current at the time; in the Old Testament these words are used in connection with the prescribed sacrifices that had to be offered at certain times of the year. For example, we read in Matthew 20:28, "The Son of Man came not to be served but to serve, and to *give* his life as a ransom for many."

When he instituted the Holy Eucharist at the Last Supper Jesus indicated the sacrificial nature of his death by the very words he used—words which are repeated by the Church each day in the Mass: "This is my body which will be *given* for you" (Lk 22:19); "This is my blood, the blood of the covenant, which is to be *poured out* for many for the forgiveness of sins" (Mt 26:28).

It should be clear, then, that Jesus' death on the Cross was a true sacrifice because it fulfilled all the requirements of a sacrificial act. As man Jesus was at the same time both sacrificing priest and sacrificial gift. As God together with the Father and the Holy Spirit, he was also the one who received the sacrifice.

The act of sacrifice consisted in the fact that Jesus, in an attitude of perfect self-surrender, voluntarily gave up his life to God by allowing his enemies to kill him, even though he could have prevented it. For, he said in John 10:18, "No one takes it (my life) from me; I lay it down of my own free will, and as it is in my power to lay it down, so it is in my power to take it up again."

31

# WHAT DO WE MEAN BY "REDEMPTION"?

In the last essay we saw that Jesus' bloody death on the Cross on Calvary was a true and proper sacrifice. At this point we might ask, "Why did Jesus die?" or "What was the purpose of his violent and sacrificial death?" Questions such as these lead us to the notion of "redemption" and "reconciliation" with God.

Because Jesus is both God and man, all of his activities have redemptive value for us. Nevertheless, the culmination of his redemptive activity is to be found in his sacrificial death on the Cross. For, it was by his death, freely and lovingly embraced in obedience to the will of the Father, that Jesus accomplished our redemption.

The official teaching of the Church is that, by his sacrifice on the Cross, Jesus redeemed us and reconciled us with God. In 1562 the Council of Trent taught that Jesus offered himself to the Father on the altar of the Cross in order to accomplish for us "an everlasting redemption".

This teaching, of course, is merely a repetition of a

truth that is often stated in the New Testament. Thus, Jesus says in Matthew 20:28, "The Son of Man came not to be served but to serve, and to give his life as a ransom (or redemption) for man." And St. Paul says in Romans 5:8, "What proves that God loves us is that Christ died for us while we were still sinners." That Jesus redeemed us from our sins by his death is a recurring theme in the letters of Paul. "Both Jew and pagan sinned and forfeited God's glory, and both are justified through the free gift of his grace by being redeemed in Christ Jesus who was appointed by God to sacrifice his life so as to win reconciliation through faith" (Rom 3:23–24).

Modern Americans often find it hard to understand clearly what is meant by the word "redemption". But it is both useful and important to grasp the idea involved in "redemption" since it is such a fundamental aspect of our Catholic faith. After all, two of the most common titles attributed to our Lord refer to this mystery; they are "Redeemer" and "Savior".

The word "redemption" means the buying back, or ransom, of a slave or captive in order to secure his freedom. In this sense it means almost the same thing as "liberation". The biblical use of "redemption" to signify the saving action of God with regard to his people has made it the term par excellence for expressing the meaning of the Cross of Christ.

What has Jesus saved us from? By his sacrificial death he has liberated us from the slavery of sin (Titus 2:14), death (2 Tim 1:10) and the devil (Col 1:13). Jesus asserts the atoning power of his death at the Last Supper: "For this is my blood, the blood of the covenant, which is to be poured out for many for the forgiveness of sins" (Mt 26:28).

Sin is the big obstacle. Because of the sin of Adam and Eve, a sin which is confirmed and repeated by the personal sins of mankind, a barrier was set up between man and God. Because of the sin of Adam death, and all the evils related to it, entered into the world. As long as sin remained, there was enmity or hostility between man and his Creator. Jesus Christ came into the world to break down the barrier, to remove the enmity and to reestablish peace and harmony between man and God. How did he do it? Certainly the Incarnation and all the acts of Jesus' life are part and parcel of our redemption, but it was specifically his sacrificial death out of love for us that accomplished our redemption. As Paul well says in Romans 5:10, "When we were reconciled to God by the death of his Son, we were still enemies; now that we have been reconciled, surely we may count on being saved by the life of his Son." The same idea appears in Colossians 1:20, "It has well pleased the Father through him (Christ) to reconcile all things to himself, making peace through the blood of his Cross."

Closely related to the notion of redemption is the idea of "reconciliation". That idea appears in four major Pauline texts in the New Testament. I suggest that you get out your Bible and look them up: 2 Corinthians 5:18–20; Colossians 1:20–22; Romans 5:10–11; Ephesians 2:11–16. But reconciliation is not just the result of redemption; it was operative during the whole life and death of Jesus, for Paul says that "God was in Christ, reconciling the world with himself" (2 Cor 5:19). When we have been finally reconciled with God, we are in a state of peace and harmony with him. The lesson is that God loved man, took the initiative and delivered him from the slavery of sin. He did this by sending his beloved Son into the world to die and to atone for the mysterious evil of sin.

St. John expresses this idea beautifully in 3:16–17, "Yes, God loved the world so much that he gave his only Son, so that everyone who believes in him may not be lost but may have eternal life. For God sent his Son into the world not to condemn the world, but so that through him the world might be saved."

## 32

## JESUS DIED NOT FOR HIMSELF BUT FOR ALL MEN

Closely related to the redemption of the human race by the sacrificial death of Jesus, which we treated in the last essay, is another truth of the holy Catholic faith, namely, that by his suffering and death Jesus rendered *vicarious atonement* to God for the sins of man. In Catholic theology, "atonement" means reparation for any wrong or injury, either material (such as the loss of something valuable) or spiritual (which is an injury or offense to another person).

Material harm requires restitution; moral injury calls for satisfaction or atonement, which is compensation for some wrong done to another. The word "vicarious" means "in the place of another". Thus, we commonly refer to our Holy Father as "the Vicar of Christ"; this means that, as the successor of St. Peter in the Chair of Rome, he takes the place of Christ as the visible head of the Church while the Lord Jesus remains the invisible Head.

On many previous occasions we have considered the sin of Adam and the disastrous consequences it had for the human race. Also, because of our weakened human nature and the influence of concupiscence, we all imitate Adam by committing personal sins. Sin, as you will recall, is an offense against God. For such an offense or injury there must be satisfaction or atonement in order to restore the original state of peace and harmony between God and man. The English word "at-one-ment" clearly expresses the revealed truth that the death of Jesus restores the oneness, concord, reconciliation between God and man. Man by himself was not able to effect adequate atonement for his sins because the guilt of sin against God incurs a guilt greater than unaided man can atone for. Sin or an offense against God takes on an aspect of the infinite because of the infinite majesty of God who is offended. Man, being wholly finite, is incapable of offering infinite satisfaction to God for sin.

It is at this point where the importance of our Redeemer, the God-man Jesus Christ, stands out. Fully human and fully divine, Jesus is able to offer himself to the Father in an oblation of love that is acceptable. Being human he can suffer and die; being divine he can offer a sacrifice of love that has infinite value.

It should be noted that Jesus' atonement was *vicarious*, that is, he offered it to God for us, on our behalf, and not for himself. Thus, the Council of Ephesus (431 A.D.) teaches with St. Cyril of Alexandria: "If anyone says that he (Christ) presented His offering for Himself as well and not solely on our behalf (for as He was sinless, He had no need of any offering): let him be anathema." And the Council of Trent said in 1547: "Our Lord Jesus Christ . . . when we were enemies (see Rom 5:10), by reason of his very great love wherewith he has loved us (see Eph 2:4), *merited justification for us* by his own most holy Passion on the wood of the cross, and made satisfaction *for us* to God the Father."

There are many passages in the New Testament that refer to the same truth. Thus, Jesus says in Matthew 20:28, "The Son of Man came not to be served but to serve, and to give his life as a ransom for many." St. John expresses the same idea in 10:15, "I lay down my life for my sheep." Also, in the Gospel passages that recount the institution of the Holy Eucharist Jesus speaks about "pouring out" his blood for us, and "giving" or "handing over" his body for us. In their own way these passages express the truth taught by the Church that Jesus offered vicarious atonement to God for the sins of man.

The basic reason for the sufficiency of Jesus' atonement lies in the Hypostatic Union. Because of the Hypostatic Union Jesus' every action possesses an intrinsic infinite value because the operating subject is the second Person of the Blessed Trinity. In fact, not only is Jesus' atonement sufficient for all the sins of the human race, it is superabundant. The reason for this is that every action of Jesus has infinite value. In the fourteenth century Pope Clement VI said that, because of the Hypostatic Union, one single drop of blood of Jesus would have sufficed for the redemption of the whole human race.

The pope was merely echoing what St. Paul had

taught centuries before: "However great the number of sins committed, grace was even greater" (Rom 5:20).

A final point to consider is that Jesus died for all men, not just for those who are saved. In 1653 Pope Innocent X condemned as heretical the proposition that Christ died for the salvation of the predestined only. And the Council of Trent taught: "God sent him forth as a propitiation by his blood through faith for our sins, not for our sins only, *but also for those of the whole world* (see 1 Jn 2:2)."

We should not forget, however, that even though salvation is available to all, each one must freely accept it by faith in Jesus Christ and by keeping his commandments.

## 33

## JESUS MERITED GRACE FOR US

Most of us use the word "merit", at least on occasion, and we all have a general idea of its meaning. Few perhaps would be able to define it or to explain it in any detail. In the Catholic tradition one often encounters expressions such as "meriting grace", "meriting eternal life" or "offering up one's merits for the poor souls in purgatory".

In fact, the Teaching Authority of the Church uses the word "merit" to describe how Jesus won grace and eternal redemption for us. The Council of Trent said that Jesus is the "meritorious cause" of our sanctification and justification because he "merited justification for us by his own most holy Passion on the wood of the cross, and made satisfaction for us to God the Father".

We might ask ourselves: "What does it mean to 'merit' something?" In Catholic theology the idea of "merit" means a work performed for the benefit of another, on whom it establishes a claim to give a reward. The idea is closely related to the notion of paying a just price for goods and services rendered. It is also connected with the right to a just wage for work done. If a girl works in a shop for eight hours and the boss has agreed to pay her $5.00 per hour, then she has a right to $40.00. We say that she deserves that because she earned it. Thus we can see that "merit" has something to do with justice and equality. We all know that if someone has done a great favor for us, we are under a certain social obligation to reciprocate the favor in the future if we can or if we are asked.

So merit is the right that one has to a reward. If it is a strict right, Catholic theology calls it *de condigno* merit (the English word is "condign", which means "deserved"). If it is a question simply of appropriateness, it is called *de congruo* merit (the English word is "congruous" or "suitable").

What has all this got to do with our Lord and Savior Jesus Christ, you might be tempted to ask? Well, it has a great deal to do with him if we want to understand how a sinful human being can escape the power of sin and attain eternal happiness with God in heaven. For, Jesus' work of redemption is both *satisfactory* (he atoned for our sins) and *meritorious*. The reason is that it both removes the relationship of guilt between humanity and God, and establishes a claim for reward on the part of God.

The Council of Trent said that original sin is removed only by the merits of Jesus Christ, and that through the Sacrament of Baptism the merits of Jesus are applied to adults and children. Even though the New Testament does not use the word "merit" with regard to Jesus, it does clearly teach the doctrine of his merits. Thus, in Philippians 2:8–9 we read: "He was obedient unto death, even death on a Cross. For this reason God exalted him." The glorification and exaltation of Jesus is the reward for his obedience in suffering. The same idea is presented in Luke 24:26, "Ought not the Christ to have suffered and so enter into his glory?" (See also Jn 17:4 and Rev 5:12).

We see therefore from the Bible that Jesus, by reason of his obedience and humility, merited for himself his own glorification at the right hand of the Father, that is, Resurrection from the dead, Transfiguration of the body and Ascension into heaven.

All of Jesus' acts, from the first moment of his conception, were meritorious. For, they were free, morally good, supernatural and performed in the state of grace. Since every act of Jesus was the act of a divine Person, each one possessed an infinite meritorious value. In confirmation of this we might note that in 1343 Pope Clement VI taught that "the merits of Christ are infinite."

One consequence of this doctrine is that Jesus merited all supernatural graces received by fallen human beings. All grace therefore is the grace of Christ. St. Peter testified before the Jewish leaders in Jerusalem: "For of all the names in the world given to men, this is the only one by which we can be saved" (Acts 4:12). And the Council of Trent taught: "No one can be just unless he is granted a share in the merits of the Passion of our Lord Jesus Christ." And St. Paul says in Romans 3:23-24, "Both Jew and pagan sinned and forfeited God's glory, and both are justified through the free gift of his grace by being redeemed in Christ Jesus."

What about our own good acts? Can they be the basis of merit? The answer is, "Yes, they can." But since grace is a completely free gift of God, we cannot merit our initial sanctification *de condigno* (i.e., we don't deserve it). St. Thomas Aquinas says that, once we possess the grace of God, we can merit eternal life *de condigno*, but we cannot so merit it for others. We can, however, merit grace for others *de congruo* (i.e., with a well-founded expectation that God will grant it). That is why it is important to pray for the conversion of sinners. And we all sense that the prayers of the saints are very efficacious.

## 34

## THE DESCENT OF CHRIST INTO HELL

All Catholics know, or at least should know, the Apostles' Creed. Have you ever wondered why the expression, "He descended into hell", is in the Creed? What does it mean? And what is Jesus, our God and Savior, doing down in *hell*? The statement puzzled me for a long time and I suspect that you have a question or two about it. In this essay I will try to set forth briefly the faith of the Church on this point.

First of all, it should be noted that the English word "hell" is somewhat ambiguous in this particular expression. It corresponds to the Hebrew "Sheol", the Greek "Hades" and the Latin *inferus* or *infernus*, and therefore simply means the abode of souls after death. In current English by the word "hell" we mean the place and state of eternal damnation for the devils and for those who have died in the state of mortal sin. So in the Apostles' Creed the word "hell" means the underworld, the dwelling place of the spirits of the dead. It does not mean the hell of damnation. Once this point is grasped it is easier to understand why the Church says that Jesus "descended into hell".

The Apostles' Creed expresses the Catholic belief that after his death Jesus' human soul, separated from his body but still united to his divine Person, passed into the abode of the dead. His soul stayed there as long as his body, which also remained united to his divine Person, lay in the tomb, that is, until the morning of his glorious Resurrection.

The New Testament affirms in a number of texts that Jesus was "raised from the dead" (Acts 3:15; 4:10; 1Th 1:10). The implication is that he sojourned among the dead in the underworld (or "hell") from the time of his death until his Resurrection. Jesus himself alluded to this truth when he said: "For as Jonah was in the belly of the sea-monster for three days and three nights, so will the Son of Man be in the heart of the earth for three days and three nights" (Mt 12:40). In that context "heart of the earth" means the underworld or Sheol.

Speaking of Jesus' Resurrection, St. Peter says, "God raised him to life, freeing him from the pangs of Hades; for it was impossible for him to be held by its power"

(Acts 2:24). Liberation from the "pangs of Hades" is a symbol of the freeing of the dead from the underworld. Likewise, St. Paul says that Jesus is "the firstborn from the dead" (Col 1:18; see also Rom 10:6ff.). These texts all point to the fact of Jesus' descent into the underworld after his death.

A number of the earlier Fathers, such as St. Ignatius of Antioch, St. Justin Martyr and St. Irenaeus speak of Jesus being "really raised from the dead". After the fourth century most of the Fathers of both East and West mention the descent of Christ into hell. The belief began to appear in the various Creeds of the Church in the fifth century. It was about that time that the Apostles' Creed as we now have it was codified.

The fact of Jesus' descent into hell is certainly an article of faith, but there is some dispute about his activity there between his death and Resurrection. The explanation of that activity given by St. Thomas Aquinas and the *Catechism of the Council of Trent* is followed by most theologians today. By his death and Resurrection Christ triumphed not only over death, but also over sin and Satan. His sacrificial death therefore reversed the sad consequences of sin. Jesus opened the gates of heaven and made the Beatific Vision a possibility for those who die in faith and charity. So the purpose of his descent into hell was the freeing of the just in limbo by the application of the fruits of the redemption, that is, by the communication of the Beatific Vision.

Jesus did not descend into hell in order to suffer there, or to convert unbelievers or those lacking charity, but to put them to shame for their unbelief and wickedness. Thus, his descent brought no deliverance to those who are in hell for their sins and lack of faith. It would seem also that the souls in the limbo of children who never had the use of reason while on earth and died in the state of original sin, lacking faith and charity, were not delivered. To the poor souls in purgatory, however, who died with faith and charity he gave the hope of attaining the Beatific Vision when they had paid their debt of temporal punishment.

The limbo of the Patriarchs contained the souls of all the saints of the Old Testament, that is, those who died in faith and charity and had paid their debt of temporal punishment. To these Jesus imparted the fruits of his passion. He bestowed on them the Beatific Vision—the vision of God in his essence. Jesus enlightened them right there in the underworld with the Light of glory. He took all of them with him when he ascended into heaven. Christ descended into all these sections of the underworld by his power. His very soul, united to his divine Person, descended into the limbo of the Patriarchs and remained there until his Resurrection on Easter morning.

## 35

## JESUS' GLORIOUS RESURRECTION

There are many unique characteristics of the Catholic faith that distinguish it from all other religions. One of the most important is the Catholic belief in Jesus' Resurrection from the dead. Belief in the Resurrection of

Christ is expressed in all the creeds and rules of faith of the ancient Church.

In the *Apostles' Creed* we pray: "the third day he arose again from the dead." Each Sunday at Mass we profess our faith in the *Nicene Creed*: "On the third day he rose again in fulfillment of the Scriptures."

The term "resurrection" means the return of a dead man to life. In the course of history many miraculous resurrections have been effected by the power of God. Jesus, for example, raised from the dead by his own power the young daughter of Jairus (Mk 5:21–42), the only son of the widow of Naim (Lk 7:11-17), and his personal friend, Lazarus (Jn 11). It is recounted of St. Peter in the Acts of the Apostles that he raised the pious woman Tabitha from the dead (9:36–42). Many other cases could be cited from the Bible and from the lives of the saints.

The resurrection of these persons, however, was very different from that of Jesus. Lazarus and the others were returned from the dead to ordinary, mortal, human life. Eventually they died a second time; their souls were separated from their bodies and their bodies corrupted in the grave just as all other bodies do.

The Resurrection of Jesus from the dead is something totally different; both his soul and his body take on a whole new mode of existence. His soul was reunited with his body on Easter morning, but this was accomplished *by his own power*. The teaching of the Catholic Church emphasizes the fact that Jesus rose by his own power (*Denzinger* 286).

Moreover, Jesus' human nature, body and soul, was *glorified* in his Resurrection. It is difficult for us to grasp completely what is meant by the word "glorified".

Some of the qualities of Jesus' glorified humanity are mentioned in the Gospels: he is no longer subject to suffering and death; his body possesses a certain radiance that flows from the supreme blessedness of his soul; he can move rapidly from one place to another merely by willing to be there; he has no need of food or sleep; he can pass through other bodies effortlessly—this is indicated in his appearances to the Apostles in the upper room when the evangelist says that the doors were bolted (Jn 20:19). The same phenomenon is alluded to at the conclusion of the story of his appearance to the two disciples on the road to Emmaus. St. Luke writes in 24:31, "Their eyes were opened and they recognized him; but he had vanished from their sight."

Beginning with Jesus' enemies in Jerusalem, there have always been those, both Christian and non-Christian, who have denied the historical reality of his Resurrection. There are many theologians and scripture scholars today who deny the bodily Resurrection of the Lord. They attempt to "spiritualize" the meaning of this revealed truth and say that archeologists may some day find the "bones" of Jesus in a tomb in Jerusalem. That is not what the Catholic Church holds.

In 1907 Pope St. Pius X condemned the following error of the Modernists, many of whom are still among us today: "The Resurrection of the Savior is not properly a fact of this historical order, but only a fact of the supernatural order that is not and cannot be demonstrated; Christian consciousness derived it gradually from other data" (*Denzinger* 2036).

Jesus clearly prophesied that he would rise from the dead on the third day after his death (see Mt 12:40; Mk 8:31; Lk 9:22; Jn 2:19). The reality of the Resurrection is proved by the fact of the empty tomb and of Jesus' many appearances to his followers during which he spoke with them, ate with them, and allowed them to touch him.

The fact of Jesus' bodily Resurrection from the dead was the central point of the preaching and teaching of the Apostles. The Apostles are primarily "witnesses" of the Resurrection. This point is stressed in many passages in the Acts of the Apostles (see chapters 1, 2, 3, 5, 10, 13). One of the principal qualifications required in the replacement for Judas among the Twelve was one who "can act with us as a witness to his Resurrection" (Acts 1:22).

For Jesus himself, the Resurrection meant his final and definitive entry into the state of glory which was the reward for his humility and obedience in suffering. The Resurrection belongs to the completeness of our redemption. The New Testament associates it with his death on the Cross as one complete whole.

Jesus' Resurrection is the model of our spiritual resurrection from sin through faith and Baptism (Rom 6:3ff.) and the pledge or assurance of the resurrection of our own bodies at the Second Coming of Christ (1 Cor 15:20ff.). It is the greatest of all Jesus' miracles; it is convincing proof of his divinity and the strongest proof of the truth of his teaching (1 Cor 15).

## 36

## THE ASCENSION OF JESUS

Our final consideration of the mysteries surrounding Christ our Lord will be on his glorious Ascension into heaven. The liturgical feast of the Ascension is celebrated each year on the fortieth day after Easter Sunday. Thus, it always falls on a Thursday, usually in the month of May; in the United States it is a Holy Day of obligation. In some dioceses the feast is transferred to the following Sunday.

The Ascension of Jesus means the transfer of his risen, glorious humanity—body and soul—to heaven, that is, to the world of the divine. St. Luke tells us that he continued to appear to the Apostles for forty days after his Resurrection and instructed them "about the kingdom of God" (Acts 1:3). At the end of this period he took them to the Mount of Olives, about one mile from Jerusalem and close to Bethany. While blessing them, he ascended into heaven and disappeared from their sight (Lk 24:50–53).

The Ascension marks the definitive conclusion of Jesus' earthly life. From that moment on he no longer associated intimately, on the physical level, with his disciples. Now the disciples must live in faith, hope and charity. Jesus is the invisible Head of the Church, gloriously reigning at the right hand of the Father. He will come again at the end of the world to judge the living and the dead.

All the Creeds of the Church affirm belief in Jesus' Ascension. We profess in the Nicene Creed: "He ascended into heaven and is seated at the right hand of the Father."

Jesus ascended into heaven by his own power on two counts. In the first place, as the second Person of the Blessed Trinity he possesses the divine power necessary to transfer his human nature from this world to the divine world. In the second place, his transfigured soul has the spiritual power to move his transfigured body wherever and however he wills.

There is no doubt that the place called "the heavens" in Scripture where Jesus is, while he waits for the Parousia, remains a mystery to us. We know that this is where God reigns in all his glory, the same place where the angels are said to stand in his presence. St. Mark says that Jesus did not just enter into the heavens, but that he sits at the right hand of God, illustrating that he is now, in all his being, as the Son made man, a partner in the divine rule over the universe.

The biblical expression "to sit at the right hand of God" alludes to Psalm 110:1; the phrase is often used in the Letters of the Apostles, for example, Romans 8:34; Ephesians 1:20; Hebrews 1:3; 1 Peter 3:22. The expression means that the glorified Christ, elevated in his humanity above all the angels and saints, participates in the glory and power of God in a very special way.

Since belief in the Ascension of Jesus is an integral part of the Creed of the Church, it follows that it is a dogmatic teaching of the Church. This great truth is solidly anchored in Holy Scripture, in the tradition of the Church, in the teachings of the Fathers, and in the liturgy.

From the point of view of the salvation of mankind, the Ascension is the ultimate accomplishment of Christ's redemptive work. As we saw in the last essay, according to the common teaching of the Church the souls of the just of the pre-Christian era accompanied the Savior into the glory of heaven: "When he ascended to the height, he captured prisoners, he gave gifts to men" (Eph 4:8).

Jesus ascended into heaven as our forerunner—to prepare a place for us (Jn 14:2ff.). He also involves us with himself to such a point that St. Paul says that God has "made us live together with Christ, and raised us up with him, and made us sit with him in the heavenly places" (Eph 2:6).

In heaven Jesus also intercedes for his followers: "He is living for ever to intercede for all who come to God through him" (Heb 7:25). From heaven he sends his gifts of grace, especially the Holy Spirit, into the hearts of the faithful (Jn 14:16; 16:7): "It is for your own good that I am going because unless I do go, the Advocate will not come to you; but if I do go, I will send him to you."

The pouring out of the Spirit on the Church by the glorified Lord is the fruit of his Ascension. One might also call it the first fruit of our perfect association with the Father who sent him to us from the height of heaven.

The Ascension of Jesus into heaven is the model and pledge of our own ascension and glorification. This was the goal of his voluntary humiliation in the redemptive Incarnation. In a certain sense we might even say that he took us with him when he ascended into heaven, for St. Paul says: "For you have died, and your life is hid with Christ in God. When Christ who is our life appears, then you also will appear with him in glory" (Col 3:3–4).

# PART V

# MARIOLOGY

I

# CHURCH TEACHING ABOUT MARY THE MOTHER OF GOD

Having completed our treatment of the main aspects of the Church's doctrine on Christ the Redeemer, we will now move on to a consideration of Mary, his mother. Step by step we will examine what Holy Scripture and the Magisterium of the Church say about her and her role in redemption. There are a number of reasons for doing this.

In the first place, Catholics have traditionally cultivated a warm devotion to Mary because she is the Mother of our Redeemer. Mary leads us to Christ and knowledge of Mary is knowledge of Jesus. She imitated him most perfectly and is the model for all Christians, the exemplar for the Church. Secondly, it is obvious to any observer of the Catholic scene since the Second Vatican Council that there has been a dramatic falling off among Catholics of devotion to Mary. For example, Marian devotions in most parish churches are now either non-existent or very rare. There are still May devotions in some places, but they are not nearly as common as they were twenty years ago. After the Council it seems that there was a serious decline in the recitation of the

Rosary. Toward the end of the 1970s, however, the Rosary started to make a strong comeback.

My third reason for writing about Mary is related to our Holy Father, Pope John Paul II. He has given fresh impetus to devotion to Mary through his frequent invocations of her and through his visits to her shrines such as Guadalupe in Mexico.

The decline in devotion to Mary after Vatican II is something of a mystery. Certainly, the reason cannot be the Council itself, since that Council was summoned by Pope John XXIII under her patronage and it spoke of her in more eloquent terms than any of the preceding Councils.

In an effort to rekindle the flames of devotion to the Mother of God our own American bishops in 1973 published a pastoral letter on her entitled "Behold Your Mother: Woman of Faith". "We desire with all our hearts", the bishops said, "that (this letter) be received into homes and rectories and seminaries, into schools and institutes of higher learning, into adult education groups, confraternity centers, campus ministries and religious communities" (No. 4).

In 1974 His Holiness, Pope Paul VI, published an Apostolic Exhortation on devotion to Mary which carries the title, *Marialis Cultus*. In that exhortation Pope Paul VI laid down the guidelines for the proper development of the devotion to Mary in our times, seeing it especially in its biblical, liturgical, ecumenical and anthropological dimensions. Touching on the basic reason for devotion to the Mother of God he said that "the ultimate purpose of devotion to the Blessed Virgin is to glorify God and to lead Christians to commit themselves to a life which is in absolute conformity with his will" (No. 39).

During the past four centuries, especially in reaction to the Protestant Reformation, there has been much development in the theology of Mary, which is usually called simply "Mariology". This has come about through a systematic meditation and reflection on Mary in the Bible and through a careful study of the writings of the early Fathers of the Church. Two specific results of this increased interest in Mary have been the infallible dogmatic definitions of her Immaculate Conception by Pope Pius IX in 1854, and of her Assumption into heaven by Pope Pius XII in 1950.

For over two centuries now Catholic theologians have tried to agree on one basic principle of Mariology which unites all the Church's teaching about her. Most have said that the basic principle is that she is the Mother of God; others call her the New Eve; one theologian stressed her bridal maternity.

The advantage of holding for the divine maternity as the basic principle is that it is a doctrine of Faith and therefore most certain. It also most clearly expresses the unique relationship of Mary to God. Finally, that Mary is the Mother of God is the source of all the other truths concerning her.

As one American theologian wrote a few years ago: "By reason of being the Mother of God, Mary is a new Eve, associate of the Redeemer, spiritual mother of the Mystical Body, queen of the kingdom of God, archetype of the Church" (Rev. E. R. Carroll in *New Catholic Encyclopedia*, vol. 9, p. 226).

2

## MARY IS A GIFT OF GOD

Mary was specially favored by God because he freely chose her to be the Mother of his Son who was to be the Redeemer of the world—the one to set men free from the steel grip of Satan and sin. Scripture tells us that Mary possessed the fullness of grace: "Rejoice, O highly favored daughter! The Lord is with you. Blessed are you among women" (Lk 1:28). This salutation of the angel Gabriel forms the beginning of one of our favorite prayers, "Hail Mary, full of grace, the Lord is with you . . . . " The point here is that God had prepared a suitable dwelling place in creation for the coming of the Redeemer—the body and soul of the immaculate Virgin Mary.

Saints, theologians (some theologians are also saints!) and popes have worked out a number of "principles" in dealing with Scripture and revelation as guidelines in speaking about the graces and gifts bestowed on Mary by God. There is, for example, the "principle of singularity" which says that, since Mary transcends all other creatures, she possesses unique gifts which have not been granted to any other. This is especially so with regard to her divine maternity and her Immaculate Conception.

The "principle of suitability" states that God endowed

Mary with all the gifts that are in accordance with her role in the plan of salvation and are not contrary to the testimony of the Bible. St. Thomas said, "Everything that is most perfect is to be found in the Blessed Virgin."

The "principle of eminence" states that all the privileges granted to all the saints were also conferred on Mary, at least in some way, since she was "full of grace". On this point St. Bonaventure said: "Whatever dignity or glory was granted partially to the saints, was granted fully to the sacred Virgin."

The theologians also speak of a "principle of association" which means that Mary was intimately associated with Jesus Christ in his work of redeeming the human race. She collaborated with him in every way—physically, morally, psychologically and spiritually. Supporting this notion, Pope Leo XIII said: "The Immaculate Virgin, beloved Mother of God, became his associate in saving the human race."

Finally, another idea often applied to Mary by the Fathers of the Church is that she stands in opposition to Eve, the first woman and the mother of the human race according to the flesh. Here the point is that everything lost by Eve has been restored abundantly by Mary. St. Augustine expressed the truth of this principle in this way: "Here we discover a great mystery: namely that through a woman we die and through a woman we are brought back to life."

Let me conclude these comments on Mary by pointing out again that she was specially chosen by God to be the Mother of the Redeemer. All her other gifts and graces are related to that primary gift in one way or another. By the expression "specially chosen", I mean that everything God gave her was a pure gift.

We know from our Catholic faith that the Incarnation of God, or the coming of the Redeemer, Jesus Christ, is intimately connected with original sin, the Fall of our first parents. St. Paul says again and again that Christ came to save us from our sins. This means then that God had decreed from all eternity that his Son would become man. But if God decided to become a man in order to save us, then he had to have a mother. This is where the Blessed Virgin Mary comes into the picture of God's salvific plan. God created Mary as a suitable dwelling place for the beginning and growth of his beloved Son.

Since Jesus is God and God cannot be tainted with sin in any way, it was fitting that the Mother of God never be subject to the power of Satan, that is, to sin. Therefore, she was created immaculate—free from every taint of sin.

Mary's fullness of grace is a gratuitous gift of God. She did nothing to merit her Immaculate Conception. She was pre-destined by God to be the Mother of his Son so he endowed her with the fullness of grace so that she could fulfill the divine will. But we must not think that Mary was an automaton, that she was not free. She was a free human person who fully cooperated with God in the divine plan. Thus, Mary freely consented to be the Mother of God when she answered the angel, "Behold the handmaid of the Lord. Be it done to me according to your word" (Lk 1:38).

3

# MARY, THE IMMACULATE MOTHER OF GOD

In order to become man and to redeem us, the Word of God (the second Person of the Blessed Trinity) had to have a human mother. Now I propose to consider one of the steps that God took in the preparation of a fitting mother for the Redeemer.

Since God detests all sin and since the purpose of the Redeemer was to liberate man from Satan and from sin, it was not proper that the Redeemer should be associated with sin in any personal way. Accordingly, in his providence God saw to it that the future mother of the Christ was never subject to sin.

What I am leading up to is the Catholic doctrine of the Immaculate Conception of the Blessed Virgin Mary. We celebrate this feast of Mary in the liturgy each year on the eighth of December. There was a time, it seems, when most Catholics had at least a basic understanding of this teaching about Mary. Today I am not so sure that most Catholics know what it refers to. There are many young Catholics who do not know the difference between the Immaculate Conception and the Virgin Birth; many of them think that the phrase "Immaculate Conception" refers to the conception of Christ by the power of the Holy Spirit. Others think that the "Virgin Birth" refers to the birth of Mary.

The doctrine of the Immaculate Conception of Mary was declared an infallible dogma of the Church by Pope Pius IX at Rome on December 8, 1854. What the doctrine means is that Mary herself was preserved from all stain of original sin from the first moment of her conception. Mary was conceived through the marital sexual union of her mother and father, to whom the tradition gives the names of Anne and Joachim.

In order to understand what the Church means by this teaching it is necessary to recall that Adam and Eve were constituted in sanctifying grace at the beginning of the human race. Being the first man and the first woman, they were the parents of us all. Adam was not just the physical head of the human race; he was also the moral head of the human family—and God tested him. By this I mean that the grace of Adam was to be transmitted to all his children if he was faithful to the God who created him. Thus, our possession of divine grace, or our lack of it, by the divine will depended on Adam's fidelity to God.

We all know what happened. Adam sinned and so lost grace not only for himself but for us also, since he was, so to speak, taking our place. As a result of the sin of Adam we are born into this world deprived of something we should have, namely, the grace of God. The Church calls this state of deprivation "original sin". It means that we are born without something we should have in order to be able to attain the end God has in mind for us, that is, eternal happiness with him in heaven. Because of the great merits of Christ, won for us by his life, passion and death, through Baptism we are restored to God's good favor and thus become children of God and heirs of heaven.

What does all this have to do with the Immaculate Conception? A great deal. For, original sin is transmitted to all of us through our natural generation from our parents. Mary was conceived and born in the natural way, so it would seem that she was subject to original sin. The Church Fathers struggled with this question for many centuries, trying to reconcile the universality of original sin with the required holiness for the Mother of God.

Original sin, though the sin of Adam and not a personal sin of each one of us, means separation from God; it means being a child of wrath and subject to the power of the devil. Some of the Fathers asked: Is it possible that Mary was, at least for a time, subject to the power of Satan?

As they reflected on this problem, more and more Catholic thinkers came to the conclusion that Mary must have been excused from the universality of original sin. There are some indications of this in the Bible, although the Bible nowhere says explicitly that Mary was immaculately conceived.

Three texts that the Fathers often cited were Genesis 3:15, Luke 1:28 and Luke 1:41. The first has to do with the Lord's prophecy to the serpent: "I will put enmity between you and the woman, and between your offspring and hers; he will strike at your head, while you strike at his heel." This is interpreted to mean that the offspring of Eve (i.e., Christ) will thoroughly defeat the devil, but the devil will have some success in injuring Christ (i.e., through sin in his followers).

It was not long before some of the early Fathers saw the "woman" in this passage as a symbol or figure for Mary, the Mother of Jesus. Many modern theologians argue, in the light of this text, that Mary's victory over Satan would not have been perfect if she had ever been under his power. Consequently, Mary must have entered this world without the stain of original sin.

# 4

# HAIL MARY, FULL OF GRACE

In the previous chapter I made a few observations about the Catholic doctrine of Mary's Immaculate Conception. In the present chapter I would like to continue the discussion. Let us consider the wording of the dogma as proclaimed by Pope Pius IX with his infallible authority. What the Pope defined is this: "The most Blessed Virgin Mary in the first instant of her conception, by a unique grace and privilege of the omnipotent God and in consideration of the merits of Christ Jesus the Savior of the human race, was preserved free from all stain of original sin."

Since Mary was a member of the human race just like you and me, she was a daughter of Adam and so should have been born with original sin. For, we all fell in Adam and, hence, we all need the redemption of Christ. But, for reasons already given, it was not fitting that the

Mother of God should ever have been under the power of sin. There are hints in Scripture that this was the case. I have already mentioned the importance of Genesis 3:15. There is also the matter of Luke 1:28 where the angel Gabriel addresses Mary, "Hail, full of grace!" The fullness of grace excludes all sin. The principal reason why the pleasure of God rests on Mary in a special way is her election to the dignity of the Mother of God. Accordingly, Mary's endowment with grace proceeding from God's pleasure must also be of unique perfection. However, it is perfect only if it extends over her whole life, beginning with the very first moment of her existence.

In Luke 1:41 Mary's cousin, Elizabeth, filled with the Holy Spirit, says to her, "Blessed are you among women, and blessed is the fruit of your womb." Mary's blessing is made parallel to the blessing of God which rests upon Christ in his humanity. This parallelism suggests that Mary, just like Christ, was free from all sin from the beginning of her existence.

Since Mary was a daughter of Adam, she needed redemption. Because of this important truth, many Fathers of the Church and great theologians, such as St. Albert the Great and St. Thomas Aquinas, taught that Mary was sanctified in the womb of her mother before her birth, just as St. John the Baptist was. Therefore, according to these thinkers, Mary was born without original sin, but she must have been conceived with it. However, there was an ancient tradition going back to the fifth century that Mary was "most pure" and never subject to sin. In the East there was even a liturgical feast of the Immaculate Conception by the eighth century; by the twelfth century it had spread to Ireland, England and the continent of Europe.

The theological solution to the problem was worked out by two Franciscans, William of Ware and John Duns Scotus. They developed the concept of "anticipatory redemption" or "preredemption". What this means is that, even though Mary should have incurred the guilt of original sin, a special divine decree kept her free from it in light of the anticipated merits of Jesus Christ who was destined to die for us on the Cross. Because of this insight which was elaborated at the beginning of the fourteenth century, Pope Pius IX said in his decree "by a unique grace and privilege of the omnipotent God and in consideration of the merits of Christ Jesus the Savior of the human race" Mary was preserved free from all stain of original sin.

Another aspect of the doctrine is that Mary was immaculately *conceived*. Pius IX said "in the first instant of her conception". This means that when God created the soul of Mary and infused it into the union of ovum and sperm prepared by her parents, she was endowed with the "fullness of grace" in view of the fact that she was to be the Mother of God. The gift was granted on the basis of the foreseen infinite merits of Jesus Christ the Savior. Thus we can in complete truthfulness say that Mary is the perfectly sinless Mother since she never came under the domination of sin, not even in the womb of her own mother.

William of Ware in the thirteenth century developed the following interesting argument in favor of the doctrine: It was fitting that Mary should have as much immunity from sin as she was capable of having. But she was able to have immunity from original sin. Therefore she did have that immunity.

Since she was to be the Mother of God it was certainly

fitting. Immunity from original sin was possible because God was able to apply to her the foreseen merits of her Son. Here is another way of stating the same thing: God could do it, he ought to do it, therefore he did it.

This theological argumentation does not give absolute certainty, but it does establish a high degree of probability for the dogma. Our certainty about the reality and truth of Mary's Immaculate Conception comes from the fact that the infallible Church of Christ teaches it as a doctrine revealed by God.

5

## MARY WAS FREE FROM ALL EVIL DESIRE

Since we are all sinners we all know what temptation is. We know what it means to have thoughts run through our minds that suggest things to us contrary to God's law and what is good for us, for example, thoughts of greed, envy, pride, lust, revenge, despair and blasphemy. We also know, or at least we should know from our catechetical instruction, that such evil thoughts are not sinful unless we give consent to them. Thus, one can sin by assenting to such thoughts interiorly, even though no external deed is performed; one also sins by both assenting to such thoughts and then proceeding to act, for example, to steal, to lie or to fornicate.

The Bible tells us (Gen 1) that God saw everything he

had made and saw that everything was good. If that is so, then man also is good; but if man is *good*, where do these evil thoughts and inclinations come from? We must not forget that God's judgment on the goodness of the world he created precedes the account of the sin of Adam and Eve (Gen 3). After the fall of Adam the history of the human race is not a pretty one. The first murder is recorded in Genesis 4 where we read about Cain killing his brother Abel.

As a result of Adam's sin (original sin) man comes under the power of evil. There is now in man what is called "evil desire", that is, an inclination to think and act contrary to the will of God. Thus, in one way or another all sin is a form of pride; it is a vain attempt on man's part to put himself in the place of God. This evil desire has been given a special name in Christian history: it is called "concupiscence". Concupiscence is a tendency or inclination to sin. It can arise in our minds suddenly and suggest something evil; we may not know where it came from or how it surfaced. Often it has been said that such ideas come from "the world, the flesh and the devil". There is much truth in that.

What is surprising about concupiscence, once you stop to think about it, is that it cannot be eliminated just by an act of the will. As we all know, temptation often persists when we try to put the evil thought out of our mind. St. Paul had the same experience, for he says: "even though I want to do what is right, a law that leads to wrongdoing is always ready at hand. My inner self agrees with the law of God, but I see in my body's members another law at war with the law of my mind" (Rom 7:21–23).

Adam did not have concupiscence before he sinned.

All of his faculties were subordinate to his mind and will, and his will was subject to his Creator. From the theological point of view, concupiscence is a result of original sin. The Council of Trent said that concupiscence is "from sin and inclines to sin" (*Denzinger* 792).

My reason for discussing concupiscence is to prepare for the following question: Did the Blessed Virgin Mary experience concupiscence? For, the descendants of Adam are burdened with it; Mary is a daughter of Adam; therefore, it would seem that she too would have concupiscence.

The answer to the question is: No, Mary did not experience concupiscence. As the Council of Trent said, it flows from original sin and leads to sin. But we showed in the last essay that Mary was immaculately conceived, that she was preserved from sin from the first moment of her existence because of the foreseen merits of her divine Son. So it follows that since she did not have original sin she also did not have the consequence of it, namely, concupiscence or evil desire.

Also, the dignity of Jesus Christ, the Son of God, required that the flesh of the Virgin, from which he was to take his own human flesh, should be most pure and therefore not only sinless but also free from all sinful desire.

One could also argue, in support of this point, that what was granted to the first Eve, namely, immunity from concupiscence, should also fittingly be granted to the second Eve, the Blessed Virgin Mary.

Before the Fall our first parents were endowed not only with sanctifying grace, but also with other special gifts. One of them was their freedom from irregular desire. Mary also had this gift, as we have shown above.

Obviously, Jesus was also free from concupiscence. But what about the other gifts of Adam and Eve, such as bodily immortality and freedom from suffering? Did Mary have those gifts too? Mary is the Sorrowful Mother; she was also mortal just as we are. So the Lord did not give her these gifts because they were not necessary for her to fulfill her role in the history of salvation.

Our suffering from concupiscence can be an occasion of merit for us, but it is not a necessary pre-condition of merit. If it were, then Jesus himself could not have merited our redemption. Mary acquired abundant merits both for herself and for all of us, not by her constant struggle against evil desire, but by her great love of God and by her sublime practice of other virtues, such as faith, humility and obedience.

So Mary was created not exactly like Adam, and not exactly like us, but in a very special way—one suited to her dignity as the Mother of God.

6

## MARY, OUR SINLESS SISTER

We have seen that the Blessed Virgin Mary began her earthly existence free from original sin (Immaculate Conception) and free from concupiscence or evil desire which is a consequence of original sin and which induces men to commit personal sins.

It is obvious that, as the result of her Immaculate Conception, her fullness of grace and her holiness, the Blessed Virgin never committed any personal mortal sins. But what about venial sins? We all commit venial sins, even the saints. A venial sin is committed if one transgresses a law of God which does not oblige seriously, such as telling a lie of convenience or stealing some object of small value; one also sins venially if he violates a law that obliges gravely, but for one reason or another lacks perfect knowledge and consent. In this sense, did the Blessed Virgin Mary ever commit any deliberate or semi-deliberate venial sins?

The answer of the Church to this question is a firm no. From the fifth to the sixteenth centuries the teaching of the Fathers and the theologians was almost unanimous on this point. How Mary was sinless was explained in different ways, but the fact of her sinlessness was rarely denied. In the sixteenth century the Council of Trent made the teaching official: "No justified person can for his whole life avoid all sins, even venial sins, except on the ground of a special privilege from God such as the Church holds was given to the Blessed Virgin." Pope Pius IX in *Ineffabilis Deus* taught that God's grace was bestowed on our Lady "in such a wonderful manner that she would always be free from absolutely every stain of sin, and that, all beautiful and perfect, she might display such fullness of innocence and holiness that under God none greater would be known." Pius XII said of the Virgin Mary in his encyclical *Mystici Corporis* that "she was immune from all sin, personal or inherited."

In the light of these statements, which in turn are based on Scripture and the tradition of the Church, Catholics believe that in consequence of a special privilege of grace from God, Mary was free from every personal sin during her whole life. Therefore, she is totally pure, the immaculate one, the sinless one.

The Archangel Gabriel's words, "Hail, full of grace" (Lk 1:28), recall a unique salutation in the Bible; they imply that Mary was adorned with an abundance of heavenly gifts from the treasury of the divinity, to a degree beyond that of all the angelic spirits and all the saints. This is supported by the statement in Genesis 3:15 that there will be perpetual hostility between "the woman" and the devil. However, neither of these statements would be wholly true if Mary had ever committed any sin, no matter how slight. Therefore, it follows that Mary was free from every personal sin during her whole life.

The Father prepared a fitting mother for his divine Son. She was immaculately conceived and full of grace from the first moment of her existence. Also, Mary's perfect sinlessness implies more than merely the absence of sin; it implies perfection in the moral order, or the actual inability to sin.

Two special factors rendered Mary impeccable or unable to sin. The first was her constant awareness of God, living always in his presence, and the second was her reception of special and extraordinary graces. These special graces made it possible for Mary to maintain a perfect harmony in her mind, will and emotions and to recognize always what was the right thing to do and then to do it.

We must not forget that Mary was "full of grace". Many of the Fathers taught that whatever graces the saints had partially, Mary possessed in their fullness. So she was interiorly fortified with abundant gifts of God.

In his providence God also protected Mary exteriorly by protecting her from all the occasions of sin.

St. Thomas Aquinas argued that Mary's complete sinlessness can be established by the theological axiom that the nearer one approaches to a principle of truth or life the more deeply one partakes of its effects. Therefore, Mary's unique proximity to God, by reason of her divine maternity, and her intimate relationship to the source of all grace made her immune to any kind of personal sin.

The Catholic belief in the sinlessness of Mary highlights another dimension of the immaculate Mother of God. It is a tribute to the grace and power of God which can accomplish such a marvel of holiness in Mary, our sister who is one of us in all things except sin. Contemplating Mary and what God did for her should give us great hope since God will also be gracious to us if we strive to imitate Mary's faith and love.

# 7

# MARY'S FULLNESS OF GRACE

In this series we have reflected on the sinlessness of Mary, our Blessed Mother. She was immaculately conceived, that is, sanctified with the fullness of grace from the first moment of her creation. God granted her this special gift because he chose her to be the Mother of his only begotten Son.

To say that Mary was "sinless" is a rather negative way of looking at her reality. From the positive point of view we know that Mary is the holiest person, outside of her divine Son, who ever lived. For, from the first moment of her conception she was "full of grace", as St. Luke tells us (Lk 1:28). To be "holy" means to be close to God, to be like God, and for Christians, to be spiritually animated or re-born through his grace which is actually, in a very mysterious way, his very life.

Accordingly, it is the constant belief of the Church that Mary possessed the *fullness of grace* from the moment of her creation. This means that whatever grace was given to individual saints in any degree was given fully to Mary. Thus Mary must have possessed a far greater degree of sanctity from the time of her conception than Adam and Eve did at the moment of their creation.

It is very difficult to speak about the holiness of Mary, the Mother of God and our Mother, without falling into expressions that sound like gratuitous exaggerations. But if you reflect for a few minutes on what it might mean to be created in grace, to be the Mother of God, to be totally identified in thought, word and deed with the divine Redeemer of all men, then you can at least be sympathetic to the extraordinary claims that have been made for Mary. These claims are suggested, in various ways, in the paintings of the Madonna by the great masters of the Renaissance.

Mary is revered by the Church as the Queen of Apostles, the Queen of angels and saints. Hers is the primacy, therefore, in all things that pertain to eternal life with God for creatures. After her divine Son, she is the pinnacle, the apex of God's creation. Thus, even before the popes approved their teaching, saints and theologians were unanimous in holding that from the first moment of her creation Mary possessed a greater degree of sanctity than any angel or other merely human being. Also, many theologians have gone further and claimed that Mary's holiness surpasses the combined holiness of all angels and saints. Such a statement will perhaps shock some of us, but reflection on the mystery of Mary will show that it is plausible. The Church does not teach this, but it is a pious opinion, held by many respected theologians, which is not forbidden by Church authority.

We must always remember that Mary is a creature; therefore she is limited and her holiness always remains finite. So her fullness of grace is not comparable to the fullness of grace of Jesus, her Son. He is the very source of grace—for us and for Mary. Since he is God, and by reason of the Hypostatic Union, from his conception our Lord possessed the infinite fullness of grace. So he was not able to increase in grace, but she was. As her life progressed she learned more and more about her Son and his mission to redeem mankind on the Cross. She also united herself ever more closely with him and so grew in grace. Therefore, when we say that Mary was "full of grace" the expression is meant in a relative, not an absolute sense.

Some theologians have claimed that Mary began to grow in grace from the first moment of her existence, since, they claim, she had the use of reason as soon as she was conceived. This is a pious opinion, but it is hard to see how it could be proved from Holy Scripture. What is certain is that she did begin to advance in faith, hope and love as soon as she reached the use of reason. When was that? We do not know exactly, but because of her many natural and supernatural endowments we can assume that it began very early in her life.

In addition to Mary's unique degree of sanctifying grace, she also surpassed all angels and saints in the reception of actual graces. Thus, the Lord granted her all the graces of intellect and will necessary to perform each action of her life with the greatest possible perfection.

Beyond her fullness of grace, our Lady received also the infused theological and moral virtues and the gifts of the Holy Spirit. Thus, Mary possessed faith, hope and charity in the highest degree. Since the infused moral virtues exist in a soul in the state of grace with a perfection in proportion to its possession of charity, Mary possessed also the virtues of prudence, justice, fortitude and temperance in an extraordinary degree.

The full array of virtues along with her special endowments constitute Mary the model of both the contemplative and the active life. Her intense love of God, her unsurpassed faith, her humble obedience and her total devotion to the Word incarnate make her the supreme exemplar of the Christian life. To imitate Mary means to imitate Christ.

8

# JOSEPH AND MARY, HUSBAND AND WIFE

Having considered various aspects of Mary's conception, development and sanctity, the next point I would propose for your meditation on the mystery of Mary is her special relationship to her adult companion, protector and supporter, namely, St. Joseph. The question I raise today is this: Were Joseph and Mary truly married? In the past many have denied that a real marriage existed between Joseph and Mary because, as the Church believes and teaches, Mary was always a virgin. Perpetual virginity seems to contradict the essence of marriage. Another way of posing the same question is to ask: Is virginal marriage possible?

The purpose of marriage embraces the generation and education of children, and the mutual love of the spouses. It is necessary to keep those points in mind when one reflects on the matrimonial relationship between Joseph and Mary.

What does the Bible say? For those who like to study it, the pertinent passages on this question will be found in Matthew 1 and 2, and Luke 1 and 2. Holy Scripture clearly states that Mary was both a virgin and the wife of St. Joseph. Matthew refers to Mary as "betrothed to Joseph" (1:18), "wife" of Joseph (1:20, 24), and to Joseph as "her husband" (1:19). Luke speaks of a virgin "betrothed to a man named Joseph" (1:27), and of Mary as the "espoused wife" of Joseph (2:5). The references in Luke to the joint action of Joseph and Mary and to Jesus' "parents" would also seem to indicate that they shared the common life of marriage (2:27, 33, 41).

The question of whether or not a genuine marriage existed between Joseph and Mary was raised by the Fathers of the Church. St. Augustine taught that they were truly husband and wife, even though the marriage was never physically consummated. In the twelfth century Peter Lombard affirmed that the mutual virginity of Joseph and Mary did not impede the genuineness of their marriage. He stressed the spiritual aspect of marriage, pointing out that the marriage contract flows from an inseparable union of souls. St. Thomas in the thirteenth century followed Lombard in this view. He added that the nuptial bond between Joseph and Mary was not vitiated by the conditional consent to exercise their conjugal rights, depending on the specific will of God concerning their marriage.

That a true marriage existed between Joseph and Mary has been the common opinion of theologians since the time of St. Thomas. To give one example, in 1889 Pope Leo XIII, reflecting this view, wrote that Joseph "indeed was the husband of Mary and the father, as was supposed, of Jesus Christ. From this arise all his dignity, grace, holiness and glory. . . ."

Over the centuries saints and scholars have elaborated many reasons why the Word of God chose to be born of a virginal mother within the context of a human family. St. Thomas lists twelve reasons why Christ chose to be born of a married virgin. Some of them are: that the marriage of Joseph and Mary might serve as an outward indication of the legitimacy of his birth; that he might have legal ancestry in the people of Israel in accordance with God's promise to Abraham; that the rearing of the infant Savior might be adequately and honorably provided for; that Mary might be respected publicly and not considered an adulteress; that God might give us an example of family life in and through the Holy Family; that St. Joseph might be an unimpeachable witness to Mary's perfect virginity and also to the Virgin Birth; finally, that the marriage of Joseph and Mary might signify the mystical union between Christ and his Church, as well as to indicate that God blessed both virginity and marriage.

If Joseph and Mary were truly husband and wife, when did their marriage take place? before or after the Annunciation by the angel Gabriel and the Incarnation of the Word in Mary? We know both from Holy Scripture and from Jewish sources that marriage consisted of two stages at the time. First came the espousal or agreement to the marriage contract; at that point the girl was still living with her parents. Some months later she would move into the home of her espoused husband and the marriage would then be consummated. According to Jewish law, the actual marriage took place at the first espousals.

According to Matthew 1:18 the conception of Jesus by the Holy Spirit occurred after Mary had been promised in marriage to Joseph "but before they lived together". When Joseph discovered that she was pregnant, he was naturally disturbed and perplexed. Being unwilling to expose her, he "decided to divorce her quietly" (Mt 1:19). These texts show that Joseph considered Mary his wife, even though she had not yet moved in with him. It would seem, then, that Jesus was conceived in Mary at a time when genuine marriage rights were considered by relatives and friends to belong to his virginal parents. Thus, our Lady was already the wife of St. Joseph at the moment when the second Person of the Blessed Trinity assumed human nature within her virginal womb.

9

# MARY, THE MOTHER OF GOD

It is clear from the Gospels that Mary is the Mother of Jesus. We know by faith that Jesus is the Son of God—that he is the second Person of the Blessed Trinity—"God from God, Light from Light, true God from true God", as we profess in the Creed at each Sunday Mass. Thus, if Mary is the Mother of Jesus and if Jesus is God, it would seem to follow that Mary is the Mother of God. That is precisely the conclusion that the Church Fathers drew and already in the third century they began to refer to her and to honor her with the title "Mother of God".

Since our childhood we have learned to speak of Mary as the Mother of God; we have seen countless statues and pictures of her with the Child Jesus in her arms; we have prayed to her under this title and asked her to intercede with God for us. But how many of us, I wonder, have reflected on the implications of the title: How can a woman be the *Mother* of God? To be a mother means to conceive, to nourish and to give birth. Through the process a child, a new human being, begins to exist. But God is eternal, infinite, omnipotent; he has no beginning or end. Therefore God does not have a mother. Perhaps then "Mother of God" when applied to Mary is used in a symbolic or poetical sense.

There have been thinkers in the history of the Church who, when confronted with these problems, have denied that Mary is the Mother of God. Nestorius, a heretic of the fifth century who tried to solve the problem, said that Mary should be called the "Mother of Christ" but not the "Mother of God".

What does the Church say to this? The Church solemnly declared against Nestorius at the Council of Ephesus in 431 that Mary is the Mother of God. That decision reflected the almost universal belief of the Church—a belief that had been proclaimed by the holy Fathers of the Church for over two centuries. As a Christian community we profess this belief in the Creed when we say "by the power of the Holy Spirit he was born of the Virgin Mary, and became man." In each of the four Eucharistic Prayers that we now use at Mass we refer to Mary as the Mother of God. Thus, we pray to "Mary, the virgin Mother of God" (Eucharistic Prayers II and III). In this regard the American bishops said in their Pastoral Letter, "Behold Your Mother: Woman of Faith" (1973): "The Church's insistence on this title, Mother of God, is understandable, since no other formula makes so evident the intimate link between devotion to the Virgin Mary and belief in the Incarnation" (#62).

What does the Bible say? In Luke 1:35 the angel says to Mary: "The Holy Spirit will come upon you and the power of the Most High will overshadow you; hence, the holy offspring to be born will be called Son of God." So Mary's son is the Son of God. Mary, therefore, must be the Mother of God. St. Paul says basically the same thing in Galatians 4:4: "God sent his Son made of a woman." Also, in Luke 1:43 Elizabeth calls Mary "the mother of my Lord". In the Jewish context of the time "Lord" is a divine name used to refer to God alone.

Of course the question still remains: How can a weak human female, who has herself existed for only a few years, be the *Mother* of God who has no beginning? The answer to this question depends on some knowledge of the Church's teaching on who Jesus is. Briefly, the Church teaches that Jesus is one Person in two natures; he has a divine nature and a human nature. The two natures, however, are united in the one Person of the Word, or second Person of the Blessed Trinity. How this can be is an absolute mystery—it is a truth that we accept by faith in the Word of God. The mystery is often referred to as the "Hypostatic Union", that is, the union of the two natures in the Person of the Word.

Jesus is both God and man; he has a divine nature and a human nature. Obviously, Mary did not give birth to the divine nature. She conceived and gave birth to Jesus in his human nature. We might ask at this point: What does a human mother give birth to? Just a human nature? Or a complete person? The answer of course is that a mother gives birth to a human person.

Now Mary gave birth to Jesus, but he is not a human person; he is a divine Person united to the human nature conceived in the womb of the Virgin Mary. Therefore, since Jesus is God and since he was born of the Virgin Mary, it clearly follows that Mary is the Mother of God.

St. Cyril of Alexandria explains the title "Mother of God" and shows that the center of attention must be Christ himself: "Nor was he first born of the holy Virgin as an ordinary man, in such a way that the Word only afterwards descended upon him; rather was he united with flesh in the womb itself, and thus is said to have undergone birth according to the flesh, inasmuch as he makes his own the birth of his own flesh.... For this reason the holy Fathers have boldly proclaimed the holy Virgin *Theotokos* (Mother of God).

10

# MARY FREELY SAID YES TO GOD

In order to nourish our faith properly it is important to realize that Mary was not just a mannequin or a lifeless puppet in the hands of the Lord. She was a warm-blooded human being like the rest of us. She had her own thoughts, desires, disappointments and anxieties just as we do. Thus, an essential aspect of the reality of Mary is the lofty way in which she responded to God.

Often Christians are tempted to think that Mary was something like a spiritless doll that was used by God in order to bring about the redemption of the human race. Nothing could be further from the truth. Mary actively cooperated in the divine plan of redemption when she uttered her "Fiat", her "Yes" to God's invitation to her to become the Mother of God. Thus, she freely consented to be the mother of the Savior.

St. Luke records the event for us in his Gospel account, 1:28–38. There we read that the angel Gabriel was sent by God to Mary to announce to her that she was chosen to be the Mother of God. Mary raises the difficulty of her virginity and the angel tells her that "The Holy Spirit will come upon you and the power of the Most High will overshadow you; hence the holy offspring to be born will be called Son of God" (1:35). As soon as Mary understands what God is asking of her she freely assents to his will and utters the words that change the whole course of human history, "Behold the handmaid of the Lord. Let it be done to me according to your word" (1:38).

When reflecting on Mary's Yes to God, it is important to remember that our Creator does nothing in vain. In other words, when he does something he does it right. Accordingly, God made man free. He did not have to create man free, but that is what he did. Also, God respects his own creation. This means that he deals with his creation according to the laws or norms he put into it.

Through the angel Gabriel, then, God approaches the holy Virgin and announces to her that she has been chosen to be the Mother of Christ. But the divine maternity is not thrust upon Mary; for the annunciation is also a request from God that she give her free consent. So in faith and loving obedience Mary utters her decisive "Fiat".

From what has been said previously, we know that Mary possessed the fullness of grace. Thus, the Holy Spirit was already present within her and with his grace enabled her to speak her Yes to God. If God had not assisted her interiorly with his grace she could not have responded to him with faith and love. God's grace elevates and assists our powers of intellect and will; it does not cancel them out. Rather, it goes right along with them, raising them to a higher level. This is especially true with regard to Mary's Yes to God. Please note this: God's grace enabled Mary to consent to God's offer that she become the Mother of God and it enabled her to give her consent *freely*.

Accordingly, Mary was not a passive agent in the drama of redemption; she was highly active. St. Augustine said that "Blessed Mary by believing conceived him (Jesus) whom believing she brought forth." Augustine also said on another occasion that Mary conceived "Christ in her mind before she conceived him in her womb", that is, she freely consented to be the Mother of God.

Similar statements about Mary's faith and love abound in the Fathers of the Church and in official teaching. Thus, St. Irenaeus in the second century said that Mary "being obedient, became the cause of salvation for herself and for the whole human race". He also said: "the knot of Eve's disobedience was untied by Mary's obedience: what the virgin Eve bound through her disbelief, Mary loosened by her faith." Comparing Mary with Eve, the Fathers call her "Mother of the living", and frequently claim: "death through Eve, life through Mary."

Referring to Mary's free consent to God, the Second Vatican Council said: "The Father of mercies willed that the Incarnation should be preceded by assent on the part of the predestined mother, so that just as a woman had a share in bringing about death, so also a woman should contribute to life" (Const. on the Church, n. 56). Again, commenting on Mary's Fiat the Council said:

> Thus the daughter of Adam, Mary, consenting to the word of God, became the Mother of Jesus. Committing herself wholeheartedly and impeded by no sin to God's saving will, she devoted herself totally, as a handmaid of the Lord, to the person and work of her Son, under and with him, serving the mystery of redemption, by the grace of Almighty God. Rightly, therefore, the Fathers see Mary not merely as passively engaged by God, but as freely cooperating in the work of Man's salvation through faith and obedience.

## 11

## THE VIRGINAL CONCEPTION OF JESUS

What does the Catholic Church understand by the phrase "Virgin Birth"? It is not unusual to find Catholic college students who mistakenly think it refers to the birth of the Virgin Mary. The expression, of course, is applied to the birth of Jesus Christ from his mother Mary, ever a virgin. The *perpetual* virginity of the Blessed Virgin Mary has been the official teaching of the Catholic Church since the fifth century.

This dogma of the Church embraces three points which I will treat in three separate parts: 1) the virginal conception of Jesus by Mary without the sexual cooperation of a human father; 2) the virginal birth of the

Child from the womb of his mother without injury to the bodily integrity of Mary; 3) Mary's preservation of her virginity afterwards throughout her earthly life.

We should always keep in mind, it seems to me, that Mary is the Mother of God, for her other graces and privileges flow from that one stupendous gift. Since she is the mother of God, we should not be surprised at her other gifts. Thus, the Fathers of the Church praised the Virgin Birth and its miraculous character less as a privilege of Mary than as a glory of Christ and the beginning of the re-created human race. If we believe in the divinity of Jesus Christ, we should not be surprised at the miraculous manner of his entry into the world and the unique woman he chose to be his mother.

When we are speaking about the "Virgin Birth" it is important to know clearly what we are talking about. By "virginity" is meant the bodily integrity of a woman, which, in most cases, is disrupted by sexual intercourse. With regard to the virginal conception of Jesus, the Church believes and teaches that Mary conceived without the sexual cooperation of a man (i.e., St. Joseph). This means that, in the conception of Jesus, the sperm, which in all other cases is supplied by the male sexual partner, was miraculously supplied by God and united to Mary's ovum. Each time we say the Apostles' Creed we profess the truth, "I believe . . . in Jesus Christ . . . who was conceived by the Holy Spirit. . . ." So Mary's bodily integrity was not affected by the conception of Jesus in her.

The doctrine of the virginal conception is clearly taught by Holy Scripture. St. Matthew teaches the virginal and supernatural conception of Jesus by clearly stating in 1:18 that after her engagement to Joseph, Mary was found pregnant through the intervention of the Holy Spirit. Joseph, much perplexed and not yet understanding, made up his mind to terminate their relationship. At this point an angel appeared to him in a dream and told him not to be afraid to take Mary as his wife, since "it is by the Holy Spirit that she has conceived this child" (1:20). Matthew saw this miraculous conception as the fulfillment of a prophecy of Isaiah 7:14: "The virgin shall be with child and give birth to a son, and they shall call him Emmanuel" (Mt 1:23).

St. Luke depicts the Annunciation scene in 1:28–38. There the angel Gabriel tells Mary that she has been chosen to be the mother of the Messiah. Mary, surprised and unclear in her mind, asks the angel, "How can this be since I do not know man?" Since Mary is already betrothed to Joseph her question seems to imply that she had already resolved to remain a virgin. In any event, there is no doubt about the answer of the angel. He tells her that the power of God will accomplish the conception of her child and that therefore the conception will be virginal, without the cooperation of a human father.

Thus, the belief in the virginal conception of Jesus was current in the time of the Apostles, since it is enshrined in two of the Gospels, Matthew and Luke. Also, early Christian writers repeated the phrase, "born of the Virgin Mary". St. Ignatius of Antioch about 110 A.D. wrote to the Christians of a town called Smyrna about "the Son of God . . . truly born of a virgin". St. Justin Martyr in the middle of the second century saw the prophecy of Isaiah 7:14 fulfilled in the Virgin Birth, and called the mother of Jesus simply "Virgin Mary". In the third century Hippolytus recorded the creed: "I believe in God, the Father Almighty, and in Christ Jesus, Son of

God, who was born from the Holy Spirit of Mary the Virgin."

In their pastoral letter "Behold Your Mother: Woman of Faith" (1973), the American Bishops have this to say about the virginal conception:

> It was prophesied in the Old Testament that the Spirit would revivify all things, would create a new people, renew the face of the earth. The overshadowing Spirit who brings about the virginal conception of the Son of Mary is the same powerful Spirit. The Virgin birth is not simply a privilege affecting only Jesus and Mary, but a sign and means for the Spirit to build the new people of God, the Body of Christ, the Church. The glorious positive sign value of the Virgin birth is the merciful and free saving grace of the Father sending His Son, conceived by the Holy Spirit, born of the Virgin Mary, that we might receive the adoption of Sons (n. 48).

# 12

# MARY'S VIRGINITY DURING CHILDBIRTH

The perpetual virginity of Mary is a certain doctrine of the Catholic faith. In the full sense this means that Mary was a virgin before, during and after the birth of Jesus. In the last chapter I explained what the Church means by the virginal conception of Jesus, namely, that Mary conceived by the power of the Holy Spirit. Here I will attempt to clarify the teaching that Mary remained a virgin during the birth of Jesus.

Simply stated, it is the common teaching of the Fathers of the Church, often repeated over the centuries, that Mary gave birth to her Son without any violation of her virginal integrity. The teaching merely asserts the *fact* of the continuance of Mary's physical virginity without determining more closely how this is to be physiologically explained. In general, the Fathers and the Scholastic theologians thought of it as non-injury to the hymen, and accordingly taught that Mary gave birth in a miraculous fashion without opening of the womb and injury to the hymen, and consequently also without the normal pains of childbirth.

Mary's virginity during childbirth, in the above sense, was rejected in the early Church by some thinkers, notably by Tertullian. However, the main current of thought supported it. Some modern theologians, relying on more accurate scientific knowledge, have insisted that the purely physical side of virginity consists in the non-performance of sexual intercourse. Thus, in their view injury to the hymen in birth does not destroy virginity. Moreover, its rupture seems to belong to complete natural motherhood. It would seem to follow from this that from the perpetual virginity of Mary one cannot conclude to the miraculous character of Jesus' birth.

It is important to recall that the Church vouches for the *fact* of Mary's virginity during the birth of Jesus; how it is to be explained has not been decided, so there is a certain freedom here for theologians. The Fathers of the Church, however, with few exceptions hold for the miraculous character of the birth. Thus, St. Ambrose and his fellow bishops wrote to Pope Siricius in 390: "This is the Virgin who conceived in her womb and as a virgin bore a son. For thus it is written: 'Behold a virgin shall conceive in the womb and shall bear a son' (Is 7:14). He has said not only that a virgin shall conceive but also that a virgin shall give birth."

About fifty years later, in 449, Pope St. Leo the Great stated: ". . . she brought Him forth without the loss of virginity, even as she conceived Him without its loss. . . . (Jesus Christ was) born from the Virgin's womb, because it was a miraculous birth." This authoritative statement of the Pope and its enthusiastic reception by the Council of Chalcedon manifests the secure acceptance of the belief at that time in both the East and West.

In 1555 Pope Paul IV condemned the denial of the virginity of Mary before, during and after the birth of Jesus. Also, in his Encyclical *Mystici Corporis* (1943) Pope Pius XII defended the miraculous character of the Virgin Birth: "It was she who gave miraculous birth to Christ our Lord."

There is no clear text in the Bible concerning Mary's virginity in childbirth. Ambrose interpreted Isaiah 7:14 to mean virginity in birth as well as in conception, but modern scholarship fails to see this meaning in the literal sense of the text. The Fathers seem to have considered this a privilege of Christ, based in anticipation on his freedom from subjection to the laws of the material world which flowed from his resurrection. Mary as the new Eve, blessed among women in contrast with the curse of the first Eve, is seen by the Fathers as free from the punishments of Genesis 3:16 which include the pangs of childbirth. Thus, they definitely assert that the birth of Christ was miraculous, just like his conception. Some have suggested that Luke was hinting at the Virgin Birth when he mentioned that Mary herself wrapped Jesus in swaddling clothes and laid him in the manger (Lk 2:7). There may be something to that, but in itself it is not convincing. Thus there are indirect hints in Scripture as a basis for the belief in Mary's virginity during the birth of Jesus, but no direct statements.

We should not forget that Mary was declared "Ever-Virgin" or "Perpetual Virgin" by the Fifth General Council at Constantinople in 553. To illustrate the mystery the Fathers and theologians use various analogies—the emergence of Christ from the sealed tomb, his going through closed doors after his resurrection, the penetration of a ray of sun through glass.

If we reflect for a moment on who Jesus is, then it should not surprise us that his birth was both miraculous and surrounded with mystery. Thus, his miraculous emergence from the intact womb of the Virgin Mother finds its ultimate explanation in the almighty power of God. St. Augustine says: "in such things the whole ground of the mystery is the power of Him who permits it to happen."

13

# WHAT ABOUT THE BROTHERS AND SISTERS OF JESUS?

Mary, the Mother of Jesus, was always a virgin. This truth was commonly asserted by the Fathers of the Church in the third and fourth centuries; in the fifth and following centuries it was incorporated into the official teaching of the Church by various Councils and Synods. The statement means that Mary remained a virgin before, during and after the birth of her Son, Jesus Christ our Lord. The first two senses have already been treated. Now I will take up the question of Mary's virginity *after* the birth of Jesus.

Mary is revered by the Church as a perpetual virgin. We refer to her as the "Blessed Virgin Mary". But there are certain statements in the Bible that seem to contradict Mary's virginity. Perhaps in the course of reading the Bible or listening to the readings at Mass you have noted these points and wondered about them. For example, on more than one occasion the Gospels mention the "brothers" of Jesus (see Mt 12:46; 13:55–56; Jn 2:12). If Jesus had brothers and sisters (Mt 13:56), does that not mean that Mary had other children after Jesus and therefore was not always a virgin?

Again, St. Luke says in 2:7 that Mary "gave birth to

her first-born son". If Jesus was the first-born, then it would seem that more came after him. Finally, Matthew in 1:25 tells us that Joseph "had no relations with her at any time before she bore a son". That seems to imply that he had relations with her afterwards.

On the basis of these statements some Christians in the third and fourth centuries held that Mary gave birth to children after Jesus and therefore was not always a virgin. Origen and some of the other early Christian writers, in order to get around this difficulty, suggested that Joseph was a widower who had other children by his first wife; this could explain, they said, why Scripture mentions the "brothers and sisters" of the Lord. This explanation is merely a hypothesis, with no evidence to support it. Also, if it were true, it would be hard to explain why Jesus left his mother in the care of John the beloved disciple (Jn 19:26f.). Moreover the Holy Family in the New Testament is always composed of just three persons.

A further difficulty centers on St. Joseph himself. In recent centuries many saints and theologians, including not a few popes, have held that St. Joseph was also a virgin and have proposed him as an exemplar of virginity and sanctity.

The perpetual virginity of Blessed Mary has been a dogma of the Catholic Church since the Second Council of Constantinople in 553 A.D. The idea of the perpetual virginity of Mary is enshrined in the prayers of the Church.

From Mary's question to the angel in Luke 1:34, "How can this be since I do not know man?" St. Augustine and many others have inferred that she had made a promise or vow of perpetual virginity, prompted by a special divine enlightenment and grace. Although many modern biblical scholars hold that a promise of virginity cannot be deduced from this text, it has been so interpreted for many centuries and still is worthy of serious consideration.

It might also help to note here the fact that Jesus on the cross entrusted his mother to the protection of the disciple John when he said, "Woman, behold your son" (Jn 19:26). That presupposes that Mary had no other children but Jesus.

With regard to the objections to Mary's perpetual virginity, they are not terribly difficult to answer. The "brothers and sisters" of Jesus are to be understood as his near relatives. To refer to cousins in this fashion was common in biblical times, and the practice is still in vogue in parts of the Middle East. We should also note that the same persons are never called "sons of Mary".

From the expression "she gave birth to her first-born son" (Lk 2:7) it cannot be inferred that Mary had more children after Jesus, since among the Jews an *only son* was also known as the "first-born son" because the first-born had special privileges and duties. Finally, the statement that Joseph "had no relations with her at any time *before* she born a son" (Mt 1:25) asserts that the marriage was not consummated up to the time of Jesus' birth and so attests to the virginal conception. However, the phrase neither states nor implies that the marriage was consummated *after* the birth of Jesus.

The American bishops in their beautiful letter on Mary (1973) give testimony to Mary's perpetual virginity:

> This teaching about Mary's lifelong virginity is an example of the Church's growth in understanding of Christian doctrine. In its ordinary teaching, reflected in catechesis and liturgy, as well as in more formal pronouncements, the Church has here recog-

nized as an aspect of "public revelation" a belief not clearly demonstrable from the Scriptures. In Mary's virginal dedication to her Son's saving work, the Church sees delineated her own mission to bear witness to values that go beyond the secular city to the city of redeemed man, the kingdom of God, in its present reality as well as in its future completion. The Dogmatic Constitution on the Church repeated this conviction, urging religious to "pattern (themselves) after that manner of virginal and humble life which Christ the Lord elected for himself and which His Virgin Mother also chose" (n. 50).

# 14

# OUR SPIRITUAL MOTHER

Having treated various aspects of Mary's perpetual virginity, the next point to consider is her spiritual maternity. In a very true sense Mary is not just the Mother of Christ; she is also our mother. Reflect for a moment on some of the titles we apply to her: we address her as "Our Lady", "Our Blessed Mother", "Mother of the Church". In the Fathers and certain Church documents we find the title "Mother of all the living".

So the question we should ask ourselves here is: In what sense is Mary our mother? The answer is not difficult to grasp: Mary is our mother because she conceived and gave birth to Jesus our Redeemer. Incorporated into him through faith and Baptism, we become members of his Mystical Body—he is the Head and we are the members. Since we are members of his Body and

Mary is his mother, it follows that Mary is also our mother, not in the physical order but in the spiritual order of grace. Hence since the second century, pious Christians, and often also the Magisterium of the Church, have referred to Mary as our spiritual mother.

Mary's spiritual maternity is rooted in two key events in her life: her Yes to God in the Annunciation that she had been chosen to be the mother of the Messiah, and her Yes to God in the shadow of the cross on Calvary when she spiritually participated in her Son's agony and death and shared in his offering to the Father for the salvation of all mankind. Without her faith and obedience there would be no Redeemer, no salvation and no Church. In each case what is transmitted is life, since that is the function of a mother—to communicate life. In a true sense, then, Mary is a source of our life of grace, our spiritual life; therefore we have the right and the privilege to call her our spiritual mother. This is what we do in fact when we refer to her as "Our Blessed Mother".

The spiritual motherhood of Mary is indicated in two places in the New Testament. In John 19:26-27 we read: "Seeing his mother there with the disciple whom he loved, Jesus said to his mother, 'Woman, there is your son.' In turn he said to the disciple, 'There is your mother.' From that hour onward, the disciple took her into his care." Many Christian writers have pointed out that the scene has a symbolic value, that is, Jesus, hanging on the cross shortly before his death, is telling us more than that John should provide shelter and a home for Mary. Thus, the disciple John stands for all of us, for the whole Church. We are all children of Mary and she is given a special role as the mother of Christians. This symbolic interpretation of the person of St. John is justified by the whole context of St. John's Gospel which is replete with symbolism and in which material things stand for spiritual realities.

In Revelation 12:1–5 we read about the mysterious woman and the dragon who is defeated by her son: "A great sign appeared in the sky, a woman clothed with the sun, with the moon under her feet, and on her head a crown of twelve stars. . . . She gave birth to a son—a boy destined to shepherd all the nations with an iron rod." In the primary sense the woman symbolizes God's people in the Old and the New Testament. The Israel of old gave birth to the Messiah and then became the new Israel, the Church, which suffers persecution by the dragon, that is, the devil.

The woman can also stand for the Mother of Christ. Since the earliest centuries the passage has been so interpreted by popes and theologians. In this sense it is Mary who defeats Satan through her divine Son who breaks his power over men and casts him down into hell. Also, she labors to bring forth all of us, that is, to bring all mankind to the knowledge and love of Christ. Faith and love are followed by God's grace which makes us children of God, brothers of Christ and co-heirs with him of the kingdom of God. Once again, if we become spiritual brothers of Christ who is the Son of Mary, we must also be her spiritual children and she our spiritual mother.

In their outstanding letter on Mary, published in 1973, our own American bishops speak about Mary as our "spiritual mother":

> Like the Savior's parable of the vine and branches, the image of the Church as "body of Christ" is a graphic reminder that the same life links members to Head, branches to Vine. From earliest Christian times the Church was regarded as "Mother

Church". Gradually, Mary's relationship to the sons and daughters of the Church came to be regarded also as that of "spiritual mother". Physically mother of Christ the Head, Mary is spiritually mother of the members of Christ. She is mother of all men, for Christ died for all. She is especially the mother of the faithful, or as Pope Paul proclaimed during the Second Vatican Council, she is "Mother of the Church" (n. 70).

# 15

# MARY, OUR GO-BETWEEN

We have seen that Mary, since she is the Mother of our Redeemer, is in a very true sense our spiritual mother. For, without her there would be no Jesus Christ and without the Christ there would be no redemption.

Mary was not just a spectator in the drama of salvation through Jesus. She actively participated in God's plan to save all mankind. St. Paul says in 1 Timothy 2:5 that Jesus Christ is the sole Mediator between God and man, since he alone, by his death on the Cross, fully reconciled mankind with God. However, this does not of itself exclude another type of mediatorship which is secondary and subordinated to Christ.

Accordingly, Catholic writers and theologians since the eighth century have reflected on the mediatorship of Mary in the divine plan of redemption and have applied to her the title of "Mediatrix" of all graces. Some of the

Fathers of the Church called her the "go-between" between man and God.

What do we mean by a mediator (mediatrix = feminine)? In general, a mediator is one who interposes his good services between two persons in order to facilitate an exchange of favors or to bring about a reconciliation between parties at variance. We are all familiar with this reality in a family context. Often a son who is at odds with his father will ask his mother to talk to dad about it and try to patch things up. Mom talks to dad and the matter is resolved. In this sequence mom is acting as a "mediatrix" between son and father.

In Catholic theology Mary is given the title "Mediatrix" for three reasons. First, because she occupies a middle position between God and his creatures; this is so because of her divine maternity and her fullness of grace. Second, because during her earthly life she contributed, by her holiness, to the reconciliation between God and man brought about by Jesus. Third, because through her powerful intercession in heaven she obtains for her spiritual children all the graces that God deigns to bestow on them.

It is important to note that Mary's mediation with God on our behalf is substantially different from that of her divine Son. St. Paul teaches us: "For there is only one God, and there is only one mediator between God and mankind, himself a man, Christ Jesus, who sacrificed himself as a ransom for them all" (1 Tim 2:5–6). Thus, Jesus' mediation is primary and absolutely necessary for men's salvation; he had first to redeem Mary and mediate for her before she could mediate for us. Mary's mediation is secondary and wholly dependent on Christ's. But just because Mary's mediation is "secondary" and "dependent on Christ's", it does not follow that it is unimportant.

In the past many Protestant theologians have objected to the Catholic insistence on the mediatorship of Mary. The basic reason for their opposition is Paul's statement that Jesus is the sole mediator between God and mankind. In its fullness, it is true that Jesus alone accomplished our reconciliation with God; but in a sublime way Mary cooperated with Jesus in the redemption of mankind, and also helped him. So in a secondary and dependent sense, it is appropriate and justified to apply to her the title of "Mediatrix".

The title of "Mediatrix" is given to Mary in numerous official Church documents. During the past hundred or more years the following popes have attributed this title to Mary: Pius IX, Leo XIII, Pius X, Benedict XV, Pius XI and Pius XII.

The Second Vatican Council also referred to Mary as Mediatrix in the following passage:

> By her maternal charity, Mary cares for the brethren of her Son who still journey on earth surrounded by dangers and difficulties, until they are led to their happy fatherland. Therefore the Blessed Virgin is invoked by the Church under the titles of Advocate, Auxiliatrix, Adjutrix, and Mediatrix. These, however, are to be so understood that they neither take away from nor add anything to the dignity and efficacy of Christ the one Mediator (The Church, n. 62).

The American Bishops in their 1973 letter, "Behold Your Mother: Woman of Faith", devote two pages to the explanation of Mary's mediatorship with God. In n. 65 of the letter they write: " 'Mediatrix' is a familiar Catholic term to describe the unique role of the Mother of Jesus in her Son's mission as Mediator."

The theological basis for calling Mary "Mediatrix" is her closeness to God and her closeness to us. She is closer to God than any other creature because she was chosen by him to be the Mother of the divine Redeemer. She is close to us because she is one of us, because she is a human being just like us, sin alone excepted. Therefore, for us she is our Mediatrix, our go-between.

## 16

## MARY COOPERATED IN OUR REDEMPTION

We have seen that Mary, because of her exalted role in the redemption of mankind, exercises a special mediatorship between God and man. In a very true sense, she is our "go-between" because she is close to God and is also at the same time one of us.

As we know, Mary was chosen by God to be the Mother of the Redeemer. When the angel Gabriel announced to her that she was to be the Mother of Christ, she freely and deliberately accepted the role in the drama of salvation that was offered to her. As St. Augustine said, she conceived him first in her mind and then in her body.

Mary was a dedicated mother who cared for her Son. She treasured in her heart what was said about him and she also pondered the meaning of his words and actions. This is clear from the incident of losing him and then finding him again in the midst of the teachers and scholars in the temple.

At the beginning of his public life, Mary shows up at the wedding feast in Cana (Jn 2). The bride or groom was probably a relative of Jesus and Mary. Concerned about the embarrassment of the couple when the wine ran short, Mary asks Jesus to do something about it and he performs his first public miracle.

Mary is very much in evidence at the foot of the Cross, along with St. John, when Jesus dies for the salvation of all mankind and offers himself totally to the Father. Mary is there not only physically, but also morally and spiritually since she shares in his sufferings and unites her act of oblation to his.

In all of this Mary cooperates fully with her divine Son in the redemption of the human race. There is no doubt from Holy Scripture and the tradition of the Church that Mary cooperated fully with Jesus in the Incarnation and Redemption. As members of the Church became more aware of Mary's cooperation with Jesus, starting in the fourteenth century various theologians and preachers coined a new title for her and began to refer to her as the "Coredemptrix" ( = Coredemptress) of the human race.

The basic justification for the title is to be found in the fact that both the Incarnation of the Son of God and the Redemption of mankind by the vicarious atonement of Christ were dependent on Mary's free assent.

The Fathers contrast Mary's obedience at the Annunciation with Eve's disobedience. Mary by her obedience became the cause of salvation, while Eve by her disobedience became the cause of death. St. Jerome said,

"By a woman the whole world was saved", and "death through Eve, life through Mary."

All the popes from Pius IX to Pius XII, that is, from 1846 to 1958, spoke about Mary's role as Coredemptrix of the human race. Because many Protestants do not accept the mediatorship of Mary and especially objected to the title "Coredemptrix", the title does not occur in the documents of the Second Vatican Council. The same doctrine, however, was asserted by the Council in these words: "In the work of the Savior, she (Mary) cooperated in an altogether singular way, by her obedience, faith, hope, and burning love, to restore supernatural life to souls" (Const. on the Church, n. 61).

By giving the title "Coredemptrix" to Mary, popes and Catholic theologians do not intend in any way to equate her efficacy with the redemptive activity of Christ, the sole Redeemer of humanity (cf. 1 Tim 2:5). Since she herself required redemption and was in fact redeemed by Christ, she could not merit the grace of redemption for others. Her cooperation in the objective redemption of Christ is indirect and subordinate to him. What it means is that she voluntarily devoted her whole life to the service of the Redeemer and, under the cross, suffered and sacrificed with him.

Christ alone truly offered the sacrifice of atonement on the cross. Mary gave him moral support during his life and in his death. As the Church teaches, Jesus Christ conquered the enemy of the human race alone. The words of Luke 1:38, "Behold the handmaid of the Lord", imply Mary's mediate and remote cooperation in the Redemption.

In recent years you have probably not heard Mary referred to as the Coredemptrix of the human race. In this age of ecumenism that title is out of favor. But the term (and the spiritual reality behind it) is too strongly embedded in the tradition of the Church for it to disappear completely. It could very well be that in a future age, when current problems in the Church and between Christians have been resolved, the title will once again come into regular use. In 1935 Pope Pius XI addressed the following words to our Lady: "O Mother of love and Mercy, who, when thy dearest Son was consummating the Redemption of the human race on the altar of the Cross, didst stand by Him, suffering with Him as a *Coredemptrix*. . . , preserve in us, we beseech thee, and increase day by day the precious fruit of his Redemption and of thy compassion."

17

## MARY PRAYS FOR ALL OF US

For many centuries Mary has been referred to by popes and theologians as "the mediatrix of all graces". As we have seen, a mediatrix is a go-between, an intercessor, an advocate. Mary is the mediatrix of all graces in the sense that she gave the Redeemer, the source of all graces, to the world; in this way she is the channel of all graces.

We should not think, however, that Mary's mediatorial role ceased with the Incarnation of God and our Redemption on the cross. It is also a point of Catholic belief that, since her Assumption into heaven, Mary is the mediatrix of all graces by reason of her intercession on behalf of all mankind before the heavenly throne. What this means is that Mary not only cooperated with Jesus fully in bringing about our Redemption, but also actively works with him in the application of grace to each individual.

It is to be noted that Mary's mediation is *universal* in that it involves the granting of every single grace without exception: sanctifying grace, the infused virtues, the gifts of the Holy Spirit and all actual graces.

The manner in which Mary discharges her office as dispensatrix of all graces is through her intercession. She intercedes for men either expressly, by asking God to bestow a certain grace on a particular person, or implicitly by praying for all of us and offering to God her previous merits on our behalf.

At first it may seem astonishing that no grace is imparted to mankind without the intercession of Mary. The implication of this doctrine is not that we are obliged to go to Mary for all graces, nor even that Mary's intercession is intrinsically necessary for the bestowal of grace, but rather that according to God's positive will, the salvific grace of Christ is conferred on nobody without the actual intercessory cooperation of Mary.

Popes during the past two centuries have declared themselves in favor of this doctrine. Thus, Leo XIII said in 1891: "From that great treasure of all graces, which the Lord has brought, nothing, according to the will of God, comes to us except through Mary, so that, as nobody can approach the Supreme Father except through the Son, similarly nobody can approach Christ except through the Mother." Pope St. Pius X called Mary "the dispenser of all gifts which Jesus has acquired for us by His death and His blood." Pius XI quoted with approval the words of St. Bernard: "Thus it is His (God's) will that we should have everything through Mary."

The liturgical books of the Church, always reliable indicators of Catholic belief, echo the ideas found in the papal documents. Thus the official prayer books of the Byzantines, Copts, Syrians and Chaldeans have many references to Mary's role as dispensatrix of all graces. In the Latin liturgy the best witness is the Mass and Office of Mary, Mediatrix of All Graces. This feast was celebrated from 1921 to 1954 on May 31. In 1954 Pope Pius XII ordered the universal observance of Mary's Queenship on August 22. As a result the feast of Mary's mediation was discontinued in some dioceses and transferred to another day in other dioceses.

The doctrine of Mary's mediatorship is taught only implicitly in Holy Scripture. Theologians point to Genesis 3:15, known as the protoevangelium, as an indication of Mary's close association with Jesus in the whole process of redemption. Since the granting of graces to members of the Mystical Body is only the specific way in which they, as individuals, benefit from the redemptive work of Jesus, it seems reasonable to infer that Mary would have a share in it. Another text that bears on the subject is John 19:26–27, where Jesus, speaking from the Cross, tells Mary that John is her son; he then tells John that Mary is his mother. Recent popes have interpreted this to mean that the dying Savior proclaimed his Mother as the Mother of the whole human race.

We refer to Mary as "Our Blessed Mother". In what sense is she our mother? She is our spiritual mother. She is our mother in the order of grace, not in the order of nature. Some of the Christian writers have referred to her as "the Mother of all the living", in the order of grace of course, just as Eve is our mother in the sense of physical life.

For over two hundred years most of the popes have honored Mary as the Mediatrix of All Graces. The doctrine has also been strongly urged by many saints, among whom I would mention St. Germanus of Constantinople (d. 733), St. Bernard (d. 1153), the Franciscan St. Bernardine of Siena (d. 1444) and St. Alphonsus Liguori (d. 1787). Like many other truths about Mary, this doctrine developed slowly over the centuries, moving from implicit faith to explicit faith.

To sum up, since Mary gave the source of all grace to us, we believe that she also now in heaven cooperates with her Son in the distribution of all graces. She does this through her intercession on our behalf. Therefore, we may fittingly honor her and pray to her under this title: "Mary, Mediatrix of All Graces, pray for us."

18

# THE DORMITION OF MARY

On August 15 each year we celebrate the feast of the Assumption of Mary into heaven. What does this doctrine of the Church mean? It means that at the completion of her life Mary was taken directly into heaven, both her body and her immaculate soul were glorified, and she was admitted to the beatific or face to face vision of God. There she now reigns as Queen of Heaven, Queen of angels and saints.

There is an ancient tradition in the Church of belief in the Assumption of Mary. In fact, it can be traced all the way back to the fifth century. It was in that century when various Fathers of the Church began to make explicit reference to the end of Mary's days on earth and her "translation" into heaven by the power of almighty God.

Before we go into the question of Mary's Assumption proper, it will help much towards the understanding of this mystery of Faith to reflect on the end of Mary's life on earth. At least since the fifth century faithful Christians have wondered about the last days of Mary. There is no mention in Holy Scripture about the death of Mary, such as is recorded of Jesus himself, St. Stephen and others. The question for us believers comes down to this: Did Mary die a natural death? or was she transferred by the power of God directly into heaven while still alive?

The common belief of Christians since the fifth century is that Mary died. By "death" we mean the separation of the animating soul from the material body. Signs of death are the absence of movement and especially the beginning of corruption. But it is quite amazing, when you stop to think about it, that there is no specific tradition about how, when or where Mary died. Both Ephesus and Jerusalem claim to be the site of the tomb of Mary, but there is no solid proof.

In Jerusalem today two sites are revered in connection with the last days of Mary. One is Dormition Abbey on top of Mount Sion, which is a Benedictine monastery. In the crypt of the Church you will find a statue of Mary, stretched out on a bier, portraying her in death before her body was assumed into heaven. In Gethsemane, near the Garden, you will find an underground shrine, filled with lanterns and *ex voto* offerings, which is honored as the tomb of Mary.

At this point you might be inclined to ask, "What's the problem? All the children of Adam die, so Mary died too." That seems very reasonable, and it is most likely true, but it ignores the fact that Mary was conceived without original sin and also never contracted any personal sin, as we have seen before. Now death is the punishment of sin; so if Mary is perfectly sinless it would seem that she is not under the common sentence of death. Perhaps, then, she went directly from this life to the next life, without actually dying. It also ignores the silence of Scripture on Mary's death and the lack of any definite details about her death.

The Bible and the early Christians often referred to death as "falling asleep". Jesus used that expression in reference to the death of his friend Lazarus in John 11. "Dormition" is from the Latin word which means "sleep". Beginning in about the fifth century the Church in the East celebrated the feast of the Dormition of Mary on August 15. At first it seems to have been a feast to celebrate the day on which Mary died. Very soon, however, the idea of her Assumption into heaven was added to the feast. It became widespread in the Eastern Empire and was kept on August 15, the same day on which we still celebrate Mary's Assumption into heaven.

In the early Middle Ages some theologians began to doubt that Mary actually died because of her sinlessness.

But from the thirteenth century to the present time the vast majority of theologians have held that Mary died. Two reasons are given: 1) Mary had a mortal human nature from Adam, just like the rest of us, even though she did not contract original sin; 2) Mary resembled her Son Jesus as closely as possible; it seems fitting, then, that since he died she also would have to die.

There is no historical evidence about the mode of her death, whether by martyrdom, sickness or old age. St. Peter Damian thought that she died from sorrow. The most common opinion among theologians is that she died from a broken heart because of the intensity of her love for God.

When Pope Pius XII in 1950 defined the doctrine of the Assumption and elevated it to an infallible dogma of the Church he did not clearly settle the question of whether or not Mary actually died. This is what he said: "The Immaculate Mother of God, the ever-Virgin Mary, *having completed the course of her earthly life*, was assumed body and soul into heavenly glory" (emphasis added). Notice that the Pope does not say "after her death". He thus left the question officially undecided, but it is clear from other parts of the same document that Pius XII himself agreed with the vast majority who hold and have held that Mary died a natural death like all the rest of us. The tradition is virtually unanimous, however, in affirming that the body of the Virgin Mary, like that of her divine Son, did not undergo corruption. Shortly after the end of her life she was assumed body and soul into heaven.

# 19

# THE ASSUMPTION OF THE BLESSED VIRGIN MARY

We considered the question of Mary's death and saw that, even though it is not a defined dogma of the Church, the common teaching of popes and theologians is that Mary died just as we do and just as Christ did. Now I propose to focus more precisely on the meaning of the Assumption of Mary—a great feast of the Church which we celebrate as a Holy Day of obligation on August 15 each year.

The word "assumption" means to be taken into heaven, not by one's own power but by the power of another; in this case it is by the power of the almighty God. Since Mary was perfectly sinless, it is clear that her soul went directly to God at the moment of her death. So the doctrine of the Assumption concerns the translation of her body to heaven, after having been re-animated by her glorified soul.

The doctrine also means that Mary's body was not subject to the general law of the corruption of bodies after death. The doctrine implies that the Assumption took place shortly after her death. How long the interval was between her death and her Assumption is not stated.

In the positive sense, the Assumption means the heavenly glorification of Mary's body and her taking an important place in heaven near her Son, in line with the assertion of St. Paul that "our present perishable nature must put on imperishability and this mortal nature must put on immortality" (1 Cor 15:53).

It is to be stressed that the bodily Assumption of Mary into heaven is a *special privilege* granted to her by God because of her unique role in the history of salvation as the Mother of God. For, her assumption is an exception from the general law according to which the bodies of all Adam's descendants must return to the dust from which they came. The Lord has promised that the just will rise from the dead, but only on the last day at the end of the world. Thus Mary's Assumption is a privilege in the sense that her bodily glorification anticipates the general resurrection and she was exempted from bodily corruption.

As I pointed out previously, there is an ancient and important tradition behind the Catholic belief in the Assumption of the Blessed Virgin. It is traceable back to the fifth century in Jerusalem and the sixth century in the East. By the seventh century it made its appearance in Rome and in Gaul or present day France. Though there was some doubt about it in the early Middle Ages, by the thirteenth century it was the general belief of Catholics both in the East and in the West. At the time of the First Vatican Council in 1869–1870 two hundred bishops requested that the doctrine be solemnly and infallibly defined by the Church. This was deferred, however, until the present century.

In 1946 Pope Pius XII, having been asked by many to proceed with the definition, sent out a request to all the bishops of the world. He asked them to report to him on what their people believed with regard to Mary's Assumption. The overwhelming number of respondents said that their people believed in the Assumption of Mary. After duly considering the pros and cons, Pius XII, in virtue of his apostolic authority as the successor of Peter and the Vicar of Christ on earth, in 1950 solemnly defined as a truth of Faith that has been revealed by God: "The Immaculate Mother of God, the ever-Virgin Mary, having completed the course of her earthly life, was assumed body and soul into heavenly glory."

The doctrine, of course, is not stated explicitly in Holy Scripture, though it is certainly implied and it is formally revealed by God. Most theologians appeal to Luke 1:28 which speaks of Mary's "fullness of grace". They also appeal to Genesis 3:15. Since by the seed of the woman they understand Christ, and by the woman, Mary, it is argued that as Mary had an intimate share in Christ's battle against Satan and in his victory over Satan and sin, she must also have participated in his victory over death.

In accordance with the above, theologians argued that the corruption of the body is a punishment for sin. Since Mary was free of all sin, it was fitting that her body should be exempted from the general law of corruption and immediately assumed into the glory of heaven, as God originally planned for all mankind. Another argument is that since the body of Christ originated from the body of Mary, it was fitting that Mary's body should share the lot of the body of Christ. Similar arguments are derived from Mary's perpetual virginity and from her close participation in the redemptive work of Christ as our "Coredemptrix".

The meaning of this truth of Faith, then, is that Mary is

one with Christ for all eternity in the fullness of her humanity, or as we commonly say, "in body and soul". She shines forth, as Vatican Council II says, "as a sign of sure hope and solace for the pilgrim People of God" (Church, n. 68).

## 20

# HAIL, HOLY QUEEN

We have already considered what the Church believes and teaches with regard to the Assumption of Mary into heaven. Now I would ask you to reflect for a moment on the fifth glorious mystery of the Rosary, namely, "The Coronation of Mary as Queen of Heaven".

One of the most ancient titles of Mary in Christian piety is that she is "Queen". The same idea is expressed in such equivalent titles as "Empress" and "Our Lady".

What do we mean by the word "queen"? There are two basic meanings. In a metaphorical sense a woman is often called a queen if she is outstanding for excellence in a particular field. Thus, for example, we speak of a "fashion queen" or a "beauty queen". In the proper sense of the word, a woman is a queen if she is the mother of a king or the wife of one. Because of her queenship, then, in a given society, such as England, the queen enjoys certain prerogatives, dignity and authority.

When Catholics refer to Mary as the Queen of Heaven and when they invoke her intercession under this title they are using the word "queen" in its proper sense. The reason is that Mary, because of her role in the history of salvation, is a queen in the full sense of that word.

The evidence in the Bible for Mary's queenship is found in St. Luke 1:30–43. There the angel Gabriel addresses Mary as the Mother of a divine King and says: "The Lord God will give him the throne of his ancestor David; he will rule over the House of Jacob for ever and his reign will have no end" (verses 32–33). Also, when Elizabeth speaks to Mary she calls her "the mother of my Lord". This is an expression from the Old Testament for the queen-mother. In Luke it reflects the faith of the early Church that Jesus is the royal Messiah.

From the fourth century to the present the writings of the Fathers of the Church, of theologians and popes offer many examples of referring to Mary as "Queen", "Mother of the King", and "Mother of the Lord".

Mary has two principal titles or claims to being called a queen. The first and most important is that she is the Mother of God. Her Son, Jesus Christ, is truly a King, in fact he is the King of kings. Therefore, since Mary is the Mother of the King, it follows that she is a Queen. In her glorious Assumption Mary is received into heaven by her divine Son. Out of filial piety Jesus grants Mary a participation in his eternal kingdom. As the Mother of the King she exercises a rule of mercy and benevolence, interceding for all God's children. Therefore she is aptly called "Mother of Mercy".

Mary's second title to queenship is based on her cooperation in our redemption. In a certain sense, she is the Coredemptrix of the human race, since she shared in

Jesus' sufferings for the salvation of all. Jesus is King not just because he is the Son of God, but also because he is the Redeemer of man. Thus Mary is queen also because of her share in our redemption.

Mary exercises her queenship not through domination but by means of her intercession with her divine Son. Her relationship to the King, of course, is not just physical; there is also a profound moral relationship. We must not forget the feminine character of all queenship. Very often a queen does not exercise her power directly over others. Her influence resides, to a great extent, in her power over the heart of the King. She does not have to be present at all deliberations; nor does she have to be a minister of government or anything like that. Take for example the wife of the president of the United States. She is not elected to any particular office; she has not been appointed by Congress, but she can, and often does, have great influence over public policy because of her influence on the heart and mind of the president. There is something similar in the relationship between Mary and her divine Son.

Our prayers are a good indication of our beliefs. From this point of view we see that Christian piety has long been accustomed to praying to Mary under the title of "Queen". One need only think of the prayers "Regina Caeli" (= Queen of Heaven) and "Hail, Holy Queen". These prayers are still sung regularly in many of our churches.

Pope Pius XII affirmed strongly the queenship of Mary. He established a special liturgical feast called "Mary Queen of Heaven". He consecrated the world to the Immaculate Heart of Mary, Mother and Queen, on October 31, 1942. In the special prayer he said: "As the

Church and the entire human race were consecrated to the Sacred Heart of Jesus . . . so we in like manner consecrate ourselves forever also to you and your Immaculate Heart, our mother and queen of the world, that your love and patronage may hasten the triumph of the kingdom of God."

## 21

## MARY IS OUR SURE WAY TO CHRIST

Over the centuries one of the major points of disagreement between Catholics and Protestants has been the veneration of the Blessed Virgin Mary, or devotion to Mary. Although Luther and some of the early Protestants in the sixteenth century praised devotion to Mary, Calvin and many others were opposed to it. In the course of the next two centuries the veneration of Mary almost disappeared in most of the Protestant groups.

The Orthodox Churches, however, have continued to foster a tender devotion to the Mother of God. This is evident to the outsider from the many beautiful icons of the Virgin which adorn their churches. Morever, the cult of Mary, common to the Catholic Church and the Orthodox Church, constitutes a close bond between the two and offers a firm motive for eventual reunion of the two bodies.

Many Protestants and non-Catholics still say and seem

to think that Catholics "worship" or "adore" the Virgin Mary. Perhaps they get this idea because they see us kneeling before the statues of Mary and offering her other forms of external reverence. Since most Protestants do not believe in the intercession of Mary and the saints in heaven, they also falsely conclude that we are showing divine honors to them when we pray to them, for example, when we say the "Hail Mary" or recite the Rosary.

Perhaps some clarification of the words we use will help. "Worship" and "adoration" mean total submission or subjection of oneself to a superior personal being as the author of all creation or as divine. Such honor, obviously, can be offered by a rational person only to God Almighty, Father, Son and Holy Spirit. Thus we adore (or worship) God; we adore Jesus because he is the second Person of the Blessed Trinity—either in his resurrected state as he exists in heaven at the right hand of the Father, or in the Holy Eucharist under the appearances of bread and wine.

Since adoration is to be shown to God alone, it is totally excluded from our relationship to the holy Mother of God. But at the same time we believe that Mary was and is highly favored by God. She is "full of grace" (Lk 1:28); she is "blessed among women" (Lk 1:42); inspired by the Holy Spirit, Mary herself proclaimed, "From this day forward all generations will call me blessed, for the Almighty has done great things for me" (Lk 1:48). Because God showered his most abundant gifts on Mary and elevated her to be the Mother of the Redeemer, we show her special honor and reverence. The Second Vatican Council calls this reverence the "cult" of Mary (Const. on Church, n. 66). The same attitude is also often spoken of as the "veneration" of Mary.

A good way to understand our devotion to Mary, and the religious foundation for it, is within the context of the communion of saints. In the Creed at Sunday Mass we profess belief in the communion of saints. Many Catholic beliefs about God and man and the world are contained in that short phrase. It means the spiritual union of all those who are in the state of grace—those in heaven, those on earth and those in purgatory. It presupposes the immortality of the human person, the reality of eternal life with God after death, the need for purification for our sins, merit before God for good works; it also implies that all the saints can pray to God for each other—that they have the right and the power to intercede with God for one another.

It is at this point that Christian tradition recognizes the special place of the Blessed Virgin Mary, Mother of God and Mother of the Church. If the saints, by reason of their closeness to God, can intercede for us, how much more effective must the prayer of Mary be, since she was so intimately associated with her divine Son in the redemption of the human race. Here I would ask you to recall what we have said before: that Mary is the Mediatrix of all graces, the Coredemptrix and the Queen of Heaven.

Mary's powerful intercession with God has been recognized by Christians since the very beginning of the Church. There are many evidences of it in the Roman catacombs going back to the second century. By the fourth century the veneration of Mary was universal among Christians. After Mary was proclaimed "Mother of God" officially by the Council of Ephesus in 431 A.D., many impressive churches were dedicated to her honor. To this day many of our greatest churches are dedicated to the honor of the Virgin: Saint Mary Major in Rome, Notre Dame in Paris, St. Mary's Cathedral in San Francisco, Church of the Immaculate Conception in Washington, D.C.

Catholics and all Christian believers should not be turned away from Mary—they should go to Mary. Veneration of Mary has been encouraged on many occasions by councils, popes and bishops. Many of our greatest saints were distinguished for their Marian piety. It is also a special characteristic of our Pope, John Paul II. St. Pius X wrote that "Mary is our sure way to Christ." According to Pope Pius XII, devotion to Mary is an indication of our firm hope of salvation. In 1947 the same Pope said that "according to the opinion of the Saints it is a sign of predestination."


22

# THE IMMACULATE HEART OF MARY

We live in an age of acronyms. Every day we read about NATO, the UN, SALT talks, HEW, WHO, ICBMs and MIRVs. Many people do not know exactly what the letters stand for. Since the Church is always influenced by the surrounding culture, it is no wonder that we have taken over this mode of writing and talking. Thus in our Catholic publications we come across such combinations as USCC/NCCB, CRS, CHD, CFM, NFP and IHMs. The point I want to make in this chapter concerns the last acronym which stands for the Immaculate Heart of Mary. In this country there are four groups of nuns designated by this name and they are often referred to simply as "the IHMs". As a sign of their devotion to the Blessed Virgin Mary they usually wear a blue habit, or at least they did at one time.

We have already considered briefly the basis and justification for our religious veneration of Mary. Since the time of St. John Eudes in the seventeenth century, that is, for the past three hundred years, there has been a steady increase in devotion to Mary from the point of view of her Immaculate Heart. We have all seen pictures and statues of Mary pointing to her glowing heart. Because of her intimate relationship to her divine Son, the Immaculate Heart of Mary is always associated with the Sacred Heart of Jesus. Mary is holy because she was specially favored by God and chosen to be the Mother of God. Hence devotion to Mary cannot and must not be divorced from devotion to Jesus.

The object of this devotion is the physical heart of Mary—that heart that burned so intensely with love for God. The aspect under which Mary's heart is revered is precisely her love for her divine Son. We honor that love and try to imitate it according to the measure of God's grace given to us. All forms of the cult of Mary, whether directed to this or that aspect of her life, are ordered to the person of Mary. Devotion to the heart of the Mother of God is most fitting, therefore, since her heart includes and represents Mary's entire sanctity and inner life, along with her various gifts and perfections which are all intimately related to her love.

Devotion to the Immaculate Heart of Mary has been approved and encouraged by many bishops and popes, including Pius VII, Pius IX and especially Pius XII. Many Protestants consider our use of material things and symbols in the worship of God as being superstitious or even idolatrous. But the Catholic Church considers it fitting to approve for veneration sensible manifestations of spiritual truth, for man himself is composed of both material and spiritual elements. Thus it is very proper that a physical element, such as Mary's heart, be chosen to represent Mary's intense love for God.

The Second Vatican Council stressed that devotion to Mary should be based on Holy Scripture. Pope Paul VI emphasized the same point in his 1974 Apostolic Exhortation "On the Cult of Mary". Mary's heart is mentioned twice in the Gospel of St. Luke: "As for Mary she treasured all these things and pondered them in her heart" (2:19; see also 2:51). Many saints and theologians in their writings and sermons have reflected on these verses and expressly spoken about Mary's heart, for example, St. Augustine, St. Albert, St. Bernard, St. Peter Canisius, and especially St. John Eudes and St. Anthony Mary Claret.

From the beginning of the twentieth century many requests were directed to the Holy See that the world should be consecrated to the Immaculate Heart of Mary. Acceding to this petition, during the World War in 1942 Pope Pius XII did consecrate the world to her and established August 22 as her feast day under this title. In 1954 the same Pontiff wrote a letter about the queenship of Mary and directed that August 22 should be dedicated to her under that title. So it is still today.

Consecration to the Immaculate Heart of Mary is a

special feature of this devotion. By an act of consecration we freely submit ourselves to God and recognize his dominion over us. Since one is consecrated to Mary only because she is the Mother of God and closely associated through her queenship of heaven with the Deity, such a consecration always refers ultimately to God himself. Queenship means some sort of dominion. Thus the proper basis for a consecration to Mary is found in her dominion over and concern for her spiritual children.

Because it embraces the whole sanctity and love of Mary for God, the devotion to the Immaculate Heart of Mary in a certain sense is the synthesis of all Marian doctrine and devotion. When Pope Pius XII established the feast of the Queenship of Mary he decreed that it should be celebrated throughout the world each year. He also decreed that on that feast "there be renewed the consecration of the human race to the Immaculate Heart of the Blessed Virgin Mary".

So the next time you see an IHM sister, or the next time you see the acronym "IHM", reflect for a moment on the noble heart of Mary which is a symbol of all that we should strive to be.

## 23

# MARY, MOTHER OF THE CHURCH

In this series of essays on the Blessed Virgin Mary I have tried to explain briefly and clearly the fundamental truths that have been revealed to us by God about the holy Mother of our Redeemer. Much more, of course, could be said about the humble Virgin of Nazareth whose life was a total response to the call from God.

Many Catholics are still familiar with the Litany of the Blessed Virgin Mary, because many still recite it after praying the Rosary. It would be possible to continue this series on Mary by writing up each of her titles mentioned in the Litany. I have decided not to do that since it would entail a great deal of repetition of what has already been said about her.

Towards the close of the Second Vatican Council Pope Paul VI officially bestowed a new title on Mary. The new title is "Mother of the Church". The Holy Father wanted to express in a single phrase the spiritual motherhood that the Mother of Jesus exercises toward the members of the Mystical Body, the Church, of which Christ is the Head. Since that time the use of the new title has become more widespread. I recall vividly that, during the 1971 Synod of Bishops in Rome, the Polish Bishops (of which Pope John Paul II was at the time a member) circulated a petition to all the other delegates from around the world, asking them to implore Pope Paul VI to create a special feast day for the universal Church in honor of Mary, Mother of the Church. This has not yet been done but it would not at all surprise me if John Paul II establishes such a feast during his pontificate.

The word "mother" has a special power in the English language, as does its equivalent in all other languages. For each of us that one word summons up a host of memories, meanings, associations, feelings and emotions. A woman can be called "mother" properly only if she has given birth to a son or daughter. That means that she is a source of a new human life. And *life* is the most important reality in the personal existence of each one of us.

Mary is the mother of Jesus in his human nature; but that Jesus is also God, Logos, the second Person of the Blessed Trinity. Therefore she is also the Mother of God —a truth that was solemnly proclaimed by the Council of Ephesus in 431 and that has been preached and defended by the Catholic Church ever since.

It is clear then that Mary is a mother. But why did the Pope call her "Mother of the Church"? The "Church" includes shepherds and flocks, pastors and people. We are accustomed to refer to Mary as "Our Blessed Mother". To say that Mary is "Mother of the Church" is really just another way of saying the same thing.

The basis or foundation for the title is the fact that Mary is the Mother of God. She responded to God's call and said Yes to being the Mother of the Redeemer. Jesus died for us on the Cross on Calvary; then he rose from the dead and ascended into heaven; on Pentecost he poured out the Holy Spirit on the disciples and Mary gathered in the upper room on Mount Sion in Jerusalem. Thus the

Church was born and began her mission of preaching the Good News of salvation to all the nations of the earth. Therefore, since Jesus is the source of our spiritual life, and since there would be no Jesus without Mary and her cooperation in the divine plan of redemption, it is fitting to address Mary under the title, "Mother of the Church".

As I have pointed out before, Mary cooperated totally with her Son in the Redemption of the human race—from Nazareth to Calvary and beyond. In their 1973 Pastoral Letter "Behold Your Mother: Woman of Faith", the U.S. Bishops wrote: "After Christ's Resurrection, surrounded by His disciples, Mary prayed for the coming of that same Spirit, in order that the Church, the Body of her Son, might be born on Pentecost. Through her faith and love, Mary's maternity reached out to include all the members of her Son's Mystical Body" (n. 115).

Mary's spiritual maternity of the Church was symbolized on Calvary when Jesus placed her under the protection of St. John as his mother. Many of the Fathers and other exegetes see in John a symbol of the whole Church, Christ's Mystical Body. Pope Paul VI said that "Jesus gave us Mary as our Mother, and proposed her as a model to be imitated." The Mother of Jesus exemplified in her own life all the teachings of her divine Son and so the Church rightly regards her as the perfect model of the imitation of Christ. She is the perfect Christian.

Mary was led by the Holy Spirit and brought forth Jesus by his power. Jesus is brought forth and lives in us through the Spirit. Mary constantly intercedes for us and helps bring us forth spiritually. Therefore she is truly "Mother of the Church".